LABRADOR PATELLA
THE ARCHIE RUMBOLT STORY
NINA RUMBOLT PYE

Published in Canada by Engen Books, Chapel Arm, NL.

Library and Archives Canada Cataloguing in Publication information is available upon request.

Print: 978-1-77478-191-3
eBook: 978-1-77478-192-0

Copyright © 2025 Nina Rumbolt-Pye

NO PART OF THIS BOOK MAY BE REPRODUCED OR TRANSMITTED IN ANY FORM OR BY ANY MEANS, ELECTRONIC OR MECHANICAL, INCLUDING PHOTOCOPYING AND RECORDING, OR BY ANY INFORMATION STORAGE OR RETRIEVAL SYSTEM WITHOUT WRITTEN PERMISSION FROM THE AUTHOR, EXCEPT FOR BRIEF PASSAGES QUOTED IN A REVIEW.

Distributed by:
Engen Books
www.engenbooks.com
submissions@engenbooks.com

First mass market paperback printing: June 2025

Cover Design: Ellen Curtis

Cover Photo:
Top: The surgery photo is from the Grenfell Archives.
Middle: The dog team is owned by Dennis Burden, who continues to carry on the tradition of using Labrador dogs. The photo credit belongs to Nikita Penney.
Bottom: My daughter, Whitney Pye, and her son Liam in 2019 at the same age that Fanny and Archie would have been when he left home.
The colours of the photo represent the colours of the Labrador Flag designed by the MHA for southern Labrador, Michael Martin, in 1973. The three colours represent the snow, land, and waters. The twig is black spruce, a common Labrador tree, and its branches symbolize Labrador's three people: the Inuit, the Innu, and the European settlers. It grows from one stalk and is meant to be a positive symbol of who we are and who we hope to be... a collective of all races.

LABRADOR PATELLA
THE ARCHIE RUMBOLT STORY
WINNER OF THE 2025 PERCY JANES FIRST NOVEL AWARD
NINA RUMBOLT PYE

Dedicated to my grandsons Ashton, Ronan, and Liam: may you always be loved in your life's journey as much as you are today

INTRODUCTION

Dad was one of the plaintiffs in the Class Action Lawsuit for Residential School survivors that was settled in 2016 for fifty million dollars. In November 2017, we traveled to Goose Bay and attended a private breakfast and a public ceremony in which Prime Minister Trudeau gave a heartfelt apology to the survivors of the residential school fiasco. Trudeau did not legally have to do this, but he did, and did it with compassion. My parents were very proud and relished the attention. They were from a generation that idolized politicians.

One year prior, on November 3, 2016, my father sat at my dining room table and recounted his story of the abuse he suffered while attending the Orphanage in St Anthony. He gazed into the distance and stopped occasionally to take deep breaths and compose himself as I recorded his story for the Residential Schools Inquiry Commission. By the time he finished talking, he was practically slumped over the table, like a balloon that had just released its air.

"Dad," I said when he finished talking. "The Commission needs to know if you want this account that I have written from your story made available to the public once they have finished their work?"

"No maid, I don't want people reading about that." He cast his eyes down as if he could still feel the shame and humiliation he had felt all those years ago. Dad was always a proud man who worked hard and never let his crippled leg prevent him from doing a regular day's work. I always assumed it was the generation he grew up in that made him that way, but now as I studied him, studiously staring at his thumbs, I realized how much he had aged just in the past hour while he told me the story. He didn't want people thinking he was weak or needed attention. As proud as he was about the Court Case finally concluding, he still felt vulnerable.

It wasn't until I glanced into the living room and saw my six-year-old grandson sitting quietly and waiting for his mom to return home from work did I realize the full impact of my father's story. Not only had the events *happened to him*, but they *happened to him* while he was far far away from his mother and family in a strange land.

"Dad," I said quietly. "The government knows hateful things were done on their watch and they have admitted it. However, the stories need to be told and people need to understand the full impact of what happened to all the children. Allowing people to know your story may not help you much now, but it may prevent this from ever happening to another child."

"What do you think I should do?" He looked up at me with round eyes, seeking direction.

"I think you should allow it to be read," I responded. "You may never know who it will touch and help heal."

He nodded sadly and I checked the disclosure box.

***

I've heard Dad tell the story of his straight leg on many occasions. Sliding accident, tuberculosis, etc. I did not realize this had occurred fifteen miles in the bay from Mary's Harbour in a long-ago abandoned place called Tooth Cove.

My father always possessed such an outgoing, friendly demeanor to strangers. I now realize why. He had been a stranger in a strange land for six and a half years. He learned how to survive by being kind and accommodating. That's why we always had a parade of politicians or workers from away staying at our house. While I was growing up there were numerous occasions when Mom would look out the window and say "Who is your father bringing home to dinner today?" It seemed he wanted to feed as many lonely souls as he could, and more than once, I slept on the couch so a stranger could have my bed.

My grandmother always radiated love and had enormous pride in her family. I'll never forget the weeks prior to leaving for university in 1982. I was at my grandmother's house and she wanted to hear all about what I was going to do. She listened intently, and when I was finished, she slipped a wad of 20-dollar bills into my palm totalling 100 dollars. This was a lot of money back then and I remember using it to purchase my suitcases. Her eyes filled with tears as she said, "When you get all that done, will you be better than the Acremans?" I smiled and said yes as I knew that's what she wanted to hear, but my generation never did view the Acremans as being better or worse, for that matter. They were just members of the community.

The Acremans came to the region in the late 1800s to work for Dr. Grenfell. In those times people who came from away were held in high esteem. Samuel Acreman was one of the brothers and his children established businesses in Mary's Harbour and lived in close proximity to my grandmother. The Acreman who lived a stone's throw away from her had married a nurse from Ohio who had come to work with the International Grenfell Association. I have no doubt that my grandmother always felt that had she been an Acreman, maybe she could have held her children tighter and they would not have had to go away. Maybe if she had the nurses training that Celeste Acreman had, she could have prevented tuberculosis from infecting her child.

What I saw growing up around my grandmother was much different. Her pantry was always full of good food, there was always a delicious meal cooked, and a cake or buns always sat waiting to be eaten if you were hungry. Her house was spotless and her clothes were always clean and ironed. In the years leading up to her death, nice dresses hung in her closet and her jewelry box held precious items; all given to her by her children as they all found good employment and showered her with items she thought she would never own. She talked with pride of each child, as if their accomplishments were her accomplishments and their successes were her successes.

As Dad recounted the story for the Residential Schools Claim, I became mesmerized in the details of not only him, but of my grandmother's heartbreak. This story is as much about Fanny as it is about Archie. It's the story of a mother and son and the intense pain of having your child whisked away at seven years old and not having him home again until he was a teenager. It's the turmoil of living on the harsh unforgiving coast of Labrador during difficult times and the heartbreak of having your children be so far away with no communication. It's the story of a family that was forever changed by a simple freak sliding accident, as they essentially lost Rita also. Rita was sent to St Anthony at the tender age of fourteen to be her mother's heart and eyes for Archie.

It was a situation that may have been common seventy years ago, but one we can't possibly imagine happening in today's world.

I'm happy my dad's family finally healed. I know they did, because in my time there wasn't much talk of that time period. However, during my interviews with my aunts and uncles about that time period, in preparation for this book, I heard the sorrow, hurt, and anger in their tones and their words. "We lit a candle every night and prayed for Archie while Mom cried," recounted my aunt Mildred. "That damn Labrador Development Company left us in the bay to starve. I watched Mom cut the last piece of bread into equal chunks for us to eat while she awaited Dad's return with more food from a 30 mile walk to and from a company store in Fox Harbour," recounted my Uncle Roy.

This story is part fiction and part fact with the history of the time interwoven to aid the reader in appreciating that era. The fiction part is basically the everyday interactions and thought processes of the people involved. Although I know no intimate details of how they interacted and felt, as a daughter who grew up in their homes and was taught the importance of family, I felt I was qualified to capture the essence of who they were. I hope I portray it as closely as possible to give meaning to the story.

Much of the historical details of the times I owe to the works of John Kennedy, Dr. Anthony Paddon, Dr. Gordon Thomas, Celeste Acreman, and George Poole for their accounts of life in Labrador and life with the Grenfell Mission. My knowledge of Nurse Jupp comes from a dissertation by Heidi Coombs-Thorne in 2001. Also, I found the accounts in *Among The Deep Sea Fishers*, a Grenfell publication, from the Memorial University archives to be an incredible resource. Plus, I must acknowledge Jim Jones and Cindy Gibbons for their tidbits of essential information and for always being there for questions about the Battle Harbour area. I also acknowledge Andrea Proctor for her help with navigation in the Provincial Archives at The Room.

I wish to acknowledge a great mentor I have been privileged to know; Matthew LeDrew. Thank you Matthew, for your relentless support and teachings. Your writing classes and the authors I met in those classes greatly aided in how my work developed into award winning material.

To my author friends Michelle Clemens, Ida Linehan Young, and Robert Lundrigan; this journey was a pleasure with you by my side, holding my hand and rooting for me.

Lastly, I cannot express enough gratitude to my incredible editor, Lisa M Daly. Her unique understanding of children voices and use of language greatly complimented her already powerful skills of grammar and punctuation. Thank you for always reminding me about the "beautiful moments" in the manuscript. This was definitely my light when times got dark.

CHAPTER 1: ARCHIE
TOOTH COVE, DECEMBER 1946

Ma was hot on my heels as I bolted through the door with my coat unbuttoned and no mitts on, but I couldn't wait another second. I sucked the fresh winter air deeply into my lungs as I pounced off the bridge and into the fluffy new fallen snow.

"Get back here you harden little martel," Ma yelled as she came to an abrupt stop at the edge of the bridge. Dad had swept it all off before he left for the mill, where he made pit props for mine shafts in Norway. I remember him swearing about the greedy merchants that owned the mill who robbed them blind and the Newfoundlander Ranger who always sided with the merchants. I knew Ma in her slippers wouldn't come any further. I giggled as I made my way down the embankment towards my brothers.

I didn't make it to the bottom of the hill before I came face to face with my stern looking older brother.

"Are you not heeding Ma?" Roy scolded as his eyes bore into mine.

"I'm not a bit cold," I stammered.

"But you will be. Now hop the dyin back up there and get yer Jesus mitts."

"No and I am tellin Pa you swore too," I stood my ground, standing taller.

"You keep yer trap shut and listen to Ma." Roy's eyes were narrowing at me now.

"You never listen to Ma."

"Listen you little brat. I am 10 and you are still 7 and I am in charge when Pa is not around, so hop da Jesus up da hill."

"No," I stared at him defiantly.

In one swift movement he grabbed me by an ear and marched me up the hill to where Ma was still standing in her dress and slippers hold-

The Rumbolts in late summer 1946. Ern, standing to the left of Fanny, holds Dorothy with Archie right in front of him and Cack hiding behind Archie. Next is John, then Roy to the far right. From the Rumbolt Family Collection.

ing my mitts. I yelped all the way and by the time I was next to Ma, it wasn't me she was angry with.

"What in the hell flames is wrong with you Roy? And that language!" She slapped the side of his head as she pulled me with the other arm into her bosom and smothered wet kisses onto my throbbing ear.

I felt her shiver as she quickly buttoned my coat and held my mittens for me to shove on. She seemed so cold while she made sure I stayed warm.

I absolutely loved being outdoors with my brothers. The smell of the crisp clean air and the space to run about was exhilarating. I loved my brothers and would be so proud when Roy would take me to the rabbit snares. Of course, he was only allowed to go to the nearby ones unless Uncle Tim or Uncle Charl was with him. It was so exciting, especially when he caught a rabbit. One day a rabbit had been alive and I watched as Roy expertly tapped it on the head like Dad had shown him to do. I was so proud. Roy and John were the closest, just being a year apart so they often spent a lot of time kicking around pieces of wood or chunks of ice pretending it was a ball.

Today they were trying to teach little Clarence, but everyone called him Cack, to play ball. Cack was five, littler than me, but we still had to share a bed.

"Too bad you can teach him how to get up to use the pot at night," I groaned.

"It's too cold," Cack whined.

"The rest of us have to get up in the cold if we have to piss," I snarled.

Roy hollered at the two of us, "Boys, stop arguing."

"Well, you sleep with him tonight then," I snapped back at Roy.

"No way," Roy laughed dismissing the argument as Losten and May came around the corner of the house. Losten was my age and May was Roy's age. Their mother Charlotte, Ma's sister, was married to Dougie McClean. Like us, they lived in cove that winter.

"There's enough snow on the bank to go randying," said May. "Want to do it?"

"In a while," said Roy. "We have to finish showing Cack how to kick the ball through the goal."

"But I want to go now," moaned Losten. He was always so impatient.

"I'll go with you," I said. "We can use Dad's water komatik." The water komatik was a tiny sled measuring three feet by five feet that Dad used to pull water from the brook to the house.

"Arch," Roy said sternly. He always called me Arch when he spoke sternly. "You will wait till we are all ready."

"That's okay," said May. "I will take them." May felt she was just as deserving to be in charge as Roy. After all, they were the same age.

"Fine," replied Roy. "Just be careful."

Off we ran, grabbed the little komatik and headed up the bank where Grandfather and Grandmother had built their house. Sister Mildred, my eldest sister, was just coming out of the house where she slept most nights. Being the first born and living with Grandmother and Grandfather for so long, she just didn't bother to leave when Dad and Ma moved out.

"Did Dad say you could have that?" she asked.

"No," I replied. "But he won't mind, we won't break it."

"Well, you better be careful," she said and headed down the little bank to our house and we headed to the hill.

"The sled isn't going to go very fast or very far," said May. "The hill is not very steep."

"Well, you two get on and I will push and jump on," I offered.

"Good idea," said May. "Losten, you sit and I will hold the rope."

May sat on the komatik with Losten sitting between her legs. She was careful to leave a few inches for me to jump on, on my knees, after pushing them to ensure a fast-starting boost. She wrapped her legs around Losten's waist and he held them while she held the rope used to pull the sled. They didn't want the rope to hang loose and slow the komatik down. We had done this many times, and finding the best ways to sit for speed was now second nature to us. There wasn't much room but the exhilaration of a ride down the hill was going to be worth all the effort and discomfort.

"Are you ready?" I yelled excitedly.

"Yes," Losten and May yelled back in unison. I held Mays shoulders and ran, pushing as hard as I could. Just before the sled got going faster than I could run, I jumped on the back on my knees.

At first, I didn't realise the pain with the excitement of speeding down the. Then excruciating pain hit and I rolled off the komatik into the snow while May and Losten careened down the hill. The komatik came to a stop near where the boys were playing ball. May and Losten screamed and laughed with excitement and looked back up the hill where I had fallen off the sled. I forced myself not to cry. The pain was unbearable. The older boys would make fun of me if I cried and would call me a cry-baby. Right now, they were all laughing at me for falling off and had no idea that I was in pain. I had no idea why there was such agony. All I knew was that I was in terrible pain and I had to get away before I started crying and they started mocking me.

I then did what any seven-year-old would do and lashed out with anger to mask my emotions. "May's big butt took up too much of the komatik for me to fit on."

"Arch, that's not nice, get into the house," yelled Roy.

I gladly obliged and headed into the house. As I marched past Rita and Ma into the bedroom I said "I hate them all." I fell onto the bed and allowed the hot tears of pain and humiliation to spill.

I heard Ma sigh. "They are always having a racket over one thing or another," she said to my sister, Rita.

"Just let them fight it out among themselves; you can't fight their battles for them," my very wise sister replied. I heard Ma emit a disgruntled puff as I cried myself into a deep sleep.

CHAPTER 2: ARCHIE
TOOTH COVE, DECEMBER 1946

I lay in bed the next morning as long as I could, lingering even though I was awake most of the night. When Ma got up at 5am to light the fire and start the breakfast she must have heard me using the pail. Usually it was John; he rarely made it through the night without having to get up to piss. She looked surprised when was the one who I limped out.

"I bet you are starved," she whispered as to not wake the others. "You didn't even get up to eat supper last night."

If it was one thing Ma hated, it was for us children to be hungry. Many times, when there was not enough food, she wouldn't have her own plate. I would watch her eat our leftovers if there were any. Dorothy and Cack would rarely eat all their food and when I knew Ma didn't have a plate, I would be sure to leave her some too and just say I wasn't hungry.

"No, not really", I replied as I sat by the stove to get warm. There were a couple of partridges hanging near the stove to thaw. I shifted to avoid their cold.

"Well, breakfast won't be very long, why don't you go back to bed till the house warms up."

"Alright," I replied, and limped back to the room.

I heard Dad come out of the room a while later and check the fire. I knew Ma was probably busy cutting small pieces of dough from the bowl that she had prepared the night before from barm and flour.

"Was that Archie?" Dad asked. "He's up early, I guess he was hungry. He must have been pretty mad at the boys to sleep through supper last night."

"He said he wasn't hungry," Ma replied. "And he was limping a bit.

He must have hurt his leg when he fell off the komatik. I will check on him when I gets straightened away."

Dad took a damper off the stove and put the kettle for tea over the hole so it would boil faster while Ma dropped palm sized pieces of dough into a hot frying pan. Even though I couldn't see them, I could hear them, and I knew their morning rituals. She would probably use up about half the bread dough to make pancakes for breakfast. Bread needed to be made every day for a family of nine. Even then, most meals were prepared with a paste over the meat or doughboys dropped into the pot to help everyone fill up. Mildred was a great help in keeping the bread made, she had been doing it since she was nine years old. Rita did it sometimes, not as much as Mildred. And Rita's bread was never very good.

Dad poured a cup of tea and moved the kettle back to the stove. Now I could hear the dough sizzling in the pan of fat and could smell the dough changing flavour as it rose in the pan. It was amazing how Ma could change it from a bitter yeasty glue to a fluffy fresh mound of deliciousness. I heard two pieces of crispy pancakes hit a plate and could picture Dad drizzling molasses over them.

"I see yer gonna cook up some of the partridges or supper," Dad commented.

"Yes. Thank God for the bit of snow yesterday so you could go for a hunt on yer day off. I cooked the last of the seal last night."

"Hopefully the bay will soon freeze enough to get out the edge of the ice and get a few more seals for the winter," Dad replied.

"And I am keeping that porcupine for Christmas dinner." I could definitely hear the smile on Ma's face as she spoke about Christmas.

I heard Dad say his goodbye and close the door as he left to trudge out to the mill on the point.

Ma's footsteps approach our room.

"Archie, are you still awake?" she said quietly.

"Yes Ma," I whispered back.

I rose and met her in the doorway and limped out to the wooden slab table. Ma kept a flowered cotton cloth over it to cover its roughness.

"Let me see what ya got done."

"It's nothing Ma."

"Well, I will see for myself."

She pulled up the left leg of my pants and gasped at what she saw.

"Oh my god... what happened?" she asked.

"I hurt it on the komatik." I hung my head, ashamed at the injury.

Ma seemed shocked at the state of my knee. It was bruised and swollen and caked with dried blood.

"You should have told me about this last night," she reprimanded.

"But Ma, I didn't think it was anything till I woke up this morning."

"Well, sit on the chair," she ordered, "and put your leg up on this chair," she said as she pulled another chair over. "I have to get it washed and see what you got done."

As she moved a pot of water over the exposed damper to boil as Roy came out of the room. "What's going on Ma?" he asked.

"Archie got his knee hurt from the komatik," she said.

"Ewww, maggoty," said Roy as he looked at my knee. "You might die from that."

"ROY!" scolded Ma. "Stop tormenting him."

"I was only carrying on," said Roy, rolling his eyes.

"Ma, I won't die, will I?" I asked, feeling miserable.

"No, of course not," said Ma. "Roy might though if he don't stop tormenting you."

Ma got to work sterilising some rags in the boiling water. She dabbed some mercurochrome on the wound. Ma explained that she hoped this would kill any germs while the cut healed. She wrapped it snugly with clean bandages and went on with her day. I didn't do much that day, just moped around the house. Ma knew it would take it a few days to heal, so she tried not to fuss too much.

The next morning, however, was a different story. Dad was up and gone to the mill before any of us children woke up and even when everyone started going out of the room for breakfast, I remained in bed. I just didn't want to get up.

After Ma dished up the rolled oats for the others, she came to check on me. I was awake but still covered up in the bed, blankets up to my face.

"What's wrong with you? Is your knee hurting?"

"Yes." I said into the blankets.

"Well, let's have a look," Ma said, as she stripped back the blankets and unbandaged my knee.

My knee was swollen and yellow pus was oozing out. Ma tried to keep a straight face but I had caught a quick glimpse of her shocked expression and was immediately alarmed.

"It's not getting better, is it Ma?" I said in a tiny voice

"It's just a little bit infected," she replied, "nothing a bit of poultice won't cure."

She helped me out to the main area and got me settled in a chair. Rita was just bringing Dorothy, our youngest sister, out of the other room where she slept in a cot next to our parents' bed. "Archie's knee getting worse?" Rita asked.

"Looks like it's a bit infected. Feed Dorothy while I make some poultice," Ma ordered.

My three brothers looked away and cringed. They have all had scrapes and cuts before and it's no fun getting it cleaned up. Ma put some dried bread in a small saucepan and poured some boiling water on it. While it was cooling, she got some clean fresh rags that she kept just for this purpose. She applied the poultice and a clean bandage and told me I would have to rest up for the day while the poultice drew out the infection. I wasn't too happy to be stuck in the house for another day, but I really wanted the pain to stop. Christmas wasn't too far away and I enjoyed that time of year when there would be lots of food and visiting.

The weather was a bit warmer today, so it meant all the youngsters, besides me, could go outside to play and Ma could get some Christmas preparations done in peace. There was extra sewing to be done and, of course, the Christmas cake had to be baked and stored so the flavours would be nice for Christmas Day. She gathered her ingredients and started mixing while I watched her from the daybed in the corner of the room. The daybed was sometimes used by Dad to take short naps if the day was extra busy, or to lay on to keep an eye on the fire on nights it was too cold to let it go out. Mostly though, it was used by the children to curl up together on rainy or boring days or to lay on while sick.

I almost drooled as I watched Ma use up the last of the dried fruit for the cake. When the fruit was first bought in the fall, we were allowed to sample some and I dearly loved the apricots. But the dried fruit was expensive and only enough was bought for a small treat and for the Christmas cake.

While the cake baked, I played with an old file and a piece of wood that Uncle Bob had given me. I was making a mending needle so I could help Dad fix the nets next summer. I loved spending time with Dad at the stage.

The cake smelled amazing and when Ma took it out of the oven and placed it on the counter, I thought I had died and gone to Heaven. There was no other smell on this earth that even compared.

The cake would take a while to cool, so Ma told me to stay put on the daybed while she ran up the hill to fetch her mother.

"What for?" I asked without looking up from my filing.

"I'm gonna get Mom to take a look at your knee. Always good to have a second opinion," she explained.

I was a bit startled when a few minutes later, the door opened and four of them entered. Ma, Grandmother, Mildred and Uncle Charl, my uncle who was the same age as my sister Mildred.

"Your Grandmother is going to take a look at that knee," Ma said. "She has tended to more than I have."

Grandmother was a small woman in stature and very soft spoken and gentle. Everyone affectionately called her Aunt Liz.

"How are you feeling, my boy?" asked Grandmother as she gently cupped my face in her hands.

"I was feeling good until all yous showed up. Is the leg gonna rot off me or what?"

Ma did a grunted laugh and Mildred commented she just wanted to have a look. Charl just remained quiet. Grandmother smiled. "Everyone is just worried, that's all. I assure you we are not going to let your leg rot off."

Grandmother unwrapped the bandage and cleaned away the poultice. "This was definitely more than a surface wound. A surface wound should be healing by now." She looked at me and asked, "So Archie, you did this on the water komatik?"

"Yes," I replied.

"Charl," she said, turning to her son who was standing by the door. "Can you go have a look at the back of the komatik to see if there is a jagged edge or anything that might explain the wound?"

Uncle Charl turned and left without even responding. He returned a few minutes later looking wide eyed.

"What is it?" his mother demanded.

"There is about an inch of a two-inch nail sticking out of the back of the komatik from a broken board."

Grandmothers remained serious. "Fanny, we're gonna need more poultice and clean rags." She turned to me. "Can you buckle your leg for me."

I winced and tried, but could only move it a little. "It hurts," I said tearfully.

"You poor thing," said Mildred as she came to me and cradled my head. "We will make it all better, won't we Ma?"

"Yes," Ma replied, but she had turned quickly towards the stove and I couldn't see her face. She busied herself with the task at hand and they had me bandaged up again in no time.

After Grandmother had gone, Ma and I had a few minutes alone before everyone came in to get settled before supper. The cake had cooled down and Ma was getting some cheesecloth soaked with rum ready to wrap it in. Rum was also a rare treat that was kept for Christmas. Ma would always sneak a bit from Dad's bottle to put on her cake, while the remainder was kept for visitors during the season.

"Ma, can I have a little bit of cake before you put it away?" I asked.

"Indeed, you cannot," she replied. "You will have some on Christmas Day with everyone else. It's only another four days away, you know."

I was disappointed, but four days wasn't that long.

CHAPTER 3: FANNY
TOOTH COVE, DECEMBER 1946

Fanny woke up a little earlier than usual. She thought she heard a sound. She lit her candle and peered into the crib where Dorothy was sleeping soundly. Then she heard it again, like a muffled moan, coming from the children's room. She quickly pushed her feet into her worn slippers and padded to their room. As she scanned the room, she saw Roy sleeping on the top bunk and Cack snuggled to Rita's back on the bottom bunk. In the bed opposite, John slept quietly but Archie was in the fetal position, shivering and moaning slightly.

She laid the candle on a shelf and gently moved John and his pillow to the foot of Rita's bed. He stirred briefly and looked at her but went back to sleep as soon as she tucked him in. She then tended to Archie. He was hot and sweaty despite the shivering.

"*Fever,*" she thought.

She had dealt with fevers on many occasions from the children having the flu. She left the room to get a cloth and some cool water. The water in the boiler on the stove was cold from the fire being out all night, so she soaked the cloth in it and squeezed out the excess. Back in the room she gently wiped Archie's face and hands. It seemed to soothe him so she left to light the fire.

By the time Ern got up a while later, she had everything ready for breakfast.

"You were up early," he said.

"Archie's got a fever." She peeked into the children's room again, then turned to go get dressed.

"His knee?"

She turned back to him. "It has to be," she said, looking worried.

He pulled her close and hugged her. "Now don't go worrying. You know it's just the body's way to fight infection. He will be fine in a couple of days."

She pulled away. She felt agitated that he never seemed to worry like she did. But she didn't want to worry him either because he didn't need to have other things distracting him while he worked. She could handle it.

"I know, and I'm alright," she said.

When Ern left for the mill, she crawled back in bed with Archie. He was still shivering a bit but relaxed when she snuggled with him.

While everyone was getting breakfast, she moved him to the daybed and gave him a little sponge bath. He barely moved as she pulled clean pants and a sweater onto his clammy little body. Dragging a chair over to the cupboard, she climbed on it and reached into the top cupboard to retrieve a box of sugar cubes. She removed one cube and replaced the box. All eyes watched; those cubes were reserved for company and sickness. Making a cup of sweet tea, she sat beside her son and attempted to spoon it into him.

"We only get molasses for our tea," whispered John to Roy, but loud enough that everyone heard anyway.

"I'd rather have molasses and be well than to be sick enough to need a sugar cube," Rita mused to herself. But again, everyone had heard and John winced uncomfortably.

Archie's head twisted from side to side to avoid the tea, but Fanny was persistent and managed to get some into him. It did seem to make him feel a bit better. She then changed the bandage on his knee. It looked different, but she couldn't tell if it was different better or different worst. She sent Roy to fetch her mother again.

"It looks about the same," Liz declared, while Fanny just sighed and looked away. "All we can do is keep dressing it and hope for the best. Even if it is getting worse, there is nothing we can do this time of year."

"We could take him to the hospital in St. Mary's," offered John.

"Not yet for a while we can't," said Roy as Rita poked him in the back to be quiet.

"Well, it's true", Roy continued. "I heard Grandfather say. There is a scum of ice from the head of the bay to Captain Jack's Island. You wouldn't get a boat through it to save ya life and it's not thick enough for the dogs to haul a komatik over."

"Roy, that's enough. Try to be a bit considerate," scolded Rita while tilting her head towards her mother.

Fanny sank into a chair and wrapped her arms around her waist. Liz stood and placed a hand on her daughter's shoulder. "Try not to worry, Fan. Everything will work out. I'll get your father to keep a close eye on the weather glass. The temperatures will surely drop soon."

Fanny jumped to her feet. "I need to go see the weather glass."

Before anyone could comment she was out the door and heading up the hill in her slippers.

Fanny burst into her parents' house with her mother not far behind and headed for the shelf that held the weather glass.

"Good morning, Fan. How is Archie this morning?" her father, Archie's namesake, asked.

"He is getting worse." Fanny didn't turn around.

"He is getting worse," repeated Mildred coming out of the pantry with floury hands.

"I need to know what the weather glass is saying," said Fanny, ignoring her daughter.

"I brought up yer boots, Fan," said Liz from the doorway.

"What the big rush to see the weather glass?" Arch asked his daughter, only now noticing that she was still in her slippers.

"The ice needs to freeze to get Archie to St. Mary's," Fanny replied curtly, staring at the glass.

"Is he that bad, Ma?" asked Mildred, still standing there with her hands dripping with dough and flour.

"He don't need to go to the Mission," Liz replied as she hung her shawl on a nail.

"There were lots of fevers before the Mission ever came," said Arch.

"And lots died from fevers too," snapped Fanny.

"He won't die, will he Ma?" Mildred's eyes were full of tears.

"No!" Liz firmly stated. "No Fan, sit down and I will get you a cup of tea and Mildred, go finish making the bread," Liz ordered.

Mildred did as she was told but Fan stayed rooted to her spot in front of the glass. "Dad, can you please come read this for me," she croaked, her voice uneven.

Arch sighed and rose from his chair to go stand next to his eldest daughter. This wasn't the first time he had seen her upset about one of her children.

"Let's see. The water is cloudy and no snowflakes so it's gonna be mild."

"No frost?" Fanny looked at him wild eyed.

"Nope. See here at the bottom," Arch pointed to the bottom of the liquid. "If there was gonna be frost there would be snowflakes down there."

Fanny let out a moan and sank into one of her mother's kitchen chairs.

Liz brought tea and placed it in front of her. "Fan, kids recovered from fevers long before the Mission came."

"Damn Mission is useless anyway. Them and the goddamned Rangers," Arch spat. "We wouldn't be up here in this god forsaken bay if it wasn't for that lot."

"We had to come up here for the work," said Mildred, coming out of the pantry while wiping her hands clean on a towel.

"No one would need any measly work if the greedy merchants would pay a fair price for fish and not charge an arm and a leg for supplies. Greedy brainless bums," he muttered under his breath.

"Arch, stop it. Nothing we can do about it now. Now we have to concentrate on getting little Archie well again."

Arch gave one last 'hmmmppptttt' and picked up a split to make shavings. Liz glared at him and then turned softly to her daughter. "Drink your tea to give you some strength for the days ahead."

Tears welled up in Fanny's eyes as she obediently sipped her tea.

The fever continued for the next three days. Archie ate very little and Fanny grew more and more worried. She prayed for the fever to end and for his little body to heal, but she equally prayed for the ice to freeze hard enough in the bay for him to be taken to the hospital.

CHAPTER 4: FANNY
TOOTH COVE, CHRISTMAS EVE 1946

By Christmas Eve, Fanny was barely functioning. She spent her days in bed with Archie and wouldn't eat unless he ate. Ern had gotten off early from the mill but instead of sprinting home like the other men, he trudged home not knowing what awaited him there. Christmas usually brought Fanny so much joy, but she was too worried to enjoy anything.

The youngsters were excited, but there was a heavy cloud over the family. As in most homes, the mother is the centre of the home and creates a warm atmosphere that makes Christmas so wonderful. Being away from a proper church or a larger community made the home even more important. Normally, Fanny would be baking cookies and sewing last minute stockings and dolls clothes, but this year she did only what was necessary. It was like she could see her son dwindling away and that damn ice outside the cove refused to freeze.

That afternoon, Fanny jumped from the bed when she heard her father's dogs go by the house. Her brothers, Charl and Tim, took the dogs to the mouth of the cove every day and tested the ice.

She was on the bridge in her slippers and shawl when they returned.

"The dogs wouldn't go on it, maid," declared Tim. "Lady just stood dumbly, at the edge of the frozen cove ice and wouldn't go any further." Fanny glared at the lead dog, and watched as it bowed its head, like she was ashamed.

"We even threw some seal out on the new ice and the bitch still wouldn't go get it," Charl added.

Fanny didn't even respond. She shuffled back inside the house.

After everyone went to bed, Ern dragged in a small tree while Fanny dug out the sparse decorations she had sewn over the years. She hung all their socks on the hooks beside the tree. Each one had a name lovingly stitched across the top.

Ern placed his hands on his hips and admired the tree while Fanny put some candy and small toys she had bought in Battle Harbour in each of the socks.

"I can't wait to see their little faces in the morning," he beamed.

Fanny didn't respond. Ern put an arm around her shoulder. "Let's have a good night's sleep. Gonna be a busy day tomorrow."

She responded by shrugging away and heading for the children's room to crawl into bed with Archie.

CHAPTER 5: FANNY
TOOTH COVE, CHRISTMAS 1946

Roy was the first one awake and woke up the rest of the youngsters just as daylight was breaking through the window. Ern had already lit the fire and cooked the rolled oats, allowing Fanny to rest.

Ern made sure they had their breakfast finished before he allowed them to have their stockings. Neither Fanny nor Archie came out of the room. Ern checked on them, but Archie was very still and Fanny was just resting on her arm watching him.

"Are you coming out?" he asked. Her response was to shake Archie a little to wake him.

He seemed awake but he didn't seem to want to move. He just shook his head and snuggled back down. Ern strode into the room, reached in over Fanny and scooped him up. Fanny sucked in a breath in surprise but didn't say anything. She just rose and followed Ern as he marched into the main area and sat with Archie on the daybed, a thick blanket wrapped around him.

"Now, do ya Christmas stuff." It was an order from Ern.

When everyone recovered from the shock of Ern's stern demand, Archie watched, just barely awake, from Ern's arms as his siblings emptied their stockings.

They excitedly displayed their gifts. Dorothy had a small doll, Cack had some jacks, John had a baseball, Roy had some new trout hooks, and Rita had a new book.

John stood up and retrieved Archie's sock from the wall and brought it to him.

"Archie, do you want to see what you got?" he asked.

Archie just stared, too exhausted to respond. John reached into the sock and pulled out the new netting needle that Archie had admired in the Battle Harbour store a few short months ago. He smiled a tiny smile before closing his eyes and laying back against his father.

"You don't even want one of your candy Archie?" John asked as he pulled out a green rubber candy, Archie's favourite. He opened his eyes again, parted his lips, and John shoved the candy inside. Archie was too weak to chew so Ern kept him upright until the candy dissolved.

Fanny stood by the stove with her arms folded, watching everyone. She loved them all so much and wanted so badly to be able to share in their excitement but couldn't.

"I hope that candy gives him enough energy to eat a bit of dinner and have some Christmas cake," she said quietly.

Dinner time, Ern placed the porcupine on the table along with a few vegetables the men at the mill had given him for his family at Christmas. Fanny wasn't hungry but tried to not spoil the dinner by not eating so she nibbled on some of the meat and some carrots. It was delicious but she insisted to the family that she wasn't hungry. She tried to get Archie to eat something, but he wouldn't and turned his head away.

"I bet you won't turn your head away when I get the cake out." She gave a tiny laugh and he smiled a tiny smile for her.

Before everyone was even done with the meal, Fanny was on her knees at the cupboard digging out the cake she had carefully stored at the bottom rear where it stayed nice and cool. She placed it on the counter, unwrapped the paper and cheesecloth and sliced it up. She knew Archie thought it smelled heavenly because he closed his eyes and sucked a deep gulp of air through his nose. It was one of the smells that everyone associated with the Christmas season and every woman had their own way of making it.

Ern walked over to help her. "My, Fan, you really outdid yourself. That looks like the best cake you ever made." She beamed up at him and proceeded to slice off a piece for each family member. Ern helped herby carefully wrapping the rest of the cake to be served to visitors who would drop by during the next few days. Life was so busy all year round so it was tradition that each home be visited by one another during Christmas to establish the comradery and fellowship of the community.

Fanny placed a piece of cake in front of everyone. "Don't anyone touch it until Archie has his first. He wanted some really bad the day I made it and I know this would bring his appetite back."

Gently pulling him to a seated position on the daybed, Fanny said softly, "Look Archie, you finally get to have some Christmas cake."

She waved it under his nose. He opened his eyes and tried to smile. She could see he wanted it so badly but didn't have the strength to open his little mouth, let alone swallow it. She pressed it a little harder against his lips and that's when he started to retch. Mostly dry heaves but she quickly took him into the bedroom before the scene spoiled the enjoyment of the cake for the rest of the family.

Fanny was devastated. She just needed to be alone. Holding Archie, she silently cursed the day she had made the cake and had refused to give him some. She regretted it to her core, and feared, as she held his tiny body in her arms, that it would remain with her until her dying day.

The rest of the week passed slowly. Archie's fever would go up and down. In the heights of delirium, he would thrash around the bed, talking all sorts of foolishness. His knee was not healing, the redness around the infection site just kept growing larger and larger, and now he remained in the foetal position at all times. It was useless to try to get pyjama pants on him so Fanny put one of Rita's old night dresses on him. Normally he would have been disgusted with wearing a nightie but he was too sick to even care. Because he hadn't eaten, there were no bowel movements and urination was also rare. What little liquids they could get into him, he was sweating out. Fanny stayed with him in his bed every night, though she hardly slept.

Ern commented that he was just as worried about Fanny as he was about Archie. "You are both getting so thin and Fan, you both have the darkest eye circles I had ever seen on two people."

During the days over Christmas week, people from the cove dropped by with food and stayed for a visit. Everyone was worried. Losten and May dropped by with their mother and May expressed how sorry she was that this had happened. Her mom said that May blamed herself for not noticing the nail. The family assured them that they need not blame themselves, this was just an unfortunate accident and the ice would be forming soon and they could get to St. Mary's.

Ern had returned back to the mill the day after Christmas, so Liz, along with Mildred and Rita, cared for us all. Fanny was so weak from not eating or sleeping that she rarely got out of bed.

By New Years Eve, Ern's worry was turning to anger and he told Fanny that he insisted she return to her own bed.

Her tried to explain his concern for her. "Archie seems to be getting no better or no worse, and you can't continue to make yourself sick or you will also need to be taken to St. Mary's when the ice forms," he said.

Rita assured her mother that her and Roy would snuggle Archie during the night and keep him warm. Reluctantly, Fanny returned to her bed. She did sleep that night but as soon as her eyes opened the next morning, she was up and into their room to check on Archie.

The next day was New Year's Day and Ern had a day off from the mill. The sun was shining and it felt like a new day even though Archie was still deathly ill. Ern decided to go hunting and Fanny, having gotten a bit of rest, had made breakfast. Mildred visited and was able to coax Fanny to leave the house and visit her own mother next door for tea.

Fanny perked up a bit, especially when Arch announced that the glass was going down. The mercury that had been stable for the past week or so had dropped a few decimals in the past 24 hours. Fanny went home very optimistic and told everyone about it. Even a little change was hopeful. But as the day wore on the air did not seem to be getting any colder, and Archie seemed to be getting worse.

"Maybe it would happen overnight," Fanny hoped.

CHAPTER 6: ERN
TOOTH COVE, JANUARY 1947

Ern woke in the middle of the night and noticed that Fanny was not beside him.

"Darn that woman," he muttered, and went to the children's room with the intention of marching her back to her own bed. She wasn't there. Archie was fitfully sleeping between his siblings. Ern tried not to panic, but if she wasn't in the house, where was she?

Opening the door, he felt a cooler blast of air than yesterday but then, it always cools during the night he reasoned. Frost had gathered on the small bridge and the path was showing her footsteps leading to the cove. Now he panicked as he realized where she had gone.

Grabbing his coat and pulling on his boots he headed out the door and down to the cove. He grabbed the lantern but didn't bother to pull on pants on over his long johns.

The ice in the cove was fairly solid and had been for a while, but outside the cove was the problem. The tides of the bay and the steep hills along the coast did not allow ice to form; not even enough to trim the shoreline. He was halfway out the cove before he spotted her, on the newly formed ice just outside the mouth of the cove. He knew it wasn't very firm yet because there had only been about an inch there on New Years Eve when Charl and Tim had checked it last.

But there she was, that stupid woman, standing on the new glassy ice, under the shiny moon. He cursed under his breath. Her arms were held out as if to balance herself and she was softly walking further out, her hair flowing freely around her shoulders. In any other scenario she would have been an angelic vision, the way that the soft rays of the moon were illuminating her. But tonight, he was beyond scared. He was afraid to scream and startle her. Afraid to turn back to even grab a rope.

He had to keep moving. He had to get to her.

When he got to the edge of the older ice, he stopped and whispered her name as loud as he dared. She heard him and stopped, but as she turned to look at him, he heard the sickening crack as the ice gave way beneath her feet. With great restraint he kept himself bolted to the spot as he couldn't risk them both being in the water.

She let out a little scream and fell flat on the ice as it started to splinter in all directions.

"Stay flat," he ordered. "Spread your arms and try to inch towards me."

Silently, Fanny followed his command. Ern took off his coat, and, holding on to one of the arms, swung it out onto the ice. He spread himself out on the new ice and creeped as far as he dared until Fanny was able to reach the jacket.

Within a few minutes he had her pulled onto the older ice and had ushered her to land. He sat her down on a rock that was protruding through the sparse snowfall.

"What the hell were you thinking?" he scolded her as he wrapped the jacket around her shoulders and held her tight.

Through her sobs she sputtered, "Dad said the glass had gone down and I thought for sure the ice would be hard enough by now." She gulped for breath and continued. "I can't take it anymore Ern, I can't stand watching him pine away. He is going to die, I know it, just like Bella," she sobbed louder.

Ern didn't know what to say. He was hurting too, and it killed him to see Fan suffering so much.

"Come on, let's get you back to the house and warmed up," he said as he picked her up and carried her back. She had been only ninety pounds when they were married and though she had put on weight with each child, tonight she felt so tiny and fragile. He had to do something soon. Ern lit the fire as soon as he got back to the house. They had made tea and snuggled on the daybed for the remainder of the night.

When the children got up, Ern told Rita to be in charge until Liz and Mildred were able to come help out because Fanny was feeling sick. Fanny had crawled in bed beside Archie as soon as Cack was up from the spot next to him.

Ern never told a soul what had happened that night and him and Fanny never spoke of it again, but the incident had really shaken him. He felt a new appreciation of how deeply Fanny loved the children and he vowed to pay more attention to her needs as a mother. One of the first things he had cherished about her was the relationship she had with her younger siblings. He always knew what a wonderful mother she would be to his children. However, with all the hardships of the fishery and the mill and just trying to survive, he had lost track of the important things in life and had taken his wife for granted. He decided then that he would make sure they stayed close as a couple and that he would take care of her.

At the mill that day there was talk of a crispness in the air that hopefully signified frost coming. Everyone had heard about how sick Archie was and many prayers were being said for frosty weather. Ern hoped they were right. By the time he left the mill at six, it was dark and drastically colder than the past few weeks.

CHAPTER 7: FANNY
TOOTH COVE, JANUARY 1947

When Ern arrived home, the house was buzzing with activity. Fanny greeted him excitedly with the news that her father's weather glass was predicting a cold night and cold for the next few days as well. Fanny busied herself by making a makeshift mattress and warm bed for Archie to go in the komatik. She wanted it to be extra soft because Archie felt so boney that she was concerned his bones would pierce his skin if he had to rest on a hard surface. A normal trip down the Bay to St. Mary's would take three hours or more, and right now having to trim the shoreline, the trip could take the better part of a full day. For a sick boy, this would be a long journey.

As Ern watched her, he said, "Fan, I'm glad to see you occupied. I've been worried about how sullen ya been over the last weeks."

Liz was in the kitchen and had made a huge pot of soup. The children were playing softly so as to not disturb Archie who was fitfully resting on the daybed. Charl and Tim had checked the ice just before dark and it seemed to be getting thicker as the temperatures dropped.

That night was bitterly cold. The fire had only been out for a few hours when Ern had to get up and light it again and stay up to watch it. Some nights they would suffer through the cold so everyone could sleep, but tonight he wanted to make sure Archie didn't get any sicker before he could get him to the hospital.

When daylight came, the single paned windows were completely glazed over with frost. The children, excited to look out, held their thumbs on the frosty pane until the warmth melted tiny holes to peep out of. They were excited that the time was coming to allow Archie to be taken to the hospital. The tension in the little house over the past few weeks had taken a toll on everyone.

Charl came in just as Fanny was dishing up the porridge. "I just took Lady to the new ice and she walked on it. We went all the way around the point and I chopped as I went. At least 3 to 4 inches has made overnight so there is 5-6 inches of ice now."

Charl was grinning from ear to ear. Fanny dropped the porridge ladle and covered her mouth. Tears sprang to her eyes and the children gave a collective cheer.

"Alright," said Ern, "Let's go." He finished eating and took the mattress out to prepare the komatik. Bob was already harnessing up the dogs. The family had three dogs, but Bill Howell had brought down two of his strongest dogs to help on the journey. As soon as they finished harnessing them, they attached the dogs to the komatik. Lady was in the lead. She wasn't the strongest or the fastest but she was reliable with good instincts and leadership. While she stood stoic and determined, the other dogs were pouncing and excited to get going. Bill had to yell and whip them a few times to settle them down.

Fanny had packed a small lunch for them of molasses bread, dried fish, and canned beans. She snuggled Archie in as many warm blankets as the household could spare. Ern carefully carried him to the komatik and settled him away with a piece of canvas over the top of him to break the wind. Fanny gave Archie a gentle kiss and went to kneel by Lady.

"You take good care of my boy," she told the dog. Lady bowed her head as if in acknowledgement.

"Let's move," ordered Ern, as he stepped on the back of the komatik with Charl. Bob took the reins and sat on the front. Fanny grabbed Ern and gave him one last kiss before the dogs bolted down the hill. She chased them until they were out of sight around the point, her coat billowing in the cold morning air.

Fanny had been praying for this moment for weeks, but now that they were gone, she found herself a whole new set of worries. She wondered if they would make it there safely, if Archie would survive the trip, and when he got there, would the hospital be able to make him well.

CHAPTER 8: ERN
DOWN THE BAY, JANUARY 1947

The wind was bitter as the dogs raced down the bay. We wore canvas cossacks to stop the wind from penetrating to our skin. The dogs, led by Lady, expertly trimmed the shoreline. Only in a few small coves did the dogs dare to go straight across. Bob let them continue, knowing they would stop when they needed a break. Their first stop was Juniper Point. Snow had crusted the rocks while chunks of ice formed into huge boulders from the rising and falling of the tidey waters here. Even in the dead of winter, no one dared to go around the point. It was said that if you were to throw a rock off the point, there would never be any ice there under the blown snow to hold it up. It would sink to the bottom. They would avoid the brackish and unpredictable ice at the point.

Bob stamped a thin layer of ice off the small brook there so the dogs could get a proper drink while Ern checked on Archie. He was sleeping but his breath was laboured. The men decided to move on.

Thy continued on and didn't stop again until the dogs refused to cross Bruce Cove. The bay was frozen over and it seemed like the same thickness of ice was everywhere, but they trusted the dogs and trimmed the cove. Going around Twelve O'clock Head was also not going to happen today. The steep shoreline made it tricky before full freeze up. A trail had been cut across the neck many years ago, but it was rough and narrow and only used when absolutely necessary. Today it was necessary.

By the time they made it through the trail it was noon, but instead of the air being warmed by a midday sun, it was getting overcast, signalling that unsavoury weather may be approaching. Ern decided not to stop and eat until they arrived in Hatters Cove. Most of the necks would have to be crossed as ice around the longer points was still not passable.

They crossed the neck between Twelve O'clock Harbour and Timothy's Creek and proceeded towards the trail going over the Lookout. This was a well traversed trail in the wintertime as Hatters Cove Point was a common route.

Today, however, it wasn't going to be an easy trail. There was still not enough snow to easily ride the komatik over so the dogs had to be untied, walked up the hill, and tied on while the komatik was carried. In some spots, trees and brush had to be removed. It was a tedious process but after a couple of hours they were over the Lookout and into Hatters Cove.

Twenty years ago, Hatters Cove had been a thriving winter settlement. Between 250 and 300 people had resided there; they even had a hospital. However, when the hospital was built at St. Mary's in 1930, people slowly migrated there and now there were just a few abandoned shacks left here that served as wood cutting shacks. They went into one and lit a fire, made a cup of tea, and had lunch. It was customary that some wood was always left in a shack in case some poor souls needed a quick shelter and fire. While Ern lit the fire and boiled the kettle, Bob collected some replacement wood. They brought Archie in and laid him on a bare wooden bunk while they ate. He woke for a moment and asked if we were at the hospital yet then dropped right back into his slumber.

"Maybe we should put up here for the night," said Charl from the doorway. At the sound of his voice, Archie stirred slightly.

"No," Ern firmly replied.

"I can see snow in the sky from the eastern," said Bob entering the cabin. "Maybe we should wait it out."

"No!" Ern shouted as he stood and faced the men. Neither of them spoke.

"What the hell is wrong with you two? We are going to be at St. Mary's tonight. Don't either of you care about what we promised your sister when we left?"

"Fan would care about us not all not getting caught out and dying in a snowstorm," stated Charl.

Looking fiercely into Charl's eyes, Ern grabbed him by the collar and pushed him up against the wall of the cabin. "No one is going to die. Do you understand?" Charl nodded and Ern released him.

After a moment's pause, Bob said, "Well, if we are going on, let's get a move on."

They had to trim in Hatters Cove as far as the island in the middle of the bay. It was the deepest cove in the bay and froze up in sections, so the outer area of the cove was still not crossable. False Cove head was also tricky, so they stayed close to the shore. The rest of the journey was fairly sheltered and we crossed two more short necks before they reached Daddy Island Steady.

By this time, it was dusk and the snow was beginning to fall. Before they reached Northeast Bottom in St. Mary's River, the wind was picking up and there was poor visibility. They got stuck at one point, and the bottom had come off Ern's boot. Bob muttered as he lashed the bottom back onto the boot with some rope.

At Northeast Bottom, they turned right and continued the short distance to the hospital. While Bob secured the dogs among the trees for the night, Ern carefully lifted his son out of the komatik and followed Charl up the steps to the long narrow porch of St. Mary's Hospital.

CHAPTER 9: NURSE JUPP
ST. MARY'S HOSPITAL, JANUARY 1947

Nurse Dorothy M. Jupp had been on the coast of Labrador for nearly nine years and Nurse in Charge at St. Mary's for four of those. It was lonely and confusing at times as she often found herself in a position of authority and a position of inferiority. She was respected by the locals as a very competent nurse, but when it came to being in charge of things that could better aid the advancement of health, like good food and solid spiritual upbringing, she was in a very inferior position inside the Grenfell Mission.

The locals kept mostly to themselves, which was fine with her. She had endured criticisms from her Grenfell Mission superiors about not visiting the locals enough and then later told she was visiting too much. It seemed there was no pleasing the Mission, but she did enjoy being around the locals and they respected her and the work she did. She gained some notoriety during the fire of 1945 in which she single-handedly evacuated the hospital and saved ten patients. The hospital had been miraculously saved but the doctors' cottage was lost and hadn't been replaced.

The hospital itself was an adequate size to house staff and patients. It consisted of a basement that held the handyman tools and supplies, plus laundry and sterilisation facilities. A main floor that held the kitchen and dining area, the clinical room, the waiting area, and the staff living room. Nurse Jupp's room and private bath were also on this floor, so she would be near the clinical room for emergencies. The second floor consisted of the patient wards and storage area, while the third floor held staff accommodations. There were always two to four girls on staff as aides, plus a cook and handyman assistant who occupied the third floor. The main handyman and groundskeeper lived in the local com-

Nurse Dorothy M. Jupp in a garden. From PANL A 116-31.

munity, so he resided with his family and didn't stay on the premises at night.

Nurse Jupp was descending the second-floor stairs when she heard the rapping on the door. As the door to the outside waiting area was almost directly across from the foot of the stairs, she was able to get to it quickly. She opened it to find a young lad in an icy, snow-covered cossack. He motioned behind him to a man about her own age who was bent over a bundle of blankets, desperately peeling back the flannel layers to uncover a young boy.

Nurse Jupp was familiar with folks simply showing up in emergencies, so this was not daunting in the least. What was daunting was that a child was involved this time. She took a deep breath and went into nurse mode.

"Good evening, I am Nurse Jupp," She introduced herself, then paused to touch the arm of the distraught gentleman. He had removed his outer snowy clothes and was now lifting the young boy into his arms.

"Archie is really sick," was all he could muster.

"Bring him to the dispensary right away," she ordered gently.

The man followed her through to the inside sitting area and they both proceeded to the next door on the left. Most locals had been in this station for one thing or another and knew exactly where the dispensary was located.

As the man laid the boy on the table, the little lad opened his eyes and asked his father if they were there yet.

"Yes Archie, we made it," he replied.

"Tell me what happened," Nurse Jupp demanded.

While Ern introduced himself and his son and recounted the events of the past two weeks, Nurse Jupp busied herself exposing the effected knee. She could tell from how the boy was curled in on himself and his presentation that he was indeed suffering from rheumatic fever.

"It's obvious your mom has been taking very good care of you," she remarked to Archie as she removed the remarkably clean bandages. She could tell the boy was in distress and needed to calm him. When the last bandage was removed, she could see that the situation was dire. The infection was so advanced she wondered how the boy had survived this long.

"Is he keeping down any liquids?" she calmly asked Ern.

"I gave him some sugar tea when we stopped in Hatters Cove, but I don't think he kept it down," answered Ern.

"It's best that I inject him with penicillin then," she replied. "At least that will work faster."

She prepared the needle and asked Ern to hold Archie still for the injection. The needle was large but all the boy was strong enough to muster was one tiny yelp.

When she was done, she asked Ern to stay with him for a few moments while she went to make arrangements for them. She returned a short while later with one of the young nursing aides and the assistant handyman. The storm was beginning to rage outside so she would not be sending the men back out in it tonight to look for shelter. She instructed the young Aide to fix them some of the leftover supper and the handyman to prepare a room for them in the basement with the mattresses they had down there in storage.

Ern didn't want to leave his son's side, but Nurse Jupp assured him that Archie would be fine.

"Only time will tell if the antibiotics will work, but for right now there is nothing else you can do. I will give him a sponge bath and attend to the knee. This will be a long night. I need you to get your rest so you can relieve me at midnight. Can you do that Mr. Rumbolt?" The firm sternness of her voice was more like telling than asking. Ern simply nodded his head.

By the time Ern the men had finished eating and had settled in, Nurse Jupp had Archie all cleaned up and settled down. He was very weak, and she told them she hoped he would sleep through the night while the antibiotics did their job. Ern had wanted to sit with him, but he also knew he needed his sleep to relieve her in a few hours. Two of the staff girls were taking shifts with them so no one had to sit up alone.

Archie slept fitfully while the storm raged outside. It always seemed that situations like this happened right in the midst of violent weather that caused even more anxiety. Nurse Jupp reminded Archie that even if the weather was perfect outside, there was absolutely nothing anyone could do. He was now at the mercy of penicillin, something he would have not had access to even a year ago.

Nurse Jupp went for Ern at twelve am, but it seemed like he hadn't slept at all and was just waiting for her to come get him. She wasn't gone long before the young Aide sitting with Ern and Archie rapped on her door to come quick. She rushed into the room to see Ern trying to hold Archie's shoulders while he thrashed around the bed.

Fever, she thought.

The nurse helped Ern hold him down while the young aide got some cool wet towels.

He wasn't due for more medication for another few hours, but Nurse Jupp made the decision to give me more right away. The situation wasn't looking good, and she sent the aide to get his uncles.

"I don't want you to be alone," she said to Ern. "Raging infections can lay dormant for days and then rear its ugly head just when you think it's over. The trip down the bay to the hospital to save his life may have awakened the bacteria before the penicillin could obliterate it."

Charl and Bob entered the room looking sullen. Archie continued to thrash on the bed. He screamed out to John. He screamed out to Roy. He screamed out for Ma. Nothing would calm him. Finally, his little body weakened, and he passed out.

Archie didn't stir as Nurse Jupp warmed the stethoscope with her breath and placed it on his back. She listened and nodded her head to Ern. Ern's rigid body slumped with relief, and she watched silent tears slide down his cheeks.

She softly explained to Ern and Archie's uncles that he was still not out of danger. "His breathing and his heart rate are very shallow. The next few hours will be critical."

Nurse Jupp put some extra chairs in the dispensary and went to make tea. The rest of the night was uneventful, but the men stayed attuned to every moan and small cough.

The next morning, Nurse Jupp determined that Archie was stable enough to be moved upstairs to a ward. He was put in the smaller, two bed ward. There was a lady in the other small ward waiting to have her baby and there were four men in the larger ward recovering from tuberculosis.

Tuberculosis had been more rampant on the north coast of Labrador than in this area. The patients still at St. Mary's had been sent there from

St. Anthony before freeze up to rest for a few months before continuing on to the north coast. Even when all signs of the disease were gone, patients were required to have up to a year of rest before returning to normal activity.

Archie was still not out of the life-threatening danger zone. His fever was still high and he was very weak, but he needed to be moved from the dispensary as this room was for consultations only and it needed to be kept sterile to prevent the spread of disease. His twelve-hour stay there meant that an Aide would spend the next three hours sterilising the room again to be ready for the next patient.

Nurse Jupp explained to Ern that he and Archie's uncles could stay if they wanted until Archie was out of danger. She went on to explain that normally visitors were discouraged from prolonged stays because it impeded the staff from doing their work and the patient from getting proper rest to ensure a full recovery.

After the men retreated to the basement to rest,, Nurse Jupp left the aides in charge of Archie and said she would try to get some rest. It seemed an impossible task as her thoughts raced. She could not get the boy out of her mind. Such a cared for little lad and loved so much. She wondered what it must feel like to be loved like that. Having grown up in a convent, she never had that experience. Is that why she came to a foreign land, to forget that awful time? Or did she simply come to be of assistance to people who really needed it? And why did people not seek her as a friend? What aura about her was telling people she was too independent to need friends? Just one friend would surely alleviate the loneliness in her heart. She lay there for a few hours just pondering while sleep would not come.

She prayed the child would never have to experience what she was living through.

CHAPTER 10: ERN
ST. MARY'S RIVER, JANUARY 1947

The storm had also settled down that morning and Ern and Fanny's brothers had left to check on the dogs and to visit relatives that resided in the harbour. Ern had returned promptly after dinner to check on his boy. Archie was improving a bit but still hadn't eaten. Nurse Jupp would not be content in his road to recovery until he had consumed some food, so Ern decided to stay another night. The weather was still not totally favourable for traversing the unknown ice conditions of the bay and he hoped Fanny wouldn't be worrying too much.

He hoped his son would have a better rest tonight than the night before. He hoped he never had to witness either of his children experience the seizures that he had watched Archie go through. The deafening screams and then the eerie silence. He didn't know what was worse, hearing the suffering or thinking he had witnessed his son's death. He had wanted to scream himself as so many thoughts flew through his mind. The worst being how he would ever tell Fan.

Ern sat with Archie throughout that day. The aides came and went, checking his temperature and telling Ern that he was welcome to go get some tea and cake. He refused; he didn't want to leave Archie's side until he could see some improvement. At exactly four in the evening, Nurse Jupp came to the ward. She told Ern that Archie's temperature had dropped, and she was going to see if he would take his four o'clock dose of penicillin by mouth. She gently shook Archie who was still on his side in the fetal position.

"Archie, it's time for your medicine, would you try to swallow it for me, or would you like another needle?"

"No more needles," he managed to reply.

Ern and the nurse helped him into a sitting position while she carefully spooned two tablespoons of the pink liquid into his mouth.

"Keep holding him for a few more moments please," she directed to Ern. To Archie she asked, "Would you like some water?"

He shook his head no so they eased him back to a lying position on his opposite side.

"Let him rest now. The cook will have supper prepared by five o'clock, would you like some?" the nurse asked Ern.

"I think I will go back up the harbour to see how Bob and Charl are doing," Ern replied. "Then I will come back to see him for a while later."

"Why don't you rest a while and come back at midnight, if you insist on staying. We can do shifts again tonight. I am hoping after tonight he will be much better," Nurse Jupp suggested.

Ern nodded. He was a man who always felt so in control, but this situation had humbled and weakened him. He hated that feeling. He worried what would happen if Archie got sicker and he wasn't here, or what if Archie got better and got scared among strangers?

"Mr. Rumbolt, I know you are worried, but everything is in God's hands now and you need your rest. A few more hours and we will know more. Until then, please go rest and pray. If anything changes for the worse, I will send for you." Nurse Jupp was comforting, but firm.

He nodded his head and gave Archie a soft kiss on the forehead before he left.

When he returned at midnight, Nurse Jupp was pleased to report that Archie was feeling much better and at ten o'clock, he drank some juice and ate a cracker.

Ern smiled a huge toothy grin. "I only wish Fan was here to hear it with me. I can't wait to get back to the cove to tell her."

Ern did sit up with him throughout the rest of the night and thanked his lucky stars that everything worked out. Nurse Jupp came at four in the morning and administered another dose of penicillin. Archie was very sleepy and swallowed it then promptly went back to sleep.

Ern was still sitting there when Archie woke at six and said, "Shouldn't you be gone to the mill?"

Ern gave him the biggest smile ever and assured him that the mill would still be there when he got back to the cove.

"Am I going home too?"

"No son, you must stay here and get well. It won't be long and you will be back in the cove, randying with the others."

"Maybe I will stick to playing ball, it's less dangerous."

Ern laughed, "You just need to watch for nails, and I will pay more attention too."

Suddenly Ern's smile vanished. "This will not happen again," he said as he looked down at his hands, holding back tears.

"Don't be sad Dad, I will get all better. You go home and take care of Ma. She will be worried." Archie's speech was slow and laboured.

"I will. She is going to be so happy that you are getting better. I want you to listen to the nurse, eat your meals, take your medicine and do what she says, ok?"

Archie nodded and drifted back to sleep. Ern went downstairs to get a cup of tea.

Upon his return, Archie was awake again so Ern told him how nice Jack Howell had been.

"Who is Jack?" Archie asked.

"He is the assistant maintenance man. The main maintenance man comes during the day and Jack stays during the nights in case the nurse or aides need anything, and he lights the fires in the morning."

"This is a big place," Archie said softly.

"It is," replied Ern. "There are many good people here that will take good care of you."

Archie remained quiet and Ern continued, "Did you know your mom was here when little Dorothy was born?"

Archie's eyes opened wide. "For how long?" he asked.

"Two weeks, I think. I remember Fan telling me she felt very safe and content here."

Archie smiled, "I wonder if she slept in this bed?"

Ern laughed, "I don't know but she must have admired the nurse because your sister was named after her."

"Nurse Jupp's name is Dorothy?" Archie said weakly; he was drifting off to sleep again.

Ern bent to kiss him on the forehead and told him he was gone to get Uncle Charl and Uncle Bob and head back up the bay. He watched Archie twist his mouth into a tiny smile and say, "Cuddle into me back, Ma."

CHAPTER 11: ARCHIE
ST. MARY'S HOSPITAL, WINTER 1947

Nurse Jupp woke me up at ten in the morning to take another dose of penicillin. I felt great. Not quite well enough to go outside playing, but I certainly felt like I could get up out of bed. It was the best I had felt in a long time, and now I was hungry.

"I want you to try and eat today," she announced.

"Yes," I replied.

She wasn't out the door very long when a young Aide came in with a small bowl of oatmeal and a glass of milk. It looked heavenly. She propped up the head of my bed but I was still in the foetal position and couldn't move my legs.

"Oh my," she said. "How can I do this?"

She buzzed for the nurse who was there almost instantly.

They moved me onto my back but my knees were still bent. Nurse Jupp had hoped that the frequent bandage changes would have relaxed the knee, but it hadn't, and my good leg was almost as bad. Both legs were fairly rigid from fever and muscle stiffness. They ended up propping pillows on either side of my legs and tucked the sheets tightly around my body to keep the legs in place while I was on my back and propped into a sitting position.

This process was painful and uncomfortable and by the time they were done, I wasn't hungry anymore, but I did manage a few spoonfuls which pleased the nurse.

The run between St. Mary's and Battle Harbour had finally frozen enough to get a message to the telegraph office to ask the doctor in Cartwright his opinion. The next day Nurse Jupp received a reply back. It was a brief message that simply said to continue with the penicillin, regular bandages, and lots of fluid and rest. She told me the doctor hoped

St. Mary's River Hospital. PANL IGA 3-30.

to be there in a few weeks.

Nurse Jupp was kind to me, but I overheard an outburst that caused me to remember what Dad had told me about heeding the nurse. One of the things I hated here was using the bedpan. The Aides would be very gentle, but it was an embarrassing occurrence that I had never had to consider before when Ma or sister Rita would help me. Every detail of this process carved itself into my head. As soon as I was all done on the pan, they would place a cloth over it and take it to the utility room to be emptied into the toilet and then cleaned with a disinfectant solution. The whole hospital and the people in it smelled like that cleaner. It was a clean smell, but certainly not the smells we had at home with Ma's cooking smells and Dad's spruce smell from working at the mill.

One of the Aids had just left my room with my full bedpan and I noticed she hadn't placed a cloth over it. I didn't pay much heed until I heard Nurse Jupp holler, "Miss Poole, may I speak with you in the utility room." It was an order, not a question.

Since the utility room was between my ward and the big ward, I could hear the conversation. When the door slammed to the utility room, Nurse Jupp continued in a menacing voice, "Do I have to remind you of proper cleaning protocol?"

"No Nurse Jupp," stammered the Aide.

"So, you are aware of your mistake?"

"Yes, Nurse Jupp, and I am terribly sorry."

"As you should be. Parading around the hospital wards with uncovered bedpans," the nurse stated, disgusted. "Not only is that a very undignified embarrassment for the patient, but a fine way to spread germs and bacteria throughout the hospital. Are you aware that airborne bacteria can cause sickness in a healthy patient?"

"Yes, Nurse Jupp," the Aide whispered.

"To ensure this does not occur in future, you will forgo your dinner break and clean this hallway from top to bottom," the nurse barked.

I didn't hear the Aide's reply, but I did hear Nurse Jupp quickly exit the utility room. I covered my head with my blanket, nervous that I might be in trouble next though I wasn't sure why, and kept my head covered until I heard Nurse Jupp descend the stairs.

For the next few weeks, I had a rigid schedule of timely medicine and bandage changes. I was fed regular meals and snacks and had regular sponge baths. The Aids flipped me from one side to the other so I wouldn't get bed sores until finally the day came when I had the strength to use my arms and move around myself.

This new mobility felt so wonderful. It was almost like I had forgotten that just one short month ago I was running and playing and now I was happy just to move myself around the bed. I was able to feed myself and lift myself onto the bedpan, but my darn legs would not straighten. So, I would sit on the edge of the bed every day until finally I got my legs at a 45-degree angle. At least now I could sit in a chair at a table if I wanted, but only for short periods because my knee still hurt and my hips ached. There was a word my Ma used to say for this harsh type of pain. "Doggish," she'd say. "God damned doggish." I smiled at the memory of it and imagined saying it to Nurse Jupp. I wonder if she would laugh or be angry. I decided I wouldn't chance the anger Sometimes she looked so stern and I had to remember what Dad told me about behaving myself.

"Good morning, Archie," came a voice from the doorway.

Nurse Jupp interrupted my daydreaming as she bustled around the room and laid a small bundle on the meal tray.

"I hear you ate a good breakfast again this morning, so I brought you a special treat."

I sat as tall as I could muster in the bed and waited while she rolled the bed table over and produced a colouring book and crayons.

"Just for me?" I said in wonder.

"Of course, just for you. We keep some on hand for special patients and you are indeed a special patient." She smiled widely.

"Thank you," I muttered softly.

"Did you think you would have to share it?"

I was still in a state of wonder. "Well, one time someone gave my family a colouring book and a pack of crayons between us all. We had to tear out pages to share around and take turns with the crayons."

Nurse Jupp laughed. "That's a lovely story Archie."

"It is?" I felt confused. "Mom said it meant we was poor but I loved the bird pictures."

"It's a wonderful story of a family sharing, Archie. You should be proud to have such memories." She patted my shoulder. "I will be back later to read you a story."

Nurse Jupp would come read to me whenever she had the chance. She was always really busy and only read bible stories. She told me she liked to be involved in the church and would take me to a service when I was feeling better if I would like to go. I liked the nurse. Sometimes she had a really gentle kind spirit, but she was also very stern and I would never want to disappoint her. I knew that she was the one who was going to make me all better so I could go back to the cove.

The hospital was a flurry of activity during the day, but at night, when it was bedtime, I really missed my family. I wouldn't care if Roy teased me, or if John stuck his cold feet on my back, or if Rita was bossy, or if Cack and Dorothy were whining. I would give anything to be back in Tooth Cove with them. And most of all I wanted to feel Ma's snuggles. I wondered when I would see them again, and most nights, I would cry myself to sleep and dream of them all.

One day, Hughlette came into my ward and asked me if I would like to have a tour of the hospital. Nurse Jupp had said it was alright and that we could use the chairs with wheels. I was so excited. For almost three weeks now this was the only room I had seen and I had no memory of the night I spent in the dispensary. Hughlett told me he was Sam's son and someday he hoped to have the job. Sam Acreman was the main maintenance man at the Hospital who had been there since the Hospital was constructed in 1930. The Acremans were a family who had come from away, so they held a special distinction among the locals.

Hughlette first took me around the floor that held the wards. The ward next to mine was also a small ward. It had three beds and currently held just one lady with the biggest belly I ever saw on a lady. Hughlette said the lady was waiting for her baby to arrive. Her ward had a door that went out onto a little bridge and steps went down. The door wasn't used in winter so we didn't go out there, but Hughlette told me that he kept it shovelled out for emergencies. Then Hughlette wheeled me back past my ward again and past the utility room which held all the supplies for patients like water jugs, thermometers, and bedpans.

Then we came to the big ward that had five beds. Four of them had men in them that were sent here to the hospital here from St. Anthony to recover from tuberculosis. They were from the North Coast of Labrador and when spring came, they would be ready to go home. They all said hello to me and seemed really friendly.

Then Hughlette showed me the operating room, the linen room, the bathroom, and the emergency room. He also showed me the stairs up to the staff quarters and told me he would take me up there after if the nurse allowed it. Then he gently lifted me up and carried me down the stairs and put me in another chair with wheels.

First, he pushed me straight ahead to the long porch. There were a couple of people sitting there that I didn't know but they said hello and I gave them a little wave. Then I was shown the inside waiting room which held a big bookshelf with lots and lots of books and a huge mahogany gramophone. Moving down the hall there was a dispensary on the left that had a window overlooking the front of the hospital. Hughlette explained to me that it was the room where Nurse Jupp saw people who just came if they were sick and told me there was someone in there now with the nurse so we couldn't look inside.

Continuing down the hallway we came to a big living room. We went inside. There were huge comfy couches and chairs, and a nice big fireplace. There was a window overlooking the front of the hospital, and next to the fireplace there was a door leading to a sun porch. Hughlett said it wasn't used this time of year. Along the right wall, upon entering the living room, there was a huge bookshelf and a table with a China tea set and a plate of cookies on a silver tray.

"Those cookies look good," I said.

"They are only for the nurse and the doctors," replied Hughlett. "This is their living room. But don't worry, I'm sure the cook will have a treat for you."

We exited the living room and went left just as an Aide came up the basement stairs in front of them with some clean bedsheets for the nurse's room. She said hello to me and said it was nice to see me out and about.

"Would you like to see Nurse Jupp's room?" she asked. Hughlett had been heading that way but didn't know if we would be allowed to go in.

"Yes please," I said eagerly.

Nurse Jupp's room was on the back left of the main floor, behind the living room. A hallway led there from the living room and the kitchen bordered the other side of that hallway. Upon entering, the bed was directly in front of me with a nightstand which held a lamp and a book. To the left was a bureau and a closet. To the right was a long narrow bathroom which would be on the back wall of the hospital. This bathroom was the only bathroom on the main floor and was only used by the nurse. Visitors and patients used the bathroom on the second floor and staff used the bathroom in the basement.

Hughlett told the Aide that he was taking Archie to the basement to show him his workroom and asked her if she would be kind enough to bring down the chair behind him.

She replied, "Most certainly." Her manner told me that the maintenance men must be next in authority to the nurse.

In the basement, I was shown all around to the laundry room, the staff bathroom, and the food storage room. The only time I had seen more food than in here was one time Dad had taken me to the shop in Battle Harbour. The autoclave room, where all the hospital instruments were sterilised, and the furnace room. There was also a long cupboard the length of the basement which was locked, but Hughlette told me that all the medicine was in there and it was all stocked in alphabetical order. My most favourite room was the room where all the tools were kept. Hughlett said that this was where he worked.

His father, Sam, was there fixing some doorknobs.

"Hello Archie," he said pleasantly as he held up one of the doorknobs. "The weather is absolutely wreaking havoc on the knobs and it seems like I'm constantly fixing them."

I looked around and couldn't believe all the tools that were in that room. Dad would be in heaven if he had a room like this. Hughlette showed me some of the tools and how they worked. I was amazed and vowed someday that I would have a room like this. I didn't want to leave that room, but Hughlett said it was time for tea.

Back up the stairs to the kitchen, Hughlette carried me and Sam carried the chair. After Hughlette had placed me back in the chair, he wheeled me to the table where the staff ate.

"Will you have tea or milk?" the cook asked.

"Tea please," I replied. I usually had milk but today I felt all grown up. Plus, it was so nice to sit at a table with people. It seemed so long since I did that. Sitting with me were the two men plus two of the staff girls.

The cook poured up tea for everyone and placed a plate with some cake on the table. Then I heard a buzz so loud it made me jump and looked questionably at Sam. Sam laughed and explained to me that it was the nurse's buzzer. It meant that she was ready for tea and was letting the cook know to deliver it to her living room. I thought that was kind of neat and watched the cook pour the nurse's tea into a China teapot on a tray along with some delicious looking cookies. She noticed I was looking longingly at the cookies and gave me one.

"I'm making an exception for you," she told me. "Because you are a special little boy."

Everyone smiled at me as I bit into the cookie.

"Oh my goodness," I whispered. It practically melted in my mouth. It was so good and I closed my eyes so I could savour the moment.

"It's delicious, isn't it?" whispered one of the girls. "It's called 'shortbread,' an English recipe. Sometimes when the cook makes them, she lets us have one too, but they are mostly for the nurses and doctors because they require a lot of butter."

I nodded and thought about Ma's molasses cake and buns. I had thought they were the most delicious things ever, until now. I hoped that when it was time to go back to Tooth Cove that I could take one for Ma.

Hughlette asked the Aides if it was alright if he took me to the top level of the hospital to see that floor as it was the only place he hadn't taken me. They said it was fine, so as soon as tea was over, up we went. Up the stairs to the floor with the wards, right turn, down the hall past the bathroom and the emergency room, and up another set of stairs. I was amazed at how huge this place actually was.

At the top of the stairs, on the top floor, there was an open area with the girls' room straight ahead. The door was open and we went in. There were four neat little single beds with nightstands beside them and a bureau. The next room to the right was the cook's room. That one had a window overlooking the front of the hospital. That floor also had a room for the maintenance helper who stayed overnight, and a room for the travelling doctor. Hughlette told me that room would soon be used as the doctor was expected to arrive any day now.

I closed my eyes and imagined that as soon as the doctor saw me, I could go home the next day. That made me smile.

CHAPTER 12: ARCHIE
ST. MARY'S HOSPITAL, WINTER 1947

I had just drifted off to sleep when I heard a ruckus coming up the stairs. I bolted up in bed and hung my legs over the side. The room was dark but the door was ajar and the hallway light was streaming in through. I heard a muffle of voices as they turned the corner on the opposite side of the stairs and continued on up.

I had been told not to ring the buzzer unless it was an emergency, but I was a bit scared and decided to ring it anyway. An Aide appeared a few minutes later and explained that the doctor had just arrived. She told me to go back to sleep, everything was alright. After that, I was almost too excited to sleep. I felt confident that the doctor was going to make me all better and I would be able to go back home with my family. Not that I didn't like it here, I did, but there is no place like home and I really missed my mom and dad and brothers and sisters.

I didn't wake the next morning until the Aide showed up with my toast and oatmeal. She helped me up and onto the bedpan to pee and then got me all straightened away to have my breakfast. While she was opening the curtains I asked what time I would see the doctor.

"I'm not sure. He has a few emergencies that he has to see first thing this morning so maybe this afternoon," she replied.

I was a bit frustrated at this. "But will there still be time for me to go home after he fixes me?"

She smiled at my innocence. "Just be patient. The doctor will fix you up, but you may have to stay a bit longer."

"We'll see," I mumbled and looked down miserably at my oatmeal. I didn't feel hungry anymore.

As she exited the room she said, "And you better eat all your breakfast or the doctor will not be happy."

The oatmeal did look really good. It always had some sugar, milk, and a dollop of butter, much different from back home. Mostly we just had a bit of molasses on our oatmeal. I didn't want to make the doctor mad so I ate it all up.

The Aide came in to get the breakfast tray and helped me get dressed. Then she got me straightened away with some crayons and a colouring book. Dinner was a bowl of soup and some crackers. She told me the doctor was still really busy and helped me over to the window to show me all the dog teams that were still waiting outside. She told me people came from all around to see the doctor. Battle Harbour, Matthew's Cove, Trap Cove, Indian Cove, Lodge Bay, Fox Harbour, and from further up in the bay. I smiled when she said there were people from the bay so she promised me she would inquire while I drank my soup.

She returned half an hour later to get the tray and to tell me she heard that there may be someone in the clinic from Tooth Cove, someone that was helping an injured worker from the mill. I knew the only man from Tooth Cove that worked in the mill and wasn't in my family was Bill Howell, so I got pretty excited that a family member might be here.

I heard a flurry of activity on the other side of the stairs and I heard Nurse Jupp giving orders. Then I heard someone outside my door.

"Archie?"

I looked up and couldn't believe my eyes, it was Uncle Bob. I was immediately excited to see a relative, but it was mixed with a bit of disappointment that it wasn't Dad.

"Hi little one," my uncle stammered and grinned.

I grinned back. Uncle Bob had a speech impediment that never stopped him from communicating but somehow seemed to make him kinder. Like he accepted you no matter what because he knew what it was like to live with a flaw.

"My, look how big you have gotten in the past few weeks, it's so good to see you looking so well," said Uncle Bob.

"Are Ma and Dad coming too?' I asked excitedly. "How long are you staying? Am I going back with you?"

My uncle laughed a genuine hearty laugh. "My it's so good to see you getting back to yourself. No, your mom and dad are not here. It's still much too cold for your mom to travel the bay yet and your dad is busy working and hunting on his day off. But they wanted me to look in at you while I was here. They will be so happy to hear how well you are doing."

My uncle was still in the doorway when he heard Nurse Jupp angrily say, "Mr. Rumbolt, I told you to go directly back downstairs. We have some very sick people in those wards who are recovering well and we want to keep it that way."

Uncle Bob hung his head and stammered, "I'm sorry," and abruptly left.

I heard them go back downstairs and I was furious. I hadn't seen a family member in weeks and Nurse Jupp had just made my uncle go away. I knew everyone was busy and it wasn't an emergency but I rang the buzzer. No one showed up right away, so I rang it again, and again. I was so mad. An Aide showed up concerned, but once she heard that I was not sick or in pain was a bit annoyed about how I was reacting. This only made me madder. I thrashed my upper body around the bed demanding to see my uncle. The Aide left to get Nurse Jupp but returned a short while later with a little cup of liquid. I had settled down and was now just quietly staring at the window.

"Nurse Jupp and the whole staff are really busy. She said for you to take this and she will come to see you a bit later."

I didn't answer.

"Are you going to take it or not?" she said as she walked towards my bed.

"No," I said firmly.

"Nurse Jupp won't be happy."

"I don't care." I continued to stare towards the window.

"The doctor won't come to see you."

The thought of not getting to see the doctor and to not be fixed up enough to go home made me rethink.

"If I take it, will I get to see my uncle?" I negotiated.

"Yes," the Aide lied.

I took the little cup and drank it down. The Aide left and I assumed she was gone to fetch my uncle. I waited and waited and eventually fell off to sleep.

It was dark outside when I was awakened by Nurse Jupp bringing in my supper tray. I was a bit stunned to realise I had slept away the whole afternoon. I remembered that my uncle was here and Nurse Jupp had sent him away. I started fuming again.

"Where is my uncle?" I asked through grinding teeth.

"Let me put your bed up and straighten you away for your supper and then we can have a little chat, ok?" She prepped my bed while I kept my head turned away.

"First," Nurse Jupp started, "let me tell you how sorry I am for not getting up to see you earlier, but I was assisting the doctor and we had a really busy day. I am only getting a little break now while the doctor is having his supper. The good news is that the doctor is going to come see you right after supper."

I brightened at this news and looked at her with hope in my eyes.

"The bad news though is that your Uncle Bob has returned back to Tooth Cove with the other injured man."

At this revelation, I didn't know if I felt anger or extreme disappointment, but whatever it was I lashed out at the nurse.

"You are all liars here," I screamed. "The other girl told me if I took the stupid medicine, I would see my uncle." I began to sob.

"She shouldn't have told you that," Nurse Jupp replied. "Please let me explain."

She sat on the edge of the bed while I wept. She reached for me, but then pulled her hand back and placed it in her lap. It wasn't the first time she seemed to want to take my hand or hold me, but stopped herself.

She handed me a cloth to dry my eyes and blow my nose and told me to sit up as straight as I could and listen to what she had to say. I did.

"Archie," she began. "The very sick man who your uncle and his colleague brought down from the mill ended up having tuberculosis."

My eyes widened. I had heard of it before and didn't know what it was but knew that it was very bad.

"Tuberculous," she continued, "is a disease that can set in a cut and is very contagious. The doctor thinks that this man contracted his through a cut in his arm that went unattended. We have him secured in our emergency room until we can get him well again, but we didn't want your uncle to come in and see you because he may have been carrying some of the tuberculosis germs and infected you. I'm very sorry you were not able to spend any time with him, but it is our duty to keep you as well as possible until you recover."

"But what if the doctor says I can go home tonight?" I asked. "Who will bring me?"

"Archie, I'm very sorry to have to tell you this, but you will be with us for a while yet. The doctor is going to see you, but you won't be going home today."

Irrationality struck me again. My eyes blazed and I raised my voice. "So I am not going home and you sent Uncle Bob home without even letting me have a visit with him?"

"I couldn't risk him infecting you," she pleaded.

"You could have gotten him some clean clothes and he could have had a bath in the big tub," I sobbed. "You are so mean. You don't know what it feels like to not see your family. I miss them all so much."

"Listen to me," she said as she held me by the shoulders and looked in my face while big tears ran down my little cheeks. "I want you to stop crying and listen."

"But you don't understand."

"I understand more than you know," she said softly, causing me to look at her a bit differently.

"What do you mean?"

"I didn't have a father growing up, or brothers and sisters. All I had was my mom and she passed away when I was just a bit older than you. I was raised by nuns and although they were good to me, no one is ever the same as your true relatives. So, yes Archie, I do understand what you are going through."

I looked down, feeling sad. I couldn't imagine not having any brothers or sisters or even a dad. And if Ma ever died it would be the end of the world. I felt pity for poor Nurse Jupp and wondered if maybe she did understand.

"Now, will you please eat your supper and let me go eat mine?" she asked.

"Yes." I mumbled.

She turned to leave, but at the doorway she turned back to me. "Oh, by the way, before your uncle left, I wrote a quick letter to your mom telling her how well you were doing and I sent some treats for your brothers and sisters."

"You did?" I replied, surprised. "What did you send? Some of those wonderful shortbread cookies? Cack and Dorothy will love them and so will the rest, even Ma."

I literally bounced on the bed with excitement about my family having some nice treats.

She smiled, "Yes, I did, and a big block of cheese, and some other goodies, I'll be back with the doctor in a little while."

CHAPTER 13: FANNY
TOOTH COVE, JANUARY 1947

It was nearly dark when Bob dropped off the package to Fanny and told her how well Archie looked when he saw him. The children crowded around her as she placed it on the table and opened it. The letter was on top, and being unable to read, she sent John to get Edith to come read it for her. The children begged her to finish opening it, but she told them they had to be patient until John and Edith returned. She knew it was about Archie and she couldn't concentrate on anything else until she knew what was in that letter.

She thought back to when Ern had returned to the cove without Archie. She hadn't eaten a bite all the while he was gone and was quite weak by the time he had returned. She had been sitting by the stove, wrapped in a shawl, when John ran in to tell her the dog team had just come around the point. She pushed on her boots, ran outdoors, and down the bank to meet them. Ern had jumped off the back of the sled when he saw her and led her back into the house saying "he's fine, he's fine" over and over until she stopped sobbing. She had expected the worst and had been so relieved to know that Archie had made it to the hospital.

Ern had explained about the new miracle drug they injected him with and how it was making him better but it was going to be a long recovery. She had heard only good things about the hospital and had been well cared for when she had been there. Yet she felt like a big piece of her heart was missing. Every night since he left, she had gathered the children around the table and they had lit a candle and said a prayer for Archie.

John and Edith arrived and Fanny handed her the letter while the children took their seats. They waited for Edith to unfold the paper and start reading.

Dear Mrs. Rumbolt;

I am writing to give you a quick update on Archie while I have a chance to send it to you.

As you know, Archie came into my care as a very sick little boy. The injury to his knee had driven bacteria too deep into his kneecap to have been drawn out by traditional means. I know you had tried everything you could, but by the time we got him here, the infection had caused a very high fever. I'm glad he arrived here when he did and that we had the new medication on hand to treat him. He will recover but it will take some time.

The doctor has yet to see him, but I know he will be recommending therapy to re-straighten both legs when the knee is totally recovered. Both his legs are still buckled on a 45-degree angle. Right now, the wound has still not fully healed, so that process cannot be started for another two weeks.

He is adjusting well to his stay. He has made friends with the aides and the maintenance men and he is enjoying colouring and having books read. He is eating well and has put back on the few pounds he had lost during his illness.

Try not to worry and I will send you another report when I can. I hope the children enjoy the treats.

Sincerely,
Dorothy M Jupp

The children had all been holding their breath and let all of the air out of their lungs at once. They all looked at their mother who had big tears running down her cheeks.

Edith also had tear filled eyes.

"Why don't I finish opening the box and give the children their treats," she suggested.

Fanny nodded and looked at her hands. Although the tears were joyful ones, she still missed her son. Ern had been sitting quietly on the daybed watching the scene unfold. Now he crossed the room and hugged her and promised her they would go visit as soon as the weather warmed up.

The children munched happily on their shortbread while Fanny rescued the cheese and other goodies to put away for later. The cheese would make a wonderful meal of macaroni and cheese for everyone tomorrow, a treat that they usually only have during the summer months when they live near the merchant store.

That night Fanny had the best night's sleep she had had in years.

CHAPTER 14: ARCHIE
ST. MARY'S HOSPITAL, WINTER 1947

I had finished my supper when I heard the doctor and Nurse Jupp come up the stairs. I heard them in the big ward talking to the men and overheard that one of the men was well enough to make the return trip with the doctor to Cartwright where he would wait to travel back to the North Coast. The man was very excited and happy to be heading home. I knew that I would be happy like that one day soon. I smiled.

The doctor finally entered my room. I took a deep breath. I didn't know what to expect but the doctor was just a normal man. He looked younger than Dad though and was dressed a lot nicer. A sports coat instead of a pullover sweater and linen pants instead of canvas ones. Dad would have called that cruising clothes and not very practical for doing a day's work. Nurse Jupp was standing slightly behind him. She had pulled herself up to her full height and had her hands folded neatly in front of her. It reminded me of when the minister would visit and my mom would stand the same way.

"Hello there Archie," said the doctor. "My name is Doctor Paddon. I have been hearing a lot about you and it's finally good to meet you. How are you enjoying your stay here at St. Mary's Hospital?"

"Good, "I said quietly. I was suddenly speechless and nervous.

"Wonderful," said Dr. Paddon. "What I am going to do is to have a look at that knee of yours and see how well it is healing and let you know what will happen from here. How does that sound?"

"Good."

"Do you have any questions for me before I begin?"

I shook my head. I did have lots of questions but was a bit too scared to ask.

Dr. Paddon lowered my bed, and he asked me to lie on my side. He

Dr. William Anthony "Tony" Paddon. From his book, Labrador Doctor: My Life with the Grenfell Mission, *published in 1989.*

then placed a pillow between my legs so that he could easily access the bent leg that was injured. He unwrapped the bandage and inspected the wound. He asked Nurse Jupp to get him a pair of gloves and he stretched the skin near the wound to have a better look. I winced.

"Am I hurting you?" the doctor asked.

I shook my head no.

"The wound is healing quite nicely and it looks like the infection is all gone. How often have you been changing the bandage?" he directed to the nurse.

"Twice daily," she replied.

"Well, let's try once daily from now on so the wound will get drier and allow the body to heal it naturally. What about antibiotics?"

"Twice daily also."

"We will cut that to once daily also and in two weeks we can begin weight therapy. You can re-bandage the knee now while I talk to Archie."

Nurse Jupp helped the doctor raise the bed back up and put me back onto my back while she went to the next room to get clean bandages. The doctor pulled up a stool and sat facing me while the nurse went to work on the knee.

"Archie," began the doctor, "you are a very lucky boy. Two years ago, the medicine that saved your life was not available in these parts. Your knee is now healing nicely but unfortunately, the joint that allows you to buckle your knee may have been permanently damaged. I am hopeful that your left knee will regain usage, but as of now the most we can hope for is to straighten your right leg."

"How will you do that?" I asked, "and when can I go home?"

Now that I was feeling a little more comfortable, the questions were coming fast.

"Let me explain one thing at a time," laughed the doctor. "I'm glad that you are warming up to me. I want you to stay in this room for two more weeks due to infection risk. There is quite a bit of tuberculosis going around and as of yet we do not have access to the medicine that can help cure it. After two weeks, when Nurse Jupp feels you are healed nicely, we will move you to the big ward. You will have lots of company then, but more importantly, we have a bed there that we can equip with

Dr. William Anthony "Tony" Paddon on board a ship. PANL MG 63.4154.213.

a bar across the top and use some weights to bear down on your legs and straighten them."

"Will it hurt?" I interrupted, suddenly feeling nervous again.

"I would love to be able to tell you that it won't hurt, but honestly, everyone is different when it comes to pain. What I will tell you is that Nurse Jupp will not let you be hurt more than you can bear. The weights will only be used for a few hours a day starting out and for really bad pain the nurse will give you some medicine. However, the faster your legs go back to normal, the faster you will get to go home."

Up until the doctor had said the last sentence, I was feeling sullen and sad, but now I perked up. My eyes widened and I smiled.

"Then I don't care how much pain I feel if it means going home. Did you hear that Nurse Jupp, I am going home," I bubbled, addressing the nurse.

Everyone laughed.

"Try to be patient little Archie. I want you to be all better when you go home so you won't have to come back. Is that alright?" said Dr. Paddon.

"Yes," I agreed, but in my mind, I was already planning how to work hard and go home soon. Ma would be so proud, and I would spend the rest of the winter randying with my brothers, but carefully. This was the best news ever. Dr. Anthony Paddon was the best doctor in the world.

CHAPTER 15: ARCHIE
ST. MARY'S HOSPITAL, WINTER 1947

The next two weeks went by rather quickly. The staff and I equally loved spending time with each other and they helped me a lot with colouring and printing. They showed me how to stay within the lines while colouring and to use soft pressure to make a soft colour and how to make my letters sit on the lines neatly. I was soon able to print all my letters and numbers and write my own name. Nurse Jupp was really impressed at how quickly I was learning. She was convinced that it was my positive attitude that was also helping me to heal quickly. My knee actually healed well in twelve days, but she kept me the extra two days in my room just to be safe.

When the moving day came, all staff were on hand to witness the excitement. I chattered about it with everyone and was convinced that it was going to be just like being back home sharing a room with my brothers. Right after breakfast, Nurse Jupp showed up with a wheelchair to help me move. One of the Aides helped her get me into the chair while another Aide was there to strip the bed and clean the room. The remaining Aide, along with Sam and Hughlett, stood outside the doorway. Even the cook had come to the top of the stairs to watch.

Nurse Jupp wheeled me down the hallway and into the ward. There were three beds on the right-hand side and two on the left. I was wheeled to the left where my new bed awaited. It was the same size as the rest of the beds, but had an overhead steel frame fitted over the entire bed. It was a bed that was commonly used for patients with leg casts as an overhead trapeze allowed them mobility by using their arms. This bed would not only be fitted with a trapeze but also some weights to bear down on my legs in order to straighten the knee joint.

I was a bit scared and a bit excited. I imagined I would have a few painful days ahead but I was excited that at the end of all the pain, I would be closer to going home. I was lifted into my bed while another Aide entered with my books and crayons and laid them on my bed stand. I eyed the bars above my bed with unease.

"Now," declared Nurse Jupp. "That's all the excitement for now. I am going to give you the rest of the morning to get acquainted with your roommates and right after dinner, Sam will be back to equip your bed with some weights and we will try you with them for an hour or so."

I took a deep breath and nodded.

I had met the other men on a couple of occasions when Hughlette had given me some tours of the hospital. Amos and Simeon were on the right side of the room. Both were pleasant looking men from Nain, always smiling. Amos was about Dad's age and Simeon was older. In the bed next to me was a young man named Jacko. Jacko was from Makkovik and about Hughlette's age. The fourth man who had been in the ward had already left with Dr. Paddon's patrol. He had been from Rigolet and was probably back home by now. All four men had been sent from St. Anthony to finish their recovery from tuberculosis. They had no infection left but the disease had taken its toll on their bodies and they needed to rest.

"You finally come to stay with us, little one," grinned Amos. "I have a little one just like you at home. I can't wait to see him." Tears welled up in his eyes.

I immediately looked at him differently. I wondered if Dad was feeling like this. It seemed awkward to even think about it. I had never seen Dad cry. He probably didn't think it was proper to get teary eyed.

Simeon jumped off his bed drawing attention to himself.

"Well, my boys are all grown up," he declared. "But I still can't wait to see them. They will have little ones of their own soon, I imagine."

Simeon was a little man, but he grinned a big happy toothless grin. On my other visits it always seemed like he tried to make the best of any situation. Anytime Amos seemed sad, Simeon would try to lighten the mood.

"Oh my god, you guys are old," laughed Jacko. "It's finally good to have a young one in here to talk to."

We all had a laugh at this, and the conversation continued about our hometowns and families until dinner arrived. It was stewed beans and buttered bread with a dish of jelly for dessert. We ate quietly and savoured the good food we were getting here but each of us would give it all up in a heartbeat to be back home.

As soon as the trays were taken away, Sam and Hughlette showed up to install the weights and the trapeze. Sam carried a big toolbox, while Hughlette wheeled in a heavy looking box with weights in it. They asked me to lie in the bed so they could get an idea about where to do the installations. The weights had to hang in the area of my knees and the trapeze in my shoulder area. The weights were flat and were attached to cables to stabilise them and to allow for more weight to be added if necessary. The trapeze was hung low enough that I could grab it during a lying position but high enough that it wouldn't be hitting me in the face when in a sitting position. When it was all complete, they rang for Nurse Jupp.

"Well, well Archie," Nurse Jupp announced as she entered the ward. "How are you feeling about finally getting those legs straightened out?" She tried to keep her tone upbeat and I knew it was to not scare me about the pain.

"Good," I replied, but still felt a bit unsure.

"Just focus on getting the job done and getting back to your family and you will be ready to go home in no time," Hughlette said.

Simeon piped up, "Your little bones are so pliable, I'm sure it won't be too painful."

The other men smiled at me, then looked away as Nurse Jupp closed the curtains around the bed to give me some privacy.

Nurse Jupp stayed on one side of the bed, while Hughlette and Sam stayed on the other. Hughlette was near the trapeze and Sam was near the weights.

"Sam and Hughlette are going to help me get you all set up," said Nurse Jupp.

First, they showed me how to reach for the trapeze and pull myself into a sitting position.

"When the weights are on your knees, you will only have mobility in your upper body and the only positions you will have are lying on your back or sitting straight up," Nurse Jupp explained.

"Alright," I said as they guided me through some practise lifting and lowering. "This did not seem too bad at all," I said.

"Now," she said, "we are going to lower the weights onto your knees and keep lowering until you cannot stand the pain, and then we will leave it for as long as you can stand, alright?"

"Yes," I tensed and waited.

The weights were currently lying at the foot of my bed. Sam lifted the first weight into place and secured it on the heavy copper coil hanging from the overhead bar. While Nurse Jupp held my knee in place with one hand under my calf and one under my thigh, Hughlette cranked the weight down while Sam held the weight steady to ensure it was secure. Hughlette kept cranking down until Archie moaned.

"Are you alright?" asked the nurse.

"Yes."

"Good," she said. "We are going to do a few more cranks until you tell us to stop, alright?"

 I nodded.

They got a couple of more cranks in before I told them to stop. They repeated the procedure on the sore knee. This time I began to pant with pain and the nurse rang the buzzer for the Aide to get some pain medication. After the medication was administered, the men secured the weights in place.

"An aide will sit with you for the whole hour today," the nurse told me. "It's so we can monitor your progress. If you do well, we will do it for the same amount of time for a few days, but if you can't handle an hour, we will cut back the time tomorrow. Understood?"

I nodded but was gritting my teeth too hard to speak. I forced myself through the hour and the Aide left the curtain closed so I wouldn't feel self-conscious about the other men viewing my pain. It was a quiet, sombre hour on the ward as the other men were well aware of the pain going on inside my curtains.

Nurse Jupp reappeared when the hour was up with the maintenance men who removed the weights. She told me I had done very well but that tomorrow she would give me the pain medication earlier so that it would be working before they started. She noted a tiny difference in my legs and said before I knew it, I would have straight legs again.

For the next 6 weeks, the process continued, adding an hour each week until the sixth week when the maximum time was reached. I was becoming accustomed to the pressure and my legs were pretty much straight. There was some movement in my good leg and Nurse Jupp encouraged me to move it as much as I could. The doctor wanted me to have a range of motion in my good leg before he put a cast on the damaged leg. This would ensure that I could move around and be mobile. Once the damaged leg was straight and a cast applied, the doctor hoped the internal healing of the knee would just be a few months. Hopefully, after the healing, the range of motion may even return to the damaged leg as I was still young and the bones were not yet fully fused. Only time would tell.

Nurse Jupp was reading me a bible story one afternoon when she stopped and suddenly looked sad.

"Are you alright?" I asked.

"Yes. I have been meaning to tell you that I received a letter from your mom."

"Ma wrote a letter! Oh my goodness. She must really miss me if she learned to write."

Nurse Jupp laughed a huge hearty laugh. "Oh, my Archie. You should see your face." She hooted laughing again. "And your eyes. They are as big as saucers." She slapped her leg and laughed again. Finally, she stopped and wiped her eyes with her hanky.

"I'm sorry Archie. That just struck me as funny and I guess I needed a stress reliever from all the tension of seeing you in pain for the past two months." She paused and collected herself. "Someone else probably wrote the letter for your mom, actually."

"Silly me. Aunt Edith usually does all our reading and writing. She is a teacher and married to my Uncle Bill. She learns us our lessons sometimes too."

"She teaches you your lessons," Nurse Jupp corrected with a smile and I blushed.

"What did Ma say in the letter?" I asked eagerly.

"Just that she misses you and she would like permission to visit."

"Oh my goodness." I covered my mouth with my hands. "Mom asks the silliest things. Sure, I am going home soon. Right Nurse Jupp?"

"Once the doctor says you can, then you will."

"I just know that he will say I can go home. I am so excited Nurse Jupp."

"I know you are, but I sure will miss you when it is time for you to leave." She turned sad again.

"Really? You will miss me?"

"I sure will. You have been a breath of fresh air this winter for all of us here at St. Mary's. I love your attitude towards learning and being respectful to everyone. I will surely miss you, as will everyone."

"I will miss everyone too. They have all been so nice. But I really miss my family. Maybe someday you will have your own little boy."

Nurse Jupp laughed again, "I don't think having a child is ever going to happen for me. I will have to be content nursing other ladies' children back to health."

"So, in a way, you are everybody's Momma." I really meant it and I gave the Nurse a huge smile. She must have remembered she had forgotten to do something because she left quickly, not even finishing reading the story.

CHAPTER 16: FANNY
TOOTH COVE, WINTER 1947

Edith came running to Fanny's house as soon as the Mailman dropped off the letter. It was a warm March day and the bright sun was melting the snow off the rooftops. Fanny was just taking bread out of the oven when Edith burst in. The boys were all outside and little Dorothy was taking a nap.

Fanny always got excited to receive a letter from Nurse Jupp. She had had several over the winter and was really appreciative. Of course, she couldn't help feeling a bit jealous that another woman was enjoying so much time with her son, but she had no doubt that the caring hands of Nurse Jupp was the sole reason her son was still on this earth.

Edith tore open the envelope and read…

Dear Mrs. Rumbolt;

I hope this letter finds you well and that your family has prospered with the help of the Good Lord this long winter.

Archie has been doing well despite the painful process to straighten his legs. He has been eating well and it seems he has put on a few pounds since his stay at St. Mary's. He is also an avid learner and his ability to read is coming along nicely. He is eager to show off his new skills to his brothers and sisters.

I will be consulting with the doctor by the end of March and I expect he will have promising news about Archie's return to Tooth Cove.

Archie is looking forward to your visit. If you come after the first week of April, we should have more news to report.

Sincerely,
Dorothy M Jupp

Fanny's heart skipped a beat with excitement as she and Edith stood grinning at each other. Edith refolded the letter and placed it back into the envelope. Fanny couldn't wait for Ern to get home from the mill to give him the good news.

The next two weeks passed painfully slow for Fanny. She was making sure that she had lots of bread baked for her mother to keep the children fed while she was away. She didn't know how long they would have to stay at St. Mary's to wait for Archie, but she knew she wasn't coming back without him. He had been away long enough. She imagined it would just be a few days, and fortunately Ern had family there they could stay with. Ern had asked her to wait until there was definite word that Archie would be ready for home, but when she looked at him with her eyes all ablaze, he knew better than to pursue it. He did tell her however that. if the wait was going to be more than a few days, she could stay and he would come back to Tooth Cove to get a few days of work in. She conceded on this point.

The trip down the bay was uneventful. A few mild days had flattened out the drift banks on the frozen ice and that had made the travel a lot easier. They had seven dogs today, so the travel was swift. Lady was in the lead and she seemed to be bursting with excitement. It was as if she knew the purpose of this trip. Fanny thought back to the day Lady and the men had returned from St. Mary's without Archie, the dog had looked so sullen she feared she might be dying.

They stopped a few times to give the dogs a rest and water, and even a quick snack for themselves, but Fanny was anxious to get to the hospital and have a visit before visiting hours were over for the night. Altogether the trip took under six hours and they arrived around three in the afternoon.

They were in the outer porch removing their heavy clothes and boots when Nurse Jupp appeared. She knew immediately who they were and noted that Ern looked much better than he had the night he arrived with Archie three months ago.

"You must be Mr. and Mrs. Rumbolt. Welcome to St. Mary's. How was your journey?"

"Good," replied Ern. Fanny was quietly eyeing the nurse. She didn't know what to say. Words could not express the gratitude she felt for this lady. Yet despite that, she felt it improper to verbalize how she felt.

"It's good to see you again Mrs. Rumbolt, may I call you Fanny?"

"Yes, of course," said Fanny.

"And you may call me Dorothy."

The glance that Ern and Fanny exchanged did not go unnoticed by the nurse.

"What is it?" she inquired.

Ern replied that their daughter's name was Dorothy. Nurse Jupp smiled. She remembered delivering the little girl on a hot July day almost three years ago and was delighted to be her namesake. Fanny smiled in remembrance. Many children were named after the nurses that brought them into the world.

"How sweet," replied Nurse Jupp. "How is the little darling doing?" She directed the question at Fanny.

"She is well and very busy at this age," Fanny laughed. She immediately felt more relaxed.

"Well, come on then, you must be excited to see your precious boy."

Nurse Jupp led them up the stairs while talking about the various treatments Archie had received. As they approached the ward, they heard a delighted squeal. Fanny, recognizing her son's exclamation, rushed into the room to give Archie a huge hug and kiss.

She held on and held on so tight, crushing his little body to hers. She finally pulled away and looked at her son with tear filled eyes.

"I wish I could just hold you forever and never let go."

Ern looked on with a smile and Fanny could tell he wanted to do the same, but he wasn't one for strong displays of emotion, so he didn't.

Amos teared up watching them and said, "Someday I will get to do the same with my boy."

"Ma," Archie whispered, "wanna see my colouring?"

Fanny was still gripping his shoulders and staring at him from outstretched arms.

"Your little face has all filled out and you don't seem as boney as you did the last time I hugged you," she said as tears escaped her eyes. She quickly wiped them away. "I'm so happy to see you, Archie. My heart is happy again."

Ern came and touched Fanny on the shoulder. "Let's see that colouring now Archie," he said.

The next hour was filled with all of Archie's stories about healing, reading, colouring, the staff, his ward mates, the doctor; anything he could think of. He showed them how he could get around with a walker and how he was getting the use of his good leg back. By the time he was finished, he was exhausted. One of the aides showed up to announce that supper would be served in ten minutes and to get washed up. She asked Fanny and Ern if they would like a plate prepared for them in the staff dining room, but Ern replied that his family was preparing a meal for them.

"Am I going with you now?" Archie asked.

"We have to talk about it with Nurse Jupp," replied Ern. "In any case, it's too late to return to the cove tonight, so you will have another night here."

Fanny could see that Archie would have liked to protest, but he was exhausted from the excitement. Fanny and Ern gave him a kiss goodbye and told him they would be back a bit later if they could.

Downstairs, Nurse Jupp beckoned them into the dispensary for a chat. She informed them that the doctor had sent word to have a cast applied and allow Archie to return home. However, it would take a couple of days for the cast to set properly, and for the boy to adjust to moving around with it on. Fanny noticed how she said "boy" instead of "Archie" and knew that Nurse Jupp was preparing to let him go, both physically and emotionally. Fanny also wanted to question whether or not two more days were necessary but was reluctant to voice her concerns due to her great debt of gratitude to this woman.

Ern told her it was fine and they would wait around for him to be ready.

"We won't be back tonight then," said Ern. "Archie was looking a little tired, so we will let him rest as well as getting some rest ourselves."

Fanny wondered how she would rest without her children under the same roof. It wasn't often that women like her got the chance to rest with the exception of waiting for a child to be born and spending time in the hospital.

"We will apply the cast first thing in the morning, so you can visit him in the afternoon," Nurse Jupp said to conclude the conversation and allow them to leave.

Fanny felt compelled to offer this woman a word of thanks but felt that mere words could not express what was in her heart.

"Thank-you so much for making Archie well again," she finally said with a shaky voice.

"It's what I came here to do," replied Nurse Jupp in a professional manner, however she instinctively knew that Fanny meant more. "Your son is a very precious boy and we will all miss him."

Fanny nodded and made a quick exit, leaving Ern a bit bewildered, but he had long ago stopped questioning the workings of the female mind.

CHAPTER 17: ARCHIE
ST. MARY'S HOSPITAL, WINTER 1947

The next morning, after the patients had all finished their breakfast and the trays had been carried back to the kitchen, Hughlett and Sam along with Nurse Jupp showed up to apply the cast to my leg. One of the Aides had already gotten my injured leg all washed and dried properly in preparation. Sam had done this work many times but he wanted his son to get trained in the procedure.

Nurse Jupp wound cotton gauze around my leg from the hip to the ankle. She explained to me that the cast would not be going that far but it was necessary to have lots of gauze at the top and bottom to provide cushioning between the cast and flesh skin after the cast hardened. Then she positioned a wooden slab underneath my leg to keep it straight and catch cast drippings.

Within an hour, all the wet gauzy strips had been carefully applied and I was instructed to stay as still as I could while the drying the plaster dried. At lunchtime, the Aides carefully propped me up and stayed while I ate.

Visiting hours were from 2pmtwo to 4pmfour unless there was an unusual circumstance like when Ma and Dad had first arrived. So promptly at 2pmtwo o'clock, my parents showed up for a visit. Ma was happy to see that the cast had been applied and that the drying had begun. Today's visit was all about hearing stories from Tooth Cove.

I loved hearing about how John got stuck in some deep snow by a tree and how Roy shot a partridge and how Cack was learning to skin rabbits. The girls' stuff wasn't as interesting, but I still liked the sewing and baking stories and looked forward to seeing them all. The two hours passed quickly and by then, the cast seemed to be dry.

Nurse Jupp came by and said although it seemed dry on the outside it would take a while to dry all the way through. She removed the wooden board and showed us how it was still quite tacky on the bottom so she had to suspend my leg off the bed to allow it to dry underneath.

Ma and Dad didn't come back that night but showed up at the same time the next day. They told me they didn't want to disturb the schedule of the hospital too much and they wanted me to have as much rest as possible because once we returned home the other children were not going to let me rest very much.

Today, they sat in the hospital's kitchen with me as I was propped up by the big pot-bellied stove. An Aide explained that Nurse Jupp wanted to be sure the cast was dried really well before I left the hospital. The cook gave me a big glass of cold lemonade to help me stay cool and hydrated. Nurse Jupp showed up after a few minutes and tapped the cast in several places while listening for the hollow sound that indicates a well-dried cast.

"What time will he be able to leave in the morning?" asked Ma.

The nurse seemed shocked. "He definitely won't be able to go tomorrow," replied Nurse Jupp.

As quickly as I deflated though, Ma straightened her spine and pulled herself as tall as her five-foot frame would allow.

"What do you mean he can't go tomorrow? Surely the cast will dry overnight," she stated, and I could see that Ma was getting a bit angry.

"Yes, the cast will dry overnight, but he still needs some practise being mobile on it before he can leave."

Ma opened her mouth again to speak but Dad beat her to it in an attempt to calm the situation. "Maybe he could do some practice tonight with us here to learn with him and a bit more early in the morning," Dad appeased. "That way we will know how to help after he gets home."

Nurse Jupp considered this and agreed to give it a try but added she would make no promises.

"If I don't feel he is ready by morning, he will have to stay," she explained.

I saw Dad nudge Ma so she would remain quiet and her only response was a huff of discontent.

"I know you need to get back to Tooth Cove, but it's my job to ensure Archie is ready to make the trip and is able to adjust to life there with his cast. Why don't you go have supper and when you come back, we can all help him with some practise," replied the nurse

When they returned after supper, the nurse had my crutches adjusted for my height and was ready to do my walking training. She was starting me in the upstairs hallway so that I could use one crutch at a time while holding the banister. I practised on the right side and then on the left while Nurse Jupp and my parents looked on. It wasn't long at all before I had the hang of it and was using both crutches to go back and forth along the hallway.

The final tests I had to pass were rising from a chair, getting out of bed, and then getting off the floor. By the time it was all completed, I was quite tired but felt I was ready to tackle the world despite the heavy leg cast. Everyone was pleased, but Nurse Jupp wanted me in bed extra early so I could have an early rise and practise what I learned. There were still no promises about going home but Ma and Dad left very confident.

A bit later when I was finally settled into bed, Nurse Jupp brought me a snack while she packed my belongings into a canvas bag. It wasn't much: a couple of outfits she had retrieved from a donation bag, and my favourite book. She packed enough colouring pages and crayons for me to share with my two younger siblings.

"I'll come back to visit lots you know," I said. "I will miss you and all the people here."

Nurse Jupp laughed. "I sure hope you don't have to visit lots for illness but I do look forward to seeing you when you return to have your cast removed."

"You look kinda sad," I said and she looked at me in surprise.

"Oh?" she laughed. "You are a very perceptive young man. Of course I will miss you. I was just concentrating on what needed to be packed, but of course I am a bit sad. It has been really nice to have you here at St. Mary's with us this winter. It's like we had sunshine inside even when it was snowing outside." She smiled a smile that didn't quite reach her sad eyes. "Good night now Archie, you will need all the rest you can get for your journey tomorrow."

I brightened. "So, it's definite then? I am going tomorrow?"

"It certainly looks that way my friend," she replied. A smile so big it hurt my cheeks erupted over my face, but rather than smile back, she turned quickly to exit the ward.

CHAPTER 18: ARCHIE
UP THE BAY, APRIL 1947

The next morning Nurse Jupp had me up bright and early to practise my movements. At one point she even dressed me in my bulky outer clothes and made me practise. It was a bit more of a challenge, but I did great.

I had barely finished my breakfast when Dad and Ma showed up, their faces full of anticipation. The big grin I gave them when they saw me told them I was going home. It looked like Ma's smile wrapped all the way around her ears.

My exit from St. Mary's that sunny April day was probably one of the most memorable send offs that the hospital had ever witnessed. Both staff and patients filled the waiting room while the nurse made a simple first aid kit of salve and bandages and the cook wrapped a package of fresh baked goodies. Everyone had their turn to give me a hug and wish me well. I knew I would be back again to visit and to get my cast removed, so the excitement I felt about going home far outweighed any feelings of sadness about leaving.

Finally, I was out the door and breathing the sweet fresh April air. There was still a chill in the air and the sun hadn't risen to its highest position in the sky, but the watery spring smell was unmistakable. Even though I had been outside on the balcony a few times in March when the days had been warm, the railings always represented a sense of imprisonment because I couldn't go sliding or play in the snow.

As Ma and Dad helped me walk towards the team of dogs, the dogs rose from their lying positions and stood to attention to await their master. Lady stood the most rigid and emitted a deep throaty growl.

"Lady!" I screamed excitedly.

Despite the crutches, I leapt off the hard packed snow and tried to go faster towards the dog. Lady also made a leap, but didn't make it far due to the tether. She yelped and jumped until I reached her and she leapt onto me knocking me to the ground. Ma and Dad momentarily froze and watched the scene play out as I squealed with laughter.

"Hey," shouted Dad as he shook his fist in the air and the dog backed off, lowering her head.

Huskies rarely defied their master, and when they did, they received a beating that made sure it didn't happen again. The Labrador lifestyle dictated that dogs were a means of survival, and they needed to know how to take orders.

Ma rushed to help me to my feet and asked if I was alright.

I was still giggling. "Oh Ma, it's so good to see Lady."

Kids were not permitted to play with the huskies as sometimes they could be quite savage. Their ancestry as part wolf made them untrustworthy to be around, especially at feeding time. Their savagery was exactly what was harnessed to create the winter workhorse necessary.

Ma spread open the layers of blankets in the komatik and got in. Dad packed the bags at the front underneath a seat he would sit on during the ride up the bay. Ma spread her knees apart so that Dad could help me into a seated position between her legs. There was just room enough for me to keep my legs straight while Ma's were a bit buckled. Dad tucked the blankets around us and proceeded to untie the dogs. Lady was still cowering but had been sneaking happy peeks at me. Once untied, she came to full attention and awaited orders for her job.

I glanced back at the hospital as we were leaving and saw Nurse Jupp in the dispensary window, watching. I couldn't tell if she was still sad or not. For me, this was the most exciting day of my life.

Dad gave the moving orders and off we went, down the road towards a barn that marked where we would travel over the neck of land leading to Daddy Island Steady. A couple of relatives were waiting with their team of dogs near the barn to travel with us to the bay. Once on the bay, it was smooth going to Tooth Cove. Getting over the land was sometimes tricky with a loaded komatik, but there always seemed to be someone who was willing to travel along and help.

The days were getting longer, but the sun was still getting low in the sky as we rounded the point going into Tooth Cove.

Even above the dogs barking, I could hear the shouts and screams of other children as we rode into the cove. John, Roy, Losten, and May met our sled even before it reached the shore and ran along beside us up the hill. Mildred was on the bridge of Grandmother's house with Grandmother. Rita held little Dorothy in her arms on Ma's bridge with little Cack by her side. Bob and Charl scurried down the path and took the dogs from Dad so he could unpack the komatik in peace by his house. Everyone was all smiles, even little Dorothy who was bouncing up and down in Rita's arms. The very first thing I noticed was how much she had grown in the past few months.

Everyone was talking at the same time until Dad hollered. Everyone went silent while Dad explained that I had had a long day and didn't need too much excitement. By this time, Mildred and Grandmother had walked down to the komatik and were helping Ma and I get untangled from the blankets on the sled. The children gaped while I was helped into the house with an oversized pair of snow pants on to fit over my cast.

Once inside, I couldn't contain his excitement any longer and told them about the goodies the cook had sent. Everyone gathered around while Mildred and Grandmother helped me out of my outer clothes. They talked excitedly in hushed voices, still in fear of upsetting Dad. Ma and Dad had busied themselves unpacking the komatik and getting out of their own clothes.

Dad was pleased to see that his wood box was filled for the night and the water barrel was full, and Ma was equally pleased to see that a big pot of rabbits simmering on the stove and enough bread had been made for that night and the next day. If it's one thing we were grateful for, it was having a large family to help us through the rough times. Ma and Dad were both suddenly so exhausted from the whole week and were ready to relax with their family all under one roof again.

Grandfather, Uncle Bill, and Aunt Edith arrived together. Edith gave me a big hug while the men gave joyful hellos and commented on how good it was to see me looking so well. I babbled to my aunt about how well I could read and write as I knew she would be pleased to hear this.

Aunt Edith gave a little laugh and told me that although I had probably had some steady education at the hospital, she would have to see how well could read and write and how much I had learned. She told me, nothing satisfied a teacher more than the excitement of a child to learn.

Dad poured tea and left with the men to the shed for a chat while Ma, with her tea, gathered around me with the women and children to hear some stories. I couldn't figure out what was better, being home and being the centre of attention, or the wonderful smell of rabbits coming from the pot. I had had rabbit at the hospital, but it never smelled as good as it smelled here at home.

Bill Howell showed up to hustle Losten and May off home for supper. The children looked disappointed, but Bill explained they would have a long day tomorrow to see me. Ma wrapped up a cookie for each of them to take home, and they were happy with that.

Supper was delicious. The rabbits were cooked to perfection and Ma had gotten home in time to put the turnip that the cook had given her in the pot. She had even had a bit of real butter to add to the paste, making it fluffy enough to melt in your mouth. After the supper and cookies, everyone was stuffed to the gills and content.

I noticed that little Cack hadn't said much since we arrived home, and he was still quietly regarding me.

"What's wrong with ya, Cack?" I asked. "Lose yer tongue?"

I was sitting on one chair with my leg resting on another and Cack was sitting on the floor on a hooked rug Grandmother had made many years ago. One leg was bent upright, and he was hugging it while staring intently at my cast.

"Does it hurt?" Cack asked solemnly.

I laughed and lifted my leg to the floor and tapped on it.

"Come feel it, it's as hard as a rock."

My pants were covering it and Cack slowly inched over and lightly touched it. I tapped it hard again.

"Just do this," I said.

Cack was unsure but did as I said, and his eyes widened.

"Wow, it is as hard as a rock," he exclaimed. Everyone was watching and hooted in laughter.

Little Dorothy, not wanting to be left out of the fun, jumped up from where she was playing with a doll and ran over and jumped on my cast.

"Dorothy jump on rock," she screamed as she pounced.

Her weight pushed the cast down hard onto my leg and I yelped with pain.

"Lord thunderin Jesus," Dad bellowed as he leapt off the daybed. "Get your arse in the bed," he yelled at Dorothy as she ran crying to the bedroom she shared with Ma and Dad.

Ma rushed to me. I was recovering from the shock, and assured Ma I was fine. Rita also rushed to help Ma got my pants off to see if any damage had been done. Everything looked fine; the cast had been well-wrapped to prevent chafing.

Ma glared at Dad who looked sullen.

"What in the hell flames is wrong with you bawling at Dorothy like that?" she cried.

Dad did not respond, just grabbed his coat and left the house muttering about not wanting me to have to go back to the hospital.

"Rita, go see if Dorothy is alright, while I settles Archie into bed. And the rest of yas best get to bed too before ya father comes back." Ma looked around as they all scurried to their room.

Ma settled me into bed with Cack.

"Ma, I mostly bawled because I was afraid I was going to have pain. It didn't hurt, honest. Don't treat little Dorothy bad, she didn't mean to hurt me," I explained.

"I know," replied Ma. "I just gotta go beat that into yer father's head. Go to sleep now."

She kissed us all and left the room just in time to meet Rita coming from hers and Dad's room. I could still hear them from my bed.

"Dorothy is asleep now. Cried herself to sleep, little darling. Why do Dad have to be so mean?" asked Rita.

"He just got a fright 'tis all, I am going out to talk to him now," Ma declared as I heard her head out the door.

CHAPTER 19: ARCHIE
TOOTH COVE, APRIL 1947

The next few weeks passed in a blur. Dad was busy at the mill, getting the pit props all stowed by the landwash for the barge that would fetch them as soon as the bay thawed out. The women were busy knitting trigger mitts and net hauling mitts for spring as well as all their other duties. My siblings loved having more time outdoors. I even got outside a lot and, a few times, I even got to go sliding.

By the end of April, the days that weren't rainy days were beautiful warm days. The snow on the land was melting away and had become crystallised with the thaw and overnight freezing of the Labrador spring. The snow has gone off the bay, leaving just the watery ice. Still good for travelling, but slippery.

Us children had been spending quite a bit of time outdoors recently, and although the nights were longer, we still went to bed early, exhausted from our adventures, and slept well.

I had been more tired recently, but Ma brushed it off from my having been cooped up in the hospital all winter. I spent a lot of time outdoors, and Dad had made a cart that the others used to push me around. There was even room in it for Dorothy and she loved being snuggled next to her big brother while being pushed around.

Today was a beautiful warm May day, and the men had left for Fox Harbour for spring supplies. You could never tell how long a Labrador spring could be. Some years it could be just a few days between winter mode of travel, meaning dogs, and summer mode of travel, meaning boats, but some years it could be weeks, so there had to be a good supply of food in stock just in case. Ma was busy making a batch of bread and Rita was on the bridge outside playing with Dorothy and her doll. Roy and John had taken Cack to the nearby rabbit snares and I was dozing on the daybed.

Mildred dropped by with a bowl to borrow some flour for Grandmother.

"She just needs a few cups to finish her bread," she explained. "Good thing the men are gone for supplies."

"Yes," replied Ma, "Everything is getting short now."

"Why isn't Archie outdoors getting some fresh air?" asked Mildred as she flicked a towel in the air above my head making a cracking sound. I pretended to be asleep so she would leave me alone.

"Let him sleep," said Ma, while I watched her through nearly closed eyes as she gave her the behave yourself look to my sister.

"Mom, that's not normal, you know. Young boy like that sleeping his life away." Mildred was always outspoken.

"It's just because he was barred up all winter in the hospital maid. It got his energy drained." Ma was saying the words, but there was no confidence in them, like she also knew my behaviour wasn't normal.

"Mom, he has been home a month now, he should be all over that." Mildred stood with her hands on her hips and glared at her mother. "Make him get up and go out. Stop babying him."

Groggily, I tried to sit up. "What's going on?" I asked.

"It's time for you to get off that daybed and go outdoors," Mildred said curtly. "Laying around in the house on a beautiful day like this." She rolled her eyes and glared back at her mother who was still kneading the bread.

"Alright, alright," I replied. I swung my legs off the daybed and grabbed my crutches. But as I tried to stand, I collapsed on the floor. Ma pulled her doughy hands out of the bread and rushed to me, but Mildred had beaten her to it and was already kneeling on the floor, pulling my head and shoulders into her lap. "Are you ok?' she asked.

"I think so," I said. "I don't know what happened."

"Well, let's get you back up on the daybed and get you some sweet tea or something. You must be getting the flu."

Ma stood watching with her doughy hands. "You are sure growing into a capable young woman, Mildred. Thank you."

"Mom, finish making the bread. He is fine. I am just going to run up home with the flour for Nan and I will be back to get some tea for

Archie."

For the few minutes she was gone, I fell back to sleep. I felt really tired. Mildred made the tea as soon as she returned and added some cold water so I could drink it right away. "When you gets that down in ya, you are going back to bed," she ordered.

When the tea was gone, I had just enough energy to go into my room with Mildred's help. As Mildred was helping me off with my pants, she accidentally tore off a piece of the gauzy cushioning around the top of my thigh. As she grabbed it to finish ripping it off, she screwed up her nose and looked serious.

"What's wrong?" I asked.

"Nothing," replied Mildred. "I just tore a bit of gauze off the cast, is all."

"Oh, that's nothing," I said. "Hopefully it will be coming off in a few weeks, before we head to Matties Cove."

CHAPTER 20: FANNY
TOOTH COVE, APRIL 1947

Mildred knew what the smell was. Fanny was just finishing wrapping the bread to put behind the stove to rise when she noticed the horrified look on Mildreds face.

"My god Mildred, what's wrong? Is Archie alright?" Fanny asked.

Mildred led her over to the corner of the kitchen, out of earshot of Archie's room, and told her mother of her concerns.

"Go on Mildred, stop being so suspicious." Even as Fanny said the words, she knew instinctively that Mildred could be right.

"Well, that man from the mill that Uncle Bob took to the hospital the winter, had the same smell on his arm, and it ended up being TB."

Now it was Fanny's turn to be horrified as she realised that it was quite possible for Archie to have caught it from either of the tuberculosis patients that frequented the hospital.

"He is going to have to go back to the hospital as soon as your father gets home," Fanny said with tears in her eyes.

Mildred hugged her mother. "He will be fine Ma. At least the going is still good to get him to St. Mary's."

After Mildred left, Fanny went into the room and sat on Archie's bed. He looked so small and fragile. Her heart ached at the thought of him having to go back to the hospital.

"Hi Ma," Archie said sleepily. "This bed is so comfy. I love how it gets all fluffed up and when you lie in it, it hugs you. At the hospital, the beds are hard and covered with plastic. Lots of nights I wished I was home in my comfy feather bed."

Fanny started to cry.

"Ma, what's the matter?"

Fanny looked away. "I think I got some smoke in my eyes from putting wood in the stove," she replied. "You go to sleep. I should go check on my bread."

She gave him a quick peck on the cheek as he snuggled back down to sleep.

It was late by the time the men returned from Fox Harbour. The children had all waited up knowing they would each be given a candy from their father. The local man that ran the store never forgot about the children. Fanny scurried around putting away the supplies while Ern ate the supper she had saved for him. Rita tucked the children away in bed, even though they were a bit excited from the candy. Ern had noticed the worry on Fan's face, but decided to wait until the house quieted down before he asked her about it.

"Mmm… this is so good. Nuttin like fresh seal and paste," he said to no one in particular.

It was seal his brothers had sent with some travellers from Matthew's Cove last week. Seal was a plentiful food source on the outside lands, but here in the bay it was a delicacy as the travel to get them was too far. Ern mentally thanked his family for always looking out after each other.

"Archie wouldn't wake up for his candy," announced Rita as she came from the room and passed her mother the wrapped candy kiss. "We even sove him the rum and butter one."

Ern looked up and didn't miss the concern on Fanny's face as she pocketed the candy in her apron and went to the children's room.

Clarence had already made himself comfortable in the bed between Archie and the wall and was drifting off to sleep with a happy grin on his face. Roy and John were settled for the night head to foot, and Rita was climbing to the bunk above them.

Fanny felt Archie's forehead. He did feel a bit warm but seemed to be breathing normally. She didn't like all the sleeping he was doing. Something was definitely wrong.

Before she had a chance to investigate further, she heard Mildred come in, talking before the door had even closed. "Ma, did all the tea get put in down here, we got none left up home and we need it for tomorrow morning."

"I think it did all get put in here for the night, Mill," replied Ern as

Fanny was coming from the room.

"Ma, did Archie eat any supper after?" Mill asked as Ern went to retrieve the tea from the bottom cupboard.

"No," Fanny replied. "He didn't even wake up for his candy."

"What's going on?" asked Ern as he walked toward Mildred with a bag of tea. Mildred said nothing, just marched past her mother and into the children's room.

She lit a candle on the window sill and spoke gently to Archie. Only Rita and Roy were still awake and they watched her curiously. wondering what Mildred was worried about. When Mildred got something into her head, she didn't stop until it was resolved, and no one dared to try and stop her. Archie didn't respond, so turning to her mother, who was now in the doorway of the room, she asked for a clean rag.

Mildred peeled back the blankets from the boy and gently pulled his pyjama pants down far enough to expose the top of the cast. Her mother handed her the rag and she stuffed it as far as she could down inside the cast. She pulled it out and handed it to her mother.

"Ask Dad to smell that," Mildred said.

The look on Ern's face as he smelled the rag then dropped it into the stove caused Fanny's legs to turn to jelly. She made it to the table and collapsed on a chair. In the bedroom, Roy and Rita watched as Mildred snuggled Archie back down under the blankets and blew out the candle. They knew it was serious when Mildred left the room, but they knew better than to ask questions.

Mildred picked up her bag of tea from the table and before exiting the house said, "I'll tell Uncle Bob to be ready for first thing in the morning."

CHAPTER 21: ARCHIE
DOWN THE BAY, MAY 1947

Ma was sullen as she watched as Dad and Uncle Bob leash up the dogs for the second day in a row.

"At least the bay is still frozen good. At least the weather is fine. At least you're not as sick as the last time you were taken down the bay." Ma just rambled on and on while she hugged her arms around her waist. I wondered if she thought we couldn't hear her because it was so unlike Ma to act like that in front of us.

Her voice turned to a whisper as she paced, still hugging her waist. "What if the tuberculosis infection is moving rapidly? What if it gets to his lungs? What if the cold air makes it worse?" She drew in fast deep breaths.

I was getting nervous now. Little Cack had already asked if I was going to die this time and the rest of the children were so quiet. I knew there were a lot of people dying from this dreadful disease but I didn't have it that bad. Did I?

Rita and John helped me outside to sit on the wood box while we waited.

Dad had the komatik tipped on its side while he leashed up the dogs so that they wouldn't run off before he was ready. The dogs bounced and yelped except for Lady. She sat solemnly watching the house, as if she knew that there was trouble.

Dad looked to Ma and nodded he was ready. I noticed Ma did a small slump before she and Mildred grabbed the bedding to put in the komatik. As Dad approached to carry me out, Ma stooped him and said, "I should have noticed him getting sick. This is all my fault. I just wanted him home."

Dad grabbed her by the shoulders and shook her. "This is no one's fault. He is going to be fine."

When Dad lowered me into the blankets, Ma wrapped me up tightly and gave me a kiss on the forehead. "I'll see you soon, alright?"

"Yeah, Ma, as soon as I get this stinky old cast off, I'm coming back home." Ma and Dad exchanged a look that screamed of hope but was full of anguish. Dad gave her a quick peck on the cheek and we were off.

I could feel Ma watching from the bank until we turned the point of the cove. Somehow, I knew she hated to go back into the house without me once again.

The trip down the bay was uneventful. As the day wore on, more water was building up on the ice, making some places slippery. Dad and Uncle Bob had pretty much decided before they reached St. Mary's that they would stay the night and get an early start when it was colder in the morning. They had told the families back in the cove that this was a possibility so no one would worry.

We reached the hospital around three in the afternoon after a very sinky, boggy ride over the neck in the softened snow. As Grandfather would have said "the bottom is coming right out of 'er." Morning would be better travelling again after a cold night.

Nurse Jupp had seen our arrival from the upstairs veranda where she was tending to patients who were getting some fresh air and sunlight. She recognized us immediately and sped through the hospital and had the door held open for Dad as he carried me up the steps.

"Is he alright? What has happened?" she asked anxiously. She was so worried that her tone wasn't the measured professional one I was used to hearing. As Dad and Uncle Bob exchanged a glance, she looked down and collected herself quickly before pulling herself to full height.

"Good day Mr. Rumbolt. Please leave Archie's outer clothes here and bring him into the dispensary for me."

Dad laid me on the bench for Uncle Bob to undress and led the nurse out of my earshot.

She did look worried when she came back to address me. "Hello again young man. How are you feeling?"

"Hello Nurse Jupp," I smiled. It was nice to see her again, but I felt too shy to say it. "I just came to get this stinky cast off."

I was happy to see her smile back. "Then we will get it done quickly and painlessly." She turned to Dad, "Can I ask you to carry Archie to the emergency room on the second floor?"

Dad nodded and picked me up. She turned to Uncle Bob and asked him to remain in the porch while she strode to the basement to fetch Sam. She came back to inform us that Sam was busy, but told her Hughlette was quite capable of removing the cast. As soon as he gathered the tools together, he would come up.

Nurse Jupp rang for an Aide and continued on to the emergency room on the second floor. She instructed Dad to go wash up in case Hughlette needed help removing the cast. The Nurse and the Aide busied themselves with removing my pants and sweater and had just had me all propped up and ready when Hughlette showed up.

Nurse Jupp unhinged a section of the bed so that my right leg dangled, giving Hughlette better access to the casted leg. The nurse ordered that we all put on masks because of the plaster dust and the possible bacteria.

"I hope it is not as bad as you think, Mr. Rumbolt. But I am concerned about how lethargic Archie is presenting," she said.

Nurse Jupp and the Aide focused on keeping me in good spirits and still. Dad held the cast so Hughlette could begin the sawing procedure. The women held my hands and they all watched as Hughlette expertly, but slowly, sawed into the cast. He never sawed completely through, just to the innermost layer and continued down the leg. It was a tedious procedure and he was about three quarters of the way done when the nurses noticed my silent tears.

"Hughlette, let's take a little break," said the nurse. "How are you feeling Archie?"

"I'm fine," I replied. "Just a bit afraid."

"Just lie back for a few moments and take a little break, alright? I'll be right back."

Nurse Jupp left the room to go downstairs to the dispensary and Hughlette followed her. When they returned, Nurse Jupp had a syringe and a bottle of penicillin on her silver medicine tray.

"How are you feeling now Archie?" she asked as she set her tray on the table. I just nodded in reply, barely keeping back the tears. "It's almost done, so let's keep going and get it over with?" I nodded again.

Hughlette finished quickly and put on a pair of gloves before he finished breaking the cast open far enough to slip it off the leg. The nurse lifted my leg by the foot so that the cast could be completely removed. She asked Dad to sit on the chair across the room while she and her Aide donned gloves to remove the gauze.

"What do it look like?" Dad asked.

"I won't be able to tell how bad it was until the gauze is off and it is cleaned," she answered.

Twenty minutes later, she had me all cleaned up and Hughlette had left with the discards of the cast to burn in the basement wood burner.

"Alright Archie, looks like you have an infection and you will have to stay with us for another little while."

I looked at her sleepily and nodded. After the day I just had with travelling and cast removal, I was just too tired to care.

"I am going to give you a dose of penicillin so it doesn't get worse and send a message to the doctor in Cartwright for advice," she said as she drew some liquid into the syringe. I was familiar with having needles but I didn't like them. Tears sprang to my eyes again as the Aide rolled me onto my side for the shot. I was so sick of being sick.

"You can rest now while I talk to your dad downstairs," Nurse Jupp said gently as everyone left the room.

CHAPTER 22: NURSE JUPP
ST. MARY'S, APRIL 1947

In the dispensary, Nurse Jupp was writing her notes while she explained to Ern about the seriousness of the infection. "He has two abscesses at the back of his knee and a pocket that has travelled up his thigh towards his hip. A tuberculosis diagnosis can only be given by a doctor, so I must wait until I hear from him. I am sending a message to Battle Harbour tonight."

"I can take it," replied Ern, wanting desperately to be useful.

"Your dogs are probably tired from the trip down the bay, so it's better if we send the mission dogs." She was just about to ring for Hughlette when there was a rap on the dispensary door. Hughlette was all dressed for travel.

"I was hearing that the run may be breaking so Henry and I are going on," he said.

She handed him the note and he left. She turned back to Ern. "Will you be returning back to Tooth Cove tonight?"

"No, we found it a bit soft coming over the neck, so we will wait for morning," he said. He hung his head and wished there was more he could do.

"Archie will be fine. He is resting comfortably now and we will sit up with him for the night to monitor him. The penicillin will help stop the spread of infection," Nurse Jupp explained.

Ern nodded but didn't say anything. Then he rose to leave.

Nurse Jupp could feel his anguish. "Try not to worry, and by all means, stop by in the morning before you leave."

"Thank you, Miss."

After he left, Dorothy sat in silence for a long time. Many times in the past few weeks since Archie had gone home, she had craved to see that beautiful little smile. She had walked by the big ward, as he called it, many times and imagined he was still in his bed. She couldn't help but wonder if he had stayed in his own little ward, if he would have been fine or if he somehow got the infection at home. There still wasn't enough research done on tuberculosis to determine if a patient was still contagious even after they no longer show symptoms. Archie had been so excited to move to the big ward and even though she had been apprehensive, she couldn't say no to the little darling. She stressed to him the importance of cleanliness, but she couldn't be there all the time watching. And what if just being in the room with the men who were recovering from TB was the issue. Cleaning may have had nothing to do with it.

She berated herself for giving in to him, but at the same time, the move had made him so happy, and he had really thrived with the company. In the time that passed, she hadn't been able to put a patient in his bed. As luck should have it, they hadn't been full since.

Archie would soon turn eight and she couldn't help but remember back to her own eighth year. Her mother had gotten sick and was taken to a hospital. As she never knew her father, and so she was sent to live with nuns in the Home of Epiphany. She could still remember vividly the day the sisters informed her of her mother's death, and it was years later before she knew it was tuberculosis that had taken her. At that time, it was referred to as consumption and it was this scary disease that led her on the path to a medical career. Now, nearly thirty years later, she was feeling the same dread and desperation.

However, as many times as she had wished to see the little boy who had stolen her heart, she never thought it would be like this. So many people had succumbed to this terrible disease and now it looked like Archie had contracted it as well. She didn't need the doctor to diagnose tuberculosis; she already knew.

She was still sitting at her desk in the dispensary when Hughlette had returned with a message from Dr. Paddon in Cartwright. He would leave in the morning to come tend to the boy. Until then she was to continue to administer the penicillin.

CHAPTER 23: FANNY
TOOTH COVE, APRIL 1947

It was past noon when Fanny heard the dogs round the point of the cove. She dropped what she was doing and rushed outside. She knew the komatik was empty even before they reached the shoreline. The team bounded up the hill and stopped by the house. Fanny couldn't help notice the sadness in Lady's eyes. It was a look she had when hungry for food, but Fanny knew it wasn't food she was keening for. Lady and Archie had always had a bond. Even when Ern jumped off and instructed Bob to go unleash the dogs, Lady whimpered and only went reluctantly.

Ern led Fanny into the house. By this time the children had gathered and Mildred and Liz had shown up.

While Ern hung his coat and hat on the nail beside the door, Fanny poured him up a cup of tea. She was anxious but knew better than to rush him into talking. She, along with the others, were literally holding their breaths.

Ern sat down and took a sip of tea, "You were right Mill, his leg was badly infected, but hopefully he will get better soon."

Everyone let the air out of their lungs. Mildred was relieved but took no pleasure at being right this time.

"Is it TB?" she asked.

"The nurse couldn't say. The doctor is on the way from Cartwright. I saw Archie before I left and he is resting well. He is gonna get good care there. All we can do now is pray for him."

Fanny silently stood by the window with her arms folded looking out. "I should have known there was something wrong."

With this Ern jumped up and pounded his fist on the table causing the tea to tip and spill.

"Dammit woman, how the hell could you have known that? It was all inside the bloody cast."

Everything went silent; even little Dorothy muffled her whimper. Ern leaned on the table with his elbows locked and head hung down, immediately regretting this outburst. He knew what his wife was feeling and it was so frustrating to see her have to go through it again.

Rita broke the silence. "Come on guys, let's go outside so Pa can eat his dinner."

As Rita hustled the children outside, Mildred looked at her mother, "It's not your fault, Mom, the damn dirt is everywhere."

"Come up for tea da once," said Liz as she left with Mildred. Liz knew this was not the time to show her compassion. Fanny needed to be alone with her husband right now.

When the door was shut, Ern glanced at Fanny. She was still staring silently out the window with her arms folded tight to her chest and her lips set in a tight line.

"I'm going to get a quick bite and go on to the mill to see what's going on over there," he said. He had to get out of the house.

"And I have to finish sewing Cack's coat", she replied as she sat and picked up her work.

Ern ate and while Fanny sewed in silence until he jumped up, grabbed his coat, and headed to the mill. Fanny could feel the rift beginning between them but was helpless to stop it.

The only thing she could think about was Archie.

CHAPTER 24: DR. ANTHONY PADDON CARTWRIGHT, APRIL 1947

The message had come through to the station at Cartwright about six thirty in the evening. The Mission Forman, Harvey Bird, found Dr. Paddon doing rounds on the TB ward.

Dr. Paddon frowned at the message. Any sign of tuberculosis was a grave matter but when it involved a seven-year-old child, it was a serious matter indeed. He also knew that Dorothy Jupp would certainly not send a note of this urgency if it were not life and death involved. He didn't need to dwell on it long. He made his decision and quickly scribbled his note to be sent back, knowing that a messenger was waiting for a reply in Battle Harbour to bring back to the nurse at St. Mary's.

He had just spent a few long months doing dog team travel north and south of Cartwright, so another trip south wouldn't be here nor there in the grand scheme of things. Plus, the trip south this winter had to be a lot easier than the trip north had been. He knew with good going and no trouble he could reach the hospital at St. Mary's in two days. He finished his rounds and went to pack some bags and to make contact with his driver.

Jim Morris, his driver, cautioned him that with the fast-approaching spring thaw, the trip may take a bit longer so extra supplies may be needed. Dr. Paddon noted that not once did Jim show any hesitation about actually making the trip. He just needed him to be prepared for a slower trip than they had had in the winter. He had enjoyed the travel with Jim and was especially taken with his lead dog, Blossom, whom he thought to be as intelligent as any human being as well as having an excellent memory of past routes and dangerous ice.

They set out early the next morning and made quick time until the midday sun turned the icy path to loose crystals. They made it to

Roaches Brook for a quick cup of tea and continued on. From here, the trail turned inland and, being sheltered in the trees, the path was a bit tougher. With the longer daylight of spring, they managed to reach Norman Bay that night. The trek across Hawkes Bay had been slushy, but there had been fresh tracks so they had proceeded. Usually, on a well beaten track, the snow would compact with the ice to create longer lasting ice paths. However, they realized that with the hot spring sun, the ice travel wouldn't last much longer. They were welcomed for the night by a lovely couple in Norman Bay and had a great feast of seal meat.

As tired as they were, they were informed that they just completed the easy section of their trip. The next portion of their journey, although a bit shorter, involved three bays that were quickly thawing.

A local trapper travelled with them to St. Michaels Bay to see them safely across. They were not able to travel on Cape Bluff Pond this time south due to a lot of soft slushy snow. The alternate route they took was still tough due to travelling early in the morning. One of the local settlers at St. Michaels Bay guided them across the bay and travelled with them till they were safely across the shinnies.

They had the same experience at Alexis Bay. A local guided them across and put them on the trail, but not until after his wife made sure they had a warm meal and a hot cup of tea. Dr. Paddon was always humbled by the kindness and generosity of the locals. They always gave of what they had, even if it was very little.

Once they were across the bay, the path through the company town of Port Hope Simpson and on to St. Lewis Bay was well beaten from the travel of men back and forth to work at mills. By the time they reached Wallmans on the north side of bay, the sun was setting low in the sky and they decided to stay with some of the workers in the camp for the night. They would leave early in the morning when the snow was firm again. They still had another 18 miles of bay, plus a couple of miles of land, before they reached the hospital at St. Mary's.

Over a delicious meal of rabbit that night, the men told Dr. Paddon that the boy whom he was on his way to cure was a young fellow from the Tooth Cove, across the bay from Wallmans. They were telling him the story of the infected knee and the cast when Dr. Paddon realized that this was the same boy he had seen on his visit a few months ago.

The little boy who was so eager to go home. The men told him of the worried father who worked in the mill at Tooth Cove and of the distraught mother who was at times inconsolable. The doctor had heard those stories of anguish many times during his time in Labrador, and although he was able to bring relief to a lot of families, there was some that, no matter how hard he tried, he could not cure. He prayed for all involved, that he was going to be able to help this boy he was travelling to see.

They rose early the next morning and one of the local men guided them across the bay and told them to stay on the well beaten path to St. Mary's, as ice conditions were quickly deteriorating. He couldn't help but look in towards Tooth Cove and think about the family who resided there who were worrying about their son. He decided he would make time to stop to give them news on his return. The path stayed firm and they reached the hospital by noon.

While Jim busied himself tying up the dogs, Hughlette helped the doctor bring his bags into the hospital. Nurse Jupp met him in the porch with a grim look on her face. She told him how happy she was to see him and inquired about his journey.

"Would you like to eat before you meet the patient?" she asked.

Dr. Paddon was well accustomed to working long hours on an empty stomach, and although he was feeling a bit hungry, decided to wait. He didn't think he would have enjoyed his meal with a boy lying sick in an upstairs room.

"I'm fine, just bring me to the boy," he said.

He followed Nurse Jupp up the staircase and made a sharp right turn down the hall to the emergency room. A gowned aide was in the room watching over the young boy. Nurse Jupp excused the aide who promptly left, giving Dr. Paddon a quick nod as she left the room.

CHAPTER 25: ARCHIE
ST. MARY'S, APRIL 1947

I was propped up slightly in the bed with a small book beside me, but I was barely awake.

"Hello there young man, it's good to see you again. Although I wish it were under better circumstances."

My eyes sprang wide open. I couldn't believe my eyes. It was Dr. Paddon. Now I knew I would get well soon and go back to the cove. I smiled as big a smile as I could for the doctor. Nurse Jupp also smiled at this.

"I see you do remember me, Archie. Do you mind if I examine your leg?" he asked.

I shook my head no and for the next twenty minutes I willed myself to stay alert while Nurse Jupp gave him the background description of my condition.

My left leg was now propped on two pillows with a space in the middle where the abscess was draining from the back of his knee. The doctor had donned gloves and was examining that area and up to my hip. When he was done, he pulled up a chair next to me to talk.

"Archie, I must tell you that you do indeed have the tuberculosis infection, and it has certainly been growing rapidly in your leg. The penicillin can only do so much to attack the bacteria, so it's only slowing it a little. I have been in touch with Dr. Thomas in St. Anthony and they are in the process of acquiring a brand-new drug that has been proven effective for combating TB. It's called streptomycin, and they have just ordered a batch from the Pfizer Company in New York, thanks to a generous $7000 donation from a Montreal family. If I can get you out to St. Anthony, we can get this infection made all better in no time."

The doctor's soothing voice and commanding tone really relaxed me, and I felt so much better now that the doctor was here. Even though I trusted and respected Nurse Jupp, there was something about the way that she acted around the doctor that gave him that extra air of superiority.

However, at the mention of going to St. Anthony, I suddenly became unnerved. I had heard people talk about it and it seemed so far away. If I went there, would I ever see his family again? It was overwhelming. Panic hit me; tears sprang to my eyes and I bolted upright.

"I can't go there, it's too far, why can't you help me here? Tell them to send the needles here," I cried, beginning to feel desperate.

"Archie, please relax. Everything is going to be fine. At St. Anthony you will have all the proper care of the best doctors in the world. It's the fastest way for you to get better, I promise."

I laid back in the bed and regarded Nurse Jupp, who just smiled and nodded. "You will love it there Archie. There are lots of other children and you can attend a proper school. The time will pass very quickly, and before you know it you will be back home."

"Alright." I consented. All I wanted to do was to go back to the cove as soon as I could and if this was the only way, I would have to make peace with the idea.

"Wonderful," declared the doctor. "Now I need to explain what I must do while I am here. You have large pockets of infection at the back of your knee and working its way to your hip area. As I already told you, the penicillin is slowing it a bit but I would like to remove it. As long as it's there it could eat away into your bones and cartilage and do permanent damage to your knee and leg bones. What I am going to do is to remove some of the infection with a syringe."

My eyes widened. "Will it hurt?" I asked.

"I will try my best to make it as painless as possible, but yes, you may have discomfort."

I glanced at Nurse Jupp. "Will Nurse Jupp be here?"

The nurse smiled and said, "I will be here holding your hand all the while."

This made me smile too. I would try his best to be brave. "Are you doing it right now?"

The doctor laughed. "Well, right now I need to have a bite to eat and freshen up a bit so I can do a proper job without distractions. So, why don't you rest a bit and I will be back in an hour."

I nodded and watched them leave. As I took deep breaths to try and calm my thudding heart, I had a sudden ache to see Ma.

While I waited, the Aide returned with Sam pushing a narrow bed on wheels. Sam steadied the bed and helped the Aide move me onto it, explaining to me that the procedure the doctor was going to do would be done in the operating room. When I was all settled onto the bed, they wheeled me down the hall, past the public bathroom and the utility room and into the OR. This room was kept very sterile and held all the instruments that the doctor would need to perform any surgery, including dentistry. The Aide covered my head with a cap and put some socks on me just in case I got cold. There wasn't much heat in the OR.

Sam left but the Aide stayed with Archie until the doctor and Nurse Jupp appeared. They were both dressed in green surgical gowns and gloves. They also had their heads covered.

Nurse Jupp gave me a mild sedative to relax me, and the doctor got to work. The syringe looked huge, but after they turned me onto my right side, I couldn't see anything except Nurse Jupp. The doctor was working behind me. I felt tiny pricks when the doctor would insert the syringe and a cooling emptiness as the doctor extracted the infection. It was strange, but it wasn't unbearable. The doctor repeated the procedure about ten times and extracted about two cups of the infectious bacteria from my knee and thigh. Nurse Jupp watched in awe as the Dr Paddon precisely and competently did his job.

"It's not often that I have the opportunity to witness this procedure as most of the TB patients I treat are lung cases," she remarked.

"I saw a lot of cases like this during the war," the doctor remarked. "This procedure was very successful in delaying infection until we got patients out of the field hospitals and into larger centres."

"You did really well, Archie," proclaimed the doctor. "I am confident that I extracted all that was possible and that if not much more develops before you get to St. Anthony, then you should be fine. At least now the infection won't reach your organs very quickly."

"I bet John would have cried like a baby," I said, still a bit fuzzy feeling because of the sedative.

The doctor and the nurse had a little laugh while I started to drift into a contented sleep.

As I was starting to drive away, I head Dr. Paddon and Nurse Jupp talking. The doctor was saying he was confident that he had done everything he could and would leave for Cartwright while winter travel was still possible.

"You can handle it from here," he said to Nurse Jupp. "Unfortunately, the only thing to do in those cases of joint TB is to let it drain and hope it would heal."

As they walked out of the room, I heard him say, "The boy really needs to get to St. Anthony and hopefully the *Maraval* will get across soon."

CHAPTER 26: FANNY
TOOTH COVE, MAY 1947

It was nearly noon when Fanny heard a dog team yelping as they rounded the point of the cove. The men were at the mill, but Charl and Roy were working at the wood and walked down to meet the two men. The travel had slowed this time of the year, and usually the only visitors to the cove was family or mail delivery, so Fanny just assumed it was mail for someone.

While she continued to watch, she saw Charl point to her house and a well-dressed man took a parcel out of the komatik and followed Charl and Roy to her house.

The blood drained from her body she slowly backed away from the window and only after Rita had exclaimed "Mom" under her breath, did Fanny realise she had whimpered. No one had to tell her what was in that parcel. She had witnessed that scene before when clergy had returned the meagre belongings of a relative to his family. She wanted to scream, to hit something, to kick something, but as she turned to face Rita, she saw Cack and Dorothy also watching her.

"They are coming here Ma," said Rita as she started towards the door.

"Do not let them in this house," Fanny barked, her fists tightly clenched to her sides. She did not want that package that held the leftovers of her son. She couldn't bear to see that little flannel shirt she had sent him to the hospital in, without him in it. She was suffocating. She couldn't breathe. Then came the knock on the door.

Rita and the children stood frozen, not knowing what to make of their mother's behaviour. Finally, Charl burst through the door and Dr. Paddon came in behind him.

"How come no one opened the door for Dr. Paddon? What was yas doin?" Charl looked from one to the other as Roy, John, Mildred, and Liz followed the doctor inside.

Fanny kept her eyes on the parcel as she slowly backed away. This didn't go unnoticed by the doctor. He held it out to her and told her it was for the children from Nurse Jupp. Fanny looked into Dr. Paddon's face and saw kindness and bewilderment; she realised her mistake. Almost at the same moment, the doctor also understood the situation.

"Mrs. Rumbolt, your boy is doing well. I just dropped by to let you know," he gushed out as quick as he could to ease her mind. Fanny grabbed the edge of the table to steady herself and finally let the air out of her lungs. Dr. Paddon touched her arm and gave her a sympathetic nod to indicate that he understood and then turned to the children.

"Who would like to have a piece of English shortbread while I talk to your mom?" he asked.

"Me," yelled Cack and Dorothy in unison, even though they didn't have a clue what it was. They did know that if Nurse Jupp sent it, then it was probably delicious.

Everyone laughed and Dr. Paddon handed the parcel to Rita to open and Mildred hurried to get a cup of tea for the doctor. Over tea and a slice of delicious molasses bread, the doctor explained to Fanny the procedure he had performed on her son, and about the new medication in St. Anthony that would cure him.

"It will all take time, Mrs. Rumbolt, and there are no guarantees, but your son had tuberculosis in the best possible place, if that makes any sense to you. Lung TB does not have a good mortality rate and brain TB and tubercular meningitis are always fatal. Your son has it in the knee and hip joint so there is a good prognosis."

Fanny listened intently, and even though she didn't understand the medical terms, she understood enough to know that her son was not in imminent danger. She would make peace with the Grenfell Mission keeping her son for as long as it took to heal him. It was possible to be happily broken-hearted, because that's exactly how she felt.

CHAPTER 27: ARCHIE ON THE *MV MARAVAL*, JUNE 1947

Nurse Jupp told me that Dr. Paddon had sent a message to Battle Harbour to be transmitted to St. Anthony before he had left for his return trip to Cartwright. His instructions were clear "to dispatch the Grenfell Schooner *Maraval* immediately to St. Mary's to transport a seven-year-old boy to St. Anthony with tuberculosis complications."

However, with ice still lingering around the shorelines, a safe passage for the *Maraval* would be delayed for a few days. Travel by sea this time of year depended on the winds and tides. The amount of lingering ice could change in mere hours or remain the same for weeks.

I had improved a bit since the cast had been removed and the draining done. Not only did my leg feel better, but I didn't feel as sluggish and sleepy. I was still on bed rest and remained in the emergency room, as Nurse Jupp was very meticulous concerning cleanliness and the spread of germs in hospital. Time was a bit long even though there was an endless supply of books and colouring books at my disposal. I longed for home and to be surrounded by family. I also longed for the outdoors. The last time I was here, I had spent some time on the balcony during warm days, but the balcony was only accessed through the big ward and Nurse Jupp felt I was too contagious to be brought through it.

Finally, the day came when Nurse Jupp announced that the *Maraval* was sailing into the harbour. The run had broken up a while ago, so we had all known that there would be no notice of the approaching vessel until it was spotted sailing in. She also knew she would have a bit of time to get me ready as the small ship had to tie up and unload a few necessities for them. There would also likely be some patients transported back this way that were ready for home from the St. Anthony Hospital. Some people from the north coast might be here for a few weeks awaiting travel north.

Archie and Selma at St. Mary's River. PANL.

I wished I could have watched, but the emergency room was located at the back of the hospital. I started feeling a bit excited mingled with a bit of sadness. Although I was excited at the prospect of seeing a place I had only ever heard about, the thought of being so far away from home was daunting. At least here at St. Mary's, my family was able to see me from time to time.

Two of the Aides showed up to get me dressed in warm clothes and to help me down the stairs. They gave me a set of crutches and I was amazed at how well I felt. My sore leg was well-bandaged, but it was nice not to have a cast on. I couldn't wait to go outside. When I hobbled through the doors with the help of the Aides and a set of crutches, I took a big deep gulp of fresh air. It was an overcast day but nice and warm. Apparently, it was the first warm day in a while because there was still a fair bit of snow lingering around. The air was so fresh that the cleaners had all the mats taken up off the porch and had them hung on the rails of the small landing. The Aides helped me down the steps as a group of people came around the small cove from the mission wharf.

My jacket felt suffocating, so I insisted that it be removed, so one of the Aides helped me take it off and she draped it over her arm. Nurse Jupp stepped out of the hospital and came down the steps behind us as the group from the *Maraval* approached. The cook even came outdoors and leaned on the rail to watch everything. I gave them all a big smile because I knew they all wanted the best for me.

Nurse Jupp greeted the group and enquired if they needed a meal or tea. One of the men named Mr. Patey declined the offer as they wanted to head on back and said that he already had dinner on the stove aboard the boat. He introduced Nurse Jupp to three of the people he had brought to St. Mary's to await transport to the north coast. I noticed that the two men and one woman had darker skin than mine and was pleasantly surprised to see a girl with them who was not much older than myself.

We eyed each other curiously. Obviously neither of us were used to seeing many children in such settings.

Mr. Patey, a tall slim young man, probably just a few years older than Hughlette, walked towards me and crouched to talk to me.

"Hello young feller, I hear you are travelling with us today back to

St. Anthony," he said in a kind voice.

I gave a slight nod and glanced nervously at Nurse Jupp.

"My name is Ted, and I'll be lookin after ya on the way back. We had a nice smooth ride over and the ice is all loose so we should not be too long going back. Are ya skerred?"

I shook my head no and glanced again at Nurse Jupp. The nurse smiled and turned to Ted. "Archie is a very special young man here at the hospital, so I trust I am leaving him in good hands."

"I've taken care of quite a few sick young lads, so he is in good hands indeed. Although I'm the cook and engineer today, so his meals may not be as good as the hospital meals," he laughed. "My young feller is actually around Archie's age," he added.

Nurse Jupp laughed, "Well at least you are not the captain too."

"No." chuckled Ted. "We are lucky to have Captain Barbour today, best on the seas in my opinion."

"Good to hear," Nurse Jupp replied then turned to me. "Now let's get you over and aboard and settled."

Mr. Patey had not failed to notice the curious looks between myself and the girl. He also turned to me and said, "Archie, this is Selma. Selma has been all cured of tuberculosis and is ready to go back home, whenever she can get a ride."

I beamed thinking that maybe soon, this would be me too. All better and ready to come home.

A man in the group with a camera said, "I need a picture of them. It's not often we make a trip like this to deliver a child and pick up another."

"Well make it quick,'" said the nurse, "I want to get him all settled."

The picture was taken and the newcomers headed into the hospital with the Aides while the rest headed around the cove. I glanced back as the girl went up the steps. I never saw her again.

My eyes widened in amazement as I was led down the wharf. Hughlette and another worker had come up behind us and carried me in the chair position while Nurse Jupp carried my small bag and crutches. I had seen similar boats at Battle Harbour, in the summer, some bigger, some smaller, but I had never been on-board one. I figured you would be able to fit three of the houses in Tooth Cove in this boat with room to spare.

Grenfell hospital ship, the MV Maraval. PANL IGA 25-138.

The vessel looked long, at least forty feet long, and had a housed area in the middle. She was low in the water; lower at the stern but higher at the bow. The bow was designed to push through the ice, and I could see the steel over the oak to help with that. She was also smaller than some of the boats I had seen, so could get into shallower coves than most boats. She was ketch rigged and had two huge masts springing up from her centre. Today, the sails were not out, which meant she was just running on the diesel engine. The name *Maraval* was painted on her bow and a big red cross was painted on the housed area to signify that it was a hospital ship. Hughlette had told me all about the ship and how she went along the Labrador coast bringing doctors, nurses, and even a dentist to all the communities.

I couldn't believe that I was actually going away on this boat. I imagined telling my brothers and sisters about it. Then I wondered when I would see them again to tell them. I was again overwhelmed with both excitement and sadness.

The men carried me up the ramp leading into the schooner. Nurse Jupp followed behind. Once inside, they carried me down a narrow hallway to the ship's dispensary. I looked around with wide eyes. I couldn't believe that I was on a boat, and how huge it was. The dispensary was just a smaller version of the dispensary in the hospital, except it had a room with a couple of bunks in it for transporting patients. Mr. Patey explained to me that the galley and eating area were just down the hall, but he would bring my dinner to me in the room so that I wouldn't have to move around much. He also told me that the captain's wheelhouse was above me so I wouldn't be scared when I heard him tramping around. I had seen the captain's wheelhouse from the wharf, so I had a good visualisation of it. Mr. Patey also explained there were two double cabins onboard, but they were below deck at the stern and to access it you had to go down a ladder from the galley.

I was speechless and in awe. He also insisted I call him Ted.

Ted left to make arrangements for the boat to leave, leaving Nurse Jupp to get me settled into the bed.

"It's been so nice having you here again Archie, but I am happy you will be getting some good help at St. Anthony. That hospital is bigger with doctors who can cure almost anything, and before you know it you will be all better and back home" she said with a warm smile.

I just nodded. I suddenly realised that I wouldn't be back to St. Mary's Hospital at all. When I recovered, I would be sent directly home. I didn't know why I felt sad about that, but when I looked back up at Nurse Jupp, I knew. I wasn't going to see Nurse Jupp again either. I saw that her eyes had gone all wet like Ma's used to get when she was really sad, and I didn't know what to say. I just threw my arms around her waist and held tight.

Nurse Jupp, still standing, hugged my head and gently kissed the top of it. I could feel that she had grown to love me too during the past five months I was under her care. I wondered if this was probably the closest she would ever come to knowing what being a mom felt like? I hoped one day she would have lots of babies to love.

She pulled away and stood straight, saying, "Have a safe journey, Archie."

I nodded and looked down again as she swiftly left. Ted came back and asked if I was alright because he had seen the nurse make a hasty exit without saying good-bye.

I looked up and gave a weak, "Yes."

"Good, cuz as soon as I finish pushing off from the wharf, I am coming back to get you to do a tour of the boat."

My eyes brightened and I gave Ted a huge toothy smile.

CHAPTER 28: ARCHIE
ST. ANTHONY, JUNE 1947

Although it was nearly six in the evening, the June sun was still high in the sky as the schooner rounded Fishing Point to enter St. Anthony Harbour. I had been dozing in my bunk when the schooner whistle sounded. Ted snuggled me into some blankets and sat me on deck so I could see the harbour as we sailed in.

Ted had shown me all around the schooner after we had left St. Mary's, and I had been very impressed. I even got to meet the captain whom Ted introduced as Captain Barbour, but the captain had insisted that I call him Stan. It felt so strange to call adults by their first names, but I tried my best.

While we sailed through the run between Caribou Island and Hare Island, on the Labrador side, Ted had dished up his famous corned beef and cabbage for dinner. I wasn't sure if it was actually great cooking or if the fresh spring breeze coming into the galley from the deck stimulated my appetite, but it was absolutely delicious. Ted was busy helping the captain look out for ice, so after the meal he had taken me back to the dispensary cabin to settle crossing the straits. I was feeling tired by then; Nurse Jupp had given me a seasick pill, and I think it was starting to take effect. I had slept the rest of the way and was now excited to be reaching my destination.

Once around the point and into the long somewhat narrow sheltered harbour, I was amazed at the number of structures and houses. The largest place I had ever visited was Battle Harbour and you could surely fit six Battle Harbours in St. Anthony and maybe more. There were at least four big merchant style wharfs on both sides of the harbour and many smaller wharfs, plus lots of houses dotting the shorelines.

We were a little more than halfway to the bottom of the harbour when the boat turned left to a huge wharf. While Ted threw ashore a rope to secure the front, a man jumped aboard and secured the stern. I remained sitting on the bench until the men had secured the boat and lowered the ramp. Two men then came aboard with a stretcher to fetch me.

As the two men moved me to the stretcher, Ted and Stan came to say good-bye and hoped I had had a good trip across.

"I loved it," I replied. "Hopefully in a few days you can bring me back," I beamed.

Ted and Stan gave each other a sad glance. Ted crouched down to my level. "You know what, if you are still here in a few days, I will bring my boy over for a visit. He is your age and you two will get along famously."

"That would be nice, but I won't be here very long. Maybe I will meet him sometime if I come back," I said confidently.

Ted stood again without responding and gave me a small pat on the shoulder.

"Good luck at the hospital," piped in Stan. I nodded and off we went.

One of the old trucks used to carry freight was waiting, and the men gently put me in the back then jumped in to escort me to the hospital. The ride was bumpy, but short. I looked all around with wonderment. The buildings were huge and there were so many of them. They were mostly wood, but the hospital was a three-story brick building and looked gigantic. I couldn't wait to get all better and explore the area on foot.

Once inside the hospital, I was taken off the mobile stretcher and placed on a bed with wheels. All staff had been made aware of my arrival and my condition, so my left leg was kept straight and not tampered with. An Aide showed the men to the ward that I would be staying in.

After I was moved to my own bed and settled, the Aide introduced me to the other boys in the room. There were eight small beds in the ward, and I was in the third bed on the left. The boy to my left in the corner was introduced as Arthur. Arthur looked to be about my age and just stared blankly at me and nodded. The boy in the bed next to me on the right was introduced as Garfield. Garfield looked a bit younger and laid in his bed with the covers up to his chest the same as Arthur. The bed by the door was empty. The two beds across from Garfield but next to the door were also empty. Directly across from him was Daniel, and in the right corner across from Arthur, was Reggie. Daniel and Reggie looked older, maybe eleven or twelve, and Reggie had casts on both legs.

Even though it was getting late, the boys were still wide awake and watched me curiously. It was always interesting when someone new came, wondering what was wrong with them, how old they were, where they came from, but most of all, if they were going to be nice or just a spoiled brat. I learned that being a young patient in a large hospital, you get to see all kinds of kids go through and most are just plain scared, but the fear presents itself in many different forms. The two older boys lost interest in the new young kid and turned back toward each other and chatted in whispers, but the other two boys just looked on, watching and waiting, while I kept my head bowed and twiddled my thumbs. It felt very awkward being in a room with boys my own age. I was thinking that it had been much more comfortable with the older men in the ward at St. Mary's.

The Aide pulled around my privacy screen, a curtain that was draped from the ceiling and circled my bed. She told me to start getting undressed while she fetched me a wash pan and pyjamas. She also told me she would get me a lunch, remarking that I must be starved from his journey, but also that I shouldn't eat too much before bed.

When the Aide returned, she was pushing a cart that was loaded with a variety of cups, pans, towels, and medical tools. She set to work getting me washed and into a nightshirt, being careful around my leg. She took my temperature and pulse and remarked about what a healthy-looking boy I was despite my troubles. When she was done, she placed a bowl of custard and jelly and a glass of milk on my meal tray and told me she would be back with a toothbrush a bit later. She opened the privacy curtain again before she exited.

I took a sip of my milk but was uncomfortable with the other boys watching me.

"Where ya from?" asked Reggie. He seemed to be the least shy of the boys.

"Tooth Cove," I replied.

"Never heard of it," Reggie laughed. "Is it really called Tooth Cove? Is it shaped like a tooth or wha?" Reggie laughed a bigger laugh while I squirmed with embarrassment.

"Thats a sin to be teasing him already," said Arthur. "He is probably still missing home yet."

"I was at St. Mary's all winter," I piped up, "so I am used to being away." I didn't want the other boys to think I was a sissy or a baby.

"I know where that is," said Arthur.

"So do I," said Reggie. "We are from the Labrador too."

"I'm from these parts," said Garfield, eager to get in on the conversation. He was a couple of years younger but really wanted to fit in with the big boys. The boys chuckled and carried on with the introductory chatter.

"Are you gonna eat that custard and jello or wha?" asked Reggie.

"No, I'm not very hungry."

"Well, can I have it?" he asked.

"I don't care," I laughed.

"Daniel?" asked Reggie.

Daniel looked over at Reggie and rolled his eyes. It took me a moment to figure out what was going on, but I soon discovered that because Daniel was the most agile in the room, with only one cast on, the other boys were always asking him to do stuff.

"Fine," he replied. "But I get half."

This time Reggie rolled his eyes. "There is always a price to Daniels favours," he noted.

Daniel hobbled over to my bed and took the bowl and spoon off the tray. He ate half and handed the bowl to Reggie and watched as he quickly gobbled it down. Daniel then quickly hobbled back to replace the empty bowl and the spoon on the tray before the Aide came back to catch him. Myself and the other boys laughed a good ole belly laugh. It was so funny to watch.

The boys carried on talking a bit longer until the nurse came and said it was time for lights out. She brought a toothbrush for me and some water and a kidney bowl to spit in. The other boys were also told to brush their teeth.

Even though I liked the boys and was happy to be with my own age group, I had a hard time getting to sleep. I felt so far away from home, and he wondered what my family was doing tonight, especially Ma. At least I would see the doctor tomorrow and hopefully not have a very long stay.

CHAPTER 29: ARCHIE
ST. ANTHONY, JUNE 1947

It seemed I had only just dropped off to sleep when a nurse came buzzing through the wards, opening the curtains on the window and announcing it was time to rise and shine. The other boys groaned as they were forced from their sleep, beds propped up, washing pans brought in for them to get washed, and bed pans for peeing.

"The doctors will be doing rounds soon and you all need to be awake and alert," she said. The nurse looked around, satisfied that everyone was awake. "I see we have a new patient today," she remarked as she walked towards my bed and read my name that was taped to the foot of the bed. "Archibald Rumbolt, all the way from St. Mary's I believe." I nodded and she continued. "I hope you slept well?" I nodded again.

The boys sleepily waited until they heard the approaching party of doctors. I watched as they made a round of the ward stopping first at Daniel's bed. I was excited, but nervous. I knew the doctors would make me better and send me home real quick. My heart pounded in my ears so loud that I couldn't even make out what was being said to Daniel or the other boys, but when they stopped at Arthur's bed and pulled back the sheets it was as if everything went dead silent for me.

Arthur was cast from his waist to his toes. I couldn't believe what I was seeing and all of a sudden I felt faint. I remembered the difficulty of having one leg cast, but from the waist down with both legs, it must have been unbearable. I suddenly felt very sad for Arthur and gave a silent prayer of thanks that I didn't have a cast like that.

Then it was my turn. Dr. Thomas was a tall man with clean cut dark hair, and the other doctor with him was introduced as Dr. Salter. Dr. Salter was a bit shorter than Dr. Thomas and his receding hairline was a bit lighter, but they were about the same age. Although both men looked

St. Anthony Hospital. PANL A 111-105.

to be smart and capable doctors, I was immediately drawn to Dr. Salter more. I didn't know what it was, but his smile was so friendly and genuine and the doctor's colouring sort of reminded me of brother Roy.

Dr. Thomas introduced the group of to himself and Dr. Salter, plus the two nurses and two visiting doctors. The nurses took notes and assisted while the two visiting doctors examined my legs. They asked me questions about my accident and about my time at St. Mary's.

They listened to my chest with a stethoscope, and I noticed that it was different from the one at St. Mary's, but I was afraid to ask about it. It felt ticklish when Dr. Thomas pressed on my belly, but I tried to stay as still as I could. I just wanted to get all this over with as quickly as possible.

When they examined my leg, they mentioned that there was swelling and tried to straighten it. It felt very painful, and they noted the fifteen-degree flexion and the twenty-degree free movement, meaning it still wouldn't move like it should. They also noted the two draining sinuses on the back of my knee.

"Well Archie," Dr. Thomas began when he had finished the examination. "It looks like I have some good news and some bad news for you. The good news is that from the waist up you are a perfectly normal healthy boy. You have a good heart rhythm of eighty-four and no murmurs. Your abdomen had a normal contour with no tenderness or rigidity and your liver and spleen seems fine. The bad news is that you definitely have tuberculosis of the left knee. Tuberculosis is never a very good thing to have but if one has to have it, it is a lot better to have it in a joint than in the lungs or the brain. We will get a cast applied to your leg right away so the knee can rest and heal. Do you have any questions?"

"Can I go back home after the cast is on?" I asked eagerly.

The doctors laughed and I felt my face redden.

"Sorry Archie," Dr. Thomas said. "It looks like you may have to stay with us for a while until you are healed. But don't worry, we will have you up and on the go in no time. With proper rest and good food and fresh air you will be as good as new."

I cast my eyes downward and fought the urge to cry. This did not go unnoticed by Dr. Salter, and he patted my hand and told me he would come back to check on me later.

Breakfast was brought in at eight, but I was too upset to eat. When the Aide came to collect the trays, she noticed the food untouched and told me that if I didn't eat, I would not heal very quickly. That made me eat a few spoonfuls of the rolled oats and a few bites of toast, but it travelled to my belly in lumps.

I just laid silently in bed listening to the boys chatter quietly. I didn't want to participate. All I could think about was not being able to go home. I was so sure I would have been on the way home today. I had the whole harbour of St. Anthony sketched inside my head so I could tell my brothers. They would be so amazed, and I would be the centre of attention for days.

Later that morning an Aide came to take me to the plaster room to have my cast put on. It was no big deal; I had had one before and this one was put on the same way. I figured I could have just as well stayed at St. Mary's because Hughlette would have done just as good a job. I just lay there and pouted while the cast dried and I refused to have any dinner.

It was almost suppertime when I was brought back to the ward. I had stubbornly decided that I would refuse to eat and maybe they would get mad at me and send me home. I knew Ma would be so happy to see me. The plan went well until an Aide came in and propped my pillow and placed a tray of fresh pork, mashed potatoes and gravy in front of me. I didn't even have time to drool before I gobbled it all up. It was so good.

I looked up from my plate to see the boys quietly watching me.

Reggie finally broke the silence, "Yas can't make fun of me no more."

The other boys hollered with laughter. I felt a bit embarrassed, but with a full belly I felt much better and just sat back to watch the other boys finish their meal.

I noticed Arthur, who was in the full body cast from the waist down, was eating but not looking at his food. I couldn't help but stare. Arthur wasn't looking at anything in particular, just staring with blank eyes.

"Whatcha lookin at," said Arthur. I looked away and immediately felt guilty.

"Nuttin," I replied.

Arthur laughed, "I can't see ya, ya know."

"You can't see what?"

"I can't see you. I can't see nuttin," he said.

"How come?"

With that, Daniel from across the room piped up, "Cuz he got that ole TB in his eyes from scratchin his leg inside his cast and then rubbin his eyes."

"Did not," Arthur retorted.

"Did so, the nurse said."

"You don't know nuttin about it, so shut yer trap." Arthur was mad so Daniel kept quiet.

After a quiet few moments, Arthur said "I can't ever remember seeing anything since I came here. I have been here for two years, and Reggie was only here one, so Daniel don't know nuttin."

"You was here two years? "I asked, my voice was barely a whisper. It was inconceivable to think about being here for two years. "You haven't seen your family in two years?"

"I couldn't see them anyway," Arthur tried to joke. The boys gave a nervous laugh and Reggie tried to change the subject.

"I wish I didn't have to look at the stupid casts they got put on my legs," Reggie said. "I swear, if the stupid legs ain't better the next time they check, I will chop them off."

Garfield whimpered. He was only five and the youngest in the room, and sometimes it made him squeamish when the boys were arguing and showing off.

"Give it up guys," commanded Daniel. He was the oldest and always felt protective over Garfield.

CHAPTER 30: ARCHIE
ST. ANTHONY, JUNE 1947

The Aides eventually took away the empty plates and by now there was just quiet chatter in the room.

The BANG happened so suddenly that I almost fell off my bed. Something had whizzed through the air, hit the wall by Arthur, then rocketed off the wall and hit Arthur's cast before falling to the floor. I ducked and pulled the sheet over my head. The boys squealed with laughter, even Arthur. I lowered the sheet slightly to see what was happening.

Dr. Salter entered the room, laughing out loud at the joy he saw on the faces of the other boys.

His wife followed him, smiling at the happy boys.

"I wish you didn't have to play so rough," she said.

He laughed. "The boys needed some roughing because before the TB had knocked them off their feet, they had all been rough young men."

He picked up the ball and tossed it at Daniel, who ducked. "I just want them to have a bit of normalcy, so they don't go back home being too coddled."

"Fine," she conceded with a smile. "Someday you will be a wonderful father. I feel it in my bones."

The boys were all yelling "me next" to get the ball thrown at them, when Mrs. Salter noticed my bed.

"Robert?" she said gently to get the doctor's attention and nodded her head toward the bed. I pulled the sheet back up over my head.

"That's the new boy," he replied, and I could hear them walking toward me. Dr. Salter came alongside the bed and pulled back the sheet. "What are you doing under there?"

"Nothing," I replied while Reggie retorted, "I think he got a scare,"

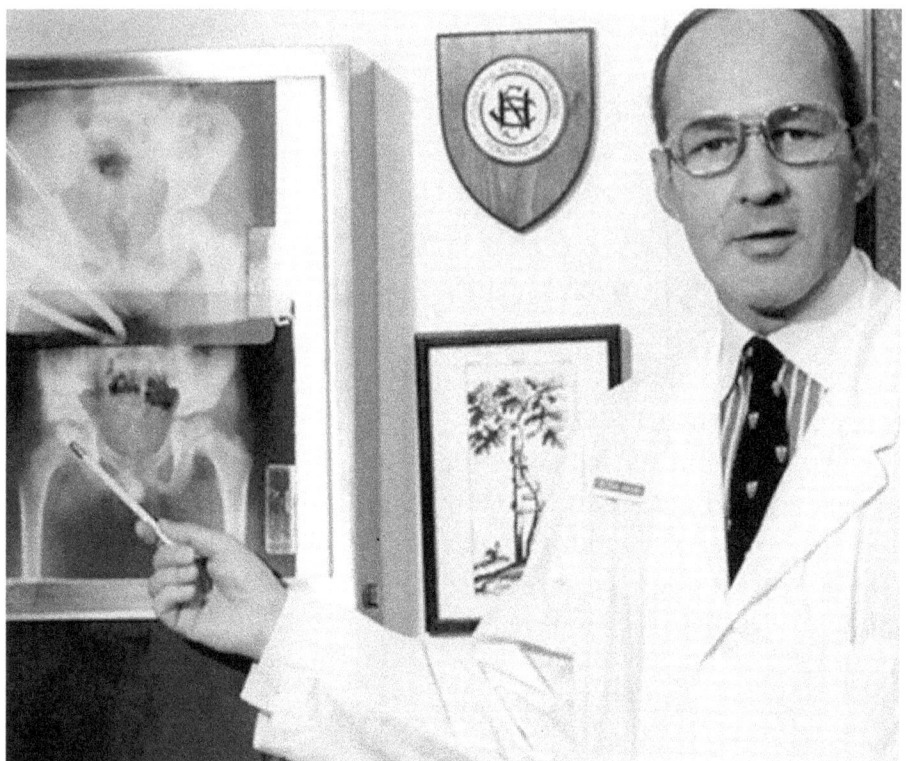

Dr. Robert Salter looking at X-rays. From The Canadian Medical Hall of Fame website.

and erupted in laughter.

At that remark Dr. Salter turned quickly and gave the rubber ball a hard toss at Reggie's cast. More screams of laughter.

I lowered the sheet a little further and took in the scene with wide eyes. I couldn't help but notice the well-dressed and coiffed young lady. Her blue dress barely covered her knees, and it buttoned up the front. A narrow white ribbon was tied in a bow at the base of the Peter Pan collar, and the short sleeves were punctuated with white bands. Her straight dark hair fell to her shoulders and was curled inwards at the ends. Archie had only ever seen ladies with long skirts and their hair pulled back in a bun, with the exception of the women from the coves who wore baggy shift dresses. I thought she was very beautiful and elegant.

Dr. Salter introduced her as Mrs. Salter, and she smiled the prettiest smile at me.

"You may call me Robina," she said.

I smiled and looked downwards. Ma would be very mad with me if I called an important lady by her first name. However, I thought it was very nice of her to say.

Dr. Salter continued tossing the ball at the boys until the head nurse appeared in the doorway with her hands on her hips. "Those boys will never settle down to sleep with you getting them all riled up like that," she scolded.

Dr. Salter pocketed the ball.

"I just dropped in to see how Archie's cast was setting," he claimed.

The nurse grunted, turned on her heels and stomped off.

The doctor turned to wink at me.

"How is your cast setting?" he asked.

"Good," I replied, although I really had no idea.

The doctor pulled back the sheets and tapped the cast. "Nice," he said, but as he was about to pull the sheet back up, he noticed redness in my right knee.

"Is your right knee hurting?" he asked.

"No, it's not hurting, just feels a bit hot," I said.

"Hmmm," pondered the doctor. "I will have the nurse put some cool cloths on it for the night and send you for an X-ray in the morning."

I sighed and hoped it was nothing.

CHAPTER 31: ARCHIE
ST. ANTHONY, JUNE 1947

On the third day of being at the hospital I had an X-ray of my right knee. In my medical chart Dr. Thomas had written:

June 27- X-ray - A.P. and lateral of right knee - there is a marked soft tissue reaction of the knee joint with narrowing of the joint space with synovial destruction. There is a reddened area on the medial side of the epiphysis of the femur and tibia.

Impression: Tuberculosis of the knee joint. Dr. Thomas

An X-ray was also done of my chest that day, which showed that everything was normal. I was had a cast put on my right leg and sent back to the ward.

Although the charts said I was comfortable, I felt worse because of the little bit of perceived freedom I felt I had was lost that day. Prior to the second cast, I had been able to manage to get to the bathroom myself even though it took me a while. Now with both legs in casts, I was confined to the bed. Still not as bad as Arthur, Garfield, and Reggie though, with their hips also cast, but when you are seven and just want to run outdoors and chase a ball and maybe go swimming on hot days, having both legs cast is like a prison sentence.

The next time Dr. Salter dropped in to see us on a social visit, he cringed to see that I had another cast applied. He said he suspected it may happen but had prayed it wouldn't. "You seem sad Archie and it makes my heart sad," he said to me.

He asked if I was in any pain, but I shook my head no, so the doctor tried to change the subject.

"I have a new stethoscope," he announced proudly, holding it up

Dr. Gordon Thomas with an unnamed patient. From his biography, From Sled to Satellite: My Years With the Grenfell Mission, *published in 1987.*

for all the boys to see.

I brightened at this as I had noticed that the first day I had met Dr. Salter. "It's not like Nurse Jupp's," I noted.

Dr. Salter smiled. "No, it certainly isn't."

He showed them how the new stethoscope had two sides instead of just one. The new one could listen to the lungs on one side and to the heart on the other. The boys were in awe, and we all had to try it out.

The doctor stopped by my bed and gave me one last try before he left. That was when I spilled my story. "A lady in the next ward left with her baby today," I said.

As I spoke, Dr. Salter's head tilted to the left and through the door acknowledging that the ladies ward was indeed next door. It was larger than the boys ward and housed the ladies who were waiting for their babies and who stayed for two weeks afterwards to rest and heal before heading home to their busy and physically demanding lifestyle. He didn't speak, instead he let me continue.

"She walked by the door, and I thought for sure it was Ma and my little sister Dorothy, but I know that Dorothy is bigger now and I know it wasn't them but for the minute I thought she had come to bring me home." The words and the tears seemed to gush out all at the same time.

Dr. Salter, feeling my pain, sat on the edge of the bed and patted my hand. "We are all doing our very best to see that you get well and get home quickly."

"I know, but she looked just like Ma, same hair and dress and everything," I sobbed.

"Why don't you just rest up. You had a long day, and after a good sleep you will feel better."

I nodded meekly.

The boys were all sombre as the doctor left. "We have all had days like that. Don't feel bad Archie," said Daniel.

Later I heard Arthur whisper, "I'm holding out my hand, can you see it?"

"Yes," I said.

"Then grab it."

I did as I was told and felt myself almost jerked off the bed as Arthur pulled me and both our beds together.

"What are you doing?" I exclaimed in a whisper.

"The last kid that used to be in your bed was about Garfield's age and we used to do this when he was sad. He had a big family and had to sleep with his brothers at home, so this used to help him get to sleep," Arthur explained.

"Well, I haven't slept with my brothers in a long time, except for the time I was at home in the spring for a while." I didn't want to seem weak, but I did find it a bit comforting to be closer to Arthur. I slept well that night.

The next three weeks passed normally. Well, as normally as one could expect in a hospital. We ate, we slept, we chatted boy talk, and the nurse would come every day with penicillin needles and cod liver oil. This was the part of the day we all disliked but it seemed to help that we were all suffering the same treatments. Dr. Salter visited regularly with his ball and his pretty wife and when the days were nice, the Aides would wheel us outside to take in the fresh air and sunlight. We especially liked the days when the staff would get together to play a game of football. We would cheer on Dr. Salter as he was an amazing player and could run really fast.

Sometimes at night, Arthur would sing for us. He had a lovely voice and would memorise songs from a radio that a nurse would sometimes bring into our ward for us to listen to. We all loved music and would try to sing or hum along with Arthur.

The coastal boats had started up again and there seemed to be a flurry of activity with people leaving to head to Labrador after being at the hospital over the winter. But with the people leaving, there were also people coming. Women who were expecting babies and people with tuberculosis made up the majority of the new patients. The boys' ward welcomed two new patients that week, a ten-year-old from Alexis Bay and an eleven-year-old from Indian Harbour.

One day, after all the new people had settled in, I heard Dr. Salter and Dr. Thomas discussing the close quarters of the hospital patients. The doctors were concerned that it could result in more infected body parts, but given the space available, could only do so much with what was available to them.

CHAPTER 32: ARCHIE
ST. ANTHONY, JULY TO SEPTEMBER 1947

By mid-July, my leg was feeling uncomfortable and on July 23, Dr. Gordon Thomas recorded this in my medical chart;

Pt. developed a slight abscess which has drained a considerable amount of pus in the right thigh, probably the result of an injection. He is on hot compresses. General condition, otherwise good. GWT

Over the next two weeks there was a flurry of excitement spreading throughout the hospital. The doctors finally came to the ward and explained that the streptomycin had finally arrived from New York. All us boys in the ward were excited that we would be cured and be able to return home. It was the medicine Dr. Paddon had told me about. The miracle drug. I could not wipe the smile from my face.

Every so often we would get a chance to sneak a look in our charts, and over the next month, the doctors had made some notes in mine.

Aug 8 - Pt. has received a month's course of streptomycin, cast is to be removed and a new one applied. GWT
September 14 – Pt. is doing well in cast.

I was slowly adjusting to hospital life. I enjoyed the company of the other boys, and because I had been bedridden for nine months now, it almost seemed as if I could never remember being any other way. None of us complained about our predicament as everyone was the same. Meals were good, and most of the staff were nice, and we got outdoors lots when the weather was good. Arthur was learning more and more songs, so he was great entertainment, and sometimes the doctors' wives brought homemade cookies for a treat.

There were also volunteers who would come from the school each day to teach lessons in reading, writing, and arithmetic, so we were kept busy and learning.

I had finished my month's dose of streptomycin, but the miracle cure I had hoped for did not occur. I became really sad about the fact that I was still not well enough to go home, but it seemed that Arthur always sensed my sad days, so we would pull their beds together and I would feel better. Having young Garfield around helped me feel better as well. I could be like a big brother to Garfield when Garfield was sad, and that helped me keep my own spirits up. It was like Cack was here with me.

On September 20th, Dr. Thomas following entries were made in my chart:

September 20 - Cast removed. New cast applied and x-rays taken. The patient has a draining sinus on both the medial and lateral side.
X-ray A.P and lateral right knee.
There is an active tuberculosis involvement of the right knee joint which seems to be progressing. There is a thinning of the synovial and destruction of the epiphysis of the tibia on the medial side and some destruction of the epiphysis of the femur on the medial side. There is also some general decalcification of the bones, possibly as a result of disuse. GWT

In one of our quiet discussions, Dr. Thomas told me that there was still a lot of work to do to get me better. He also said he had sent a report to Nurse Jupp at St. Mary's, and that she would send a letter to Ma to let her know. When he told me that it was unlikely that I would get to go home before the freeze up, I cried. I would be stuck at the hospital all winter and wouldn't be able to go home until the spring thaw.

.

CHAPTER 33: FANNY
MATTHEW'S COVE, SEPTEMBER 1947

Fanny had just finished placing the dishes on the table for supper when John burst through the door waving an envelope. "Ma, Ma, one of the sharemen from Battle Harbour just dropped this off for you on his way back from St. Mary's," he cried.

Fanny dropped what she was doing and grabbed the letter, immediately recognizing Nurse Jupp's familiar scrawl on the envelope. Her heart pounded as she tore it open and tried to read the words. This letter was the third one that Nurse Jupp had sent her since Archie had been sent to St. Anthony. The last one in August had informed her of the new drug that Archie would be receiving that was helping people get better from the dreaded tuberculosis. She was hoping this letter was going to be good news at last.

She could only recognize a few words, 'Archie, tuberculosis, winter.'

"Go get Edith", she demanded.

John sprinted to the next house as fast as he could and was back in record time with Edith. The girls and Cack followed behind. Edith had been teaching them lessons again. Rita had been learning well, and Mildred was even progressing, despite being more interested in cooking and sewing.

Edith sank breathlessly into the nearest chair and held out her hand. She was pregnant with her first child and was just beginning to show, so she was out of breath easily.

"John said you had a letter," she said between breaths.

Fanny reluctantly pulled it out of her apron pocket and handed it to Edith. She was excited to hear the contents of the letter but was also scared it might be sad news.

Edith unfolded the letter and read aloud:

Dear Mr. and Mrs. Rumbolt,

I received news today from Dr. Thomas and I only wish it could be better.

As I informed you in the last letter, the tuberculosis has spread to his right knee, infecting that as well as his left. It has been getting progressively worse.

Thankfully, the infection is maintained solely in the legs and not spreading into his chest cavity where it could be a lot worse. Hopefully, the new drug, streptomycin, will take care of it in time, but for right now we'll all have to be patient and let nature take its course.

I regret to inform you that Dr. Thomas doesn't expect him to be well enough to come home before the last steamer, so it will be spring before he could possibly be back home again.

He has the best doctors, Dr. Thomas and Dr. Salter, and I have no doubt he will recover and be a healthy boy again someday.

I will continue to keep you informed whenever I get news, and I will pray for your son's speedy recovery.

Dorothy M Jupp

There was silence as Fanny dropped to the nearest chair. She placed her head in her hands, just as Ern and Roy entered the house for supper. Ern was startled as he viewed the scene before him. Edith noticed this immediately and assured him that Archie was fine.

"He's not getting home this winter," John blurted out, half crying.

Mildred wiped her eyes as Rita pulled up a chair and sat down, facing her mother. "Ma, I want to go to St. Anthony so he won't be all alone this winter," she said.

Rita kept her eyes focused on her hands that were folded in her lap. She had no idea how her mother was going to respond. She had thought about nothing else all summer, ever since Archie had left. The thought of him all alone every night in that hospital so far away was almost more than she could bear. She had even asked around about how aides get work in the hospitals. There were many who were no older than her, usually girls and young women. Most women married young and couldn't work after marriage, having to focus instead on the children and the household.

Fanny looked up at Rita like she had just sprouted ten heads. "What's the matter with you maid? Is ya gone off yer head, or wha? Go get supper on the table and stop talking foolishness." Anger flared in her eyes as she glared at her daughter.

Rita didn't move.

"I am not off my head, Ma," she said gently but firmly. "I have been thinking about this for a while." Rita was always the gentle caring one. She was the one who doted on the children. She realized how angry her mother could get but she was determined to stand her ground. "Please Ma," she said while looking at her mother.

Fanny jumped to her feet nearly knocking over her chair. "No!" she shouted. "Now do as you are told."

Fanny looked around at the rest of her family who had gone quiet with their heads bowed, and at Ern, who just looked very sad. Dorothy broke the silence with a little whimper and Edith mumbled that she best be getting back to get Bill some supper. She handed Fanny back the letter and Fanny put it in her apron pocket.

Rita gave her father a pleading look, but he glanced away. He was hurting too. He knew it was no use to try to talk to Fan when she got like this, especially when it involved the children.

The supper was dished up by Mildred and Rita, and the children all sat around the table. Ern took his seat at the head of the table. "Sit down Fan and eat your supper," he commanded.

The children all kept their heads bowed. As hungry as they were, there was a general feeling of sadness now that they knew their brother would not be coming home. They also knew that this news would have consequences for the stability of their day-to-day lives. Usually, Ern got his own way when it came to commanding the household, but when Fanny got stubborn, there was no backing down. The children braced themselves for the storm.

Fanny's response was to grab her coat and storm out. "I'm going for a walk while you eat," she said before the door closed behind her.

Ern looked around the table and said, "Eat your supper. We still got work to do tonight to get ready to move into the bay in a few days."

"We are still going in the bay?" asked Roy.

"Yes," barked Ern. "Now eat."

Everyone ate in silence. None of them were very hungry anymore, but they knew there would be nothing else until tomorrow, so they ate.

Ern finished quickly and left the house while Mildred and Rita cleaned up. Rita was still fuming. "I'm fourteen, I'm plenty old to go to St. Anthony and go to work."

"Just give Mom time to cool down."

"She can be so stubborn," Rita huffed.

"This is all new to her," said Mildred, with a touch of grace that rarely coloured their conversations since before Archie had left. "She thought for sure he would be coming home, and even though you have had this in your mind for a while, this is the first she is hearing of it. Give it time, maid."

"Well, we are soon going to be moving in the bay. It will be too late then," pouted Rita.

While the girls were cleaning, Ern found Fanny right where he expected to; On the ragged beach area near Capstan's Cove. She was seated on a flat rock that could only be reached by jumping a small gorge. It was a great place to pick Alexander in July, but other times she would just go there a lot after visiting her baby sister's grave.

Fanny heard Ern approaching but didn't turn around. He sat on the rock across the small gorge. "It's getting dark," he said quietly.

"I'm not blind," she answered stubbornly.

"Fan, Archie is going to be fine. He is a lot better off over there than he is back here until he gets well."

"I'm not stun either." She still didn't look around.

"Well maid, you're certainly acting like it. You got six more youngsters back at home and we got to worry about getting them into the bay soon."

"Five more," she said quietly.

"What?" he asked.

"Five more. I'm sending Rita to St. Anthony too." She said this with such conviction that he was momentarily taken aback.

After a long pause he said, "Where will she go? Where will she stay?"

"On our way into the bay, I am going to stop at the hospital and talk to Nurse Jupp."

In his heart he knew it was the right thing to do, but he didn't know if he could consent. Archie had no choice but to be there, but sending

Rita? At this moment it seemed inconceivable.

"Can we sleep on it?"

"We can, but my mind is made up," she countered, looking at him, daring him to argue.

He stood and reached out his hand. She stood, took his hand, and jumped across. They walked silently home.

Fanny decided not to get Rita's hopes up until she talked to Nurse Jupp. The next few days preparing for the move flew by, even with Rita marching around pouting and shooting daggers with her eyes at her mother whenever she got the chance.

They told the children they would be staying with Ern's family at St. Mary's for a night before continuing to their final destination in the bay for the winter. This year they would be residing at Wallmans on the north side of the bay as the mill operation in Tooth Cove was over. Every season, they followed the work, leaving old homes behind.

They left early in the morning to make their way to the harbour at St. Mary's. Ern dropped Fanny off at the Mission Wharf and continued into the harbour with the children. The motorboat was filled to the brim with all their meagre belongings. Mill had asked to go with her grandparents, but Fanny insisted she come with them as she wanted Rita to say proper good-byes if Nurse Jupp could arrange a job. She has already told her mother and brothers of her plan and Rita hadn't seemed to notice the extra tight hugs they gave her when they left earlier that morning.

Fanny walked purposefully to the hospital and up the steps. No one had seen her coming and an aide greeted her at the long porch.

"Are you ill?" the girl asked.

"No, but I need to see Nurse Jupp," Fanny stated, standing tall.

Nurse Jupp came to the door and beckoned Fanny into the dispensary. The nurse assumed Fanny wanted to ask about Archie. With tears in her eyes, Fanny explained the situation. The nurse listened and understood Fanny sadness but was intrigued by the request. The hospital in St. Anthony was always looking for girls to help in the kitchen. It seemed as soon as they would find someone, she would be whisked off and married. It was unusual that this girl was only fourteen, but she knew with a good recommendation from her, Rita would be considered.

"I can't promise anything Mrs. Rumbolt, but I will keep her here with me for a few days until the steamer comes and if I think she can do the work, I will send her over. But, if I think she can handle the work, I will send her to you at Wallmans," Nurse Jupp decided.

"I will bring her to you in the morning when we leave," Fanny said as she stood to leave.

"Fanny," began Nurse Jupp. "I can only imagine how difficult this is for you. To not only have one child gone for the winter, but two."

Fanny kept her composure and did not miss the fact that the nurse had addressed her by her first name. It did make her feel better. Like the nurse understood her anguish. "I just want Archie to not be lonely," she said.

The walk up the harbour gave her the opportunity to compose and calm herself. When she reached her destination, the children were roaming the hills with their cousins. She found Rita and told her of her talk with Nurse Jupp.

Rita's eyes grew wide in astonishment, and she could not contain herself. She hugged her mother tightly and thanked her profusely. "I will not let you down Ma," she stammered. "And I will make sure that Archie is well taken care of."

"I know you will," Fanny said but her heart was breaking. Rita ran off excited to tell her siblings.

That night was another sombre night for the Rumbolts as they prepared to bid farewell to yet another family member.

CHAPTER 34: RITA
ST. MARY'S, OCTOBER 1947

Rita stayed at St. Mary's Hospital for six days before Nurse Jupp put her on the steamer to St. Anthony. Nurse Jupp was very impressed with the skills Rita showed in the nursery and gave her a letter for Dr. Curtis recommending that she be given work with children. However, if there were no positions available for that type of work, she could be given work in the kitchen.

Rita was both nervous and excited during the trip to St. Anthony. Nurse Jupp had personally paid her passage on the *Kyle* and given her some pocket money for when she arrived. She also had a letter to deliver to Dr. Curtis. Rita not only learned cooking and cleaning skills at St. Mary's, but also how to conduct herself around people. She still wasn't a very good baker, but she could peel and chop and help prepare meals. She studied Nurse Jupp intensely and admired her no-nonsense demeanour. However, Rita also saw that the nurse had a deep love for the people in her care. This insight would prove to serve her well in future years.

Rita arrived in St. Anthony at noon on a crisp sunny October day. She made her way to the hospital and enquired for Dr. Curtis. The nurses looked at her strangely, but she curtly told them she had a letter for Dr. Curtis.

Rita may have been raised poor, but she was proud of her upbringing and held her head high. Her mother had instilled in her the attitude that she was as good as anyone else on the coast of Labrador, especially some of the merchant children that came to Battle Harbour every year to look down their noses at the locals. Her mother insisted she was never to be brazen or ignorant, but that was always to remember that she should never feel inferior. She was told to be polite and respectful but to never be degraded. She would remember with humour how Mill would put some of the local girls in their place when they got too high and mighty. She knew she could do the same if she had to.

She sat across from Dr. Curtis as he read the letter from Nurse Jupp. She knew from the way he snorted and rolled his eyes that he did not respect the nurse very much and she suddenly felt very nervous.

She watched as he folded the letter and returned it to the envelope. He crossed out his name and replaced it with Dr. Thomas. He informed her he was soon leaving St. Anthony, and she was to give Dr. Thomas the letter. He told her where to find him and sent her on her way.

Dr. Thomas was younger and more understanding and regarded her with sad eyes. He quickly wrote a note for the kitchen manager and sent her to the basement of the hospital. After a thorough interrogation, she was offered a job peeling potatoes the following morning and was given a place to sleep on the top floor of the hospital with other staff.

She was ecstatic but very tired from all the events and by now it was five in the evening. However, she needed to find her brother and the prospect of finally getting to see him again after five long months gave her renewed energy. She found Archie just as supper was being delivered.

Rita deposited her little suitcase by the wall and as she entered all the boys looked up from their meal. She was plainly but elegantly dressed, and her youthful glow and natural beauty caused her to turn heads wherever she went, especially in a hospital ward of young boys,

She made a beeline for Archie and squealed with delight as she embraced him. She was amazed at how he had grown but was saddened at the two casts on his legs.

Archie was so happy to see her and started asking questions as soon as she let him out of her hug. "Where did you come from? How did you get here? Did Ma come too?" The questions bubbled out and everyone laughed.

"Matthies Cove, *Kyle* and no, Ma couldn't come...just me," she answered, smiling. The rapid-fire questions kept coming.

"How come you're here?"

"I came to work in the kitchen."

"For how long?"

"I don't know."

"Why didn't Ma come?"

"They are all moved up in the bay now."

"Tooth Cove?"

"No, Wallmans this year."

"How come?"

"I think the Tooth Cove mill is finished."

"Oh. Is our house still there?"

"Yes, but not much left now. Dad was going to move it over to Wallmans. Honey, maybe you should finish your supper before it gets cold. Do you need some help?"

"Alright," Archie consented, and Rita finished feeding him the last of his mashed potatoes and gravy.

"Rita, I hear your belly rumbling. Did you eat today?"

"No, but I am fine. I will eat later."

"No way. Here, have my fruit," Archie offered.

"I can't take your fruit," she laughed.

"She can have mine too," echoed the other boys in unison.

"I'm fine," she laughed again. "But thank you all so much. I can see that my brother has acquired a new family." Archie beamed with pride to have his sister with him, while Rita noted that all the other boys smiled shyly at her.

"Are you going back before the last steamer goes? I am hoping to," Archie said.

"We will talk about it later? I need to get some supper and find my room."

Rita hugged her brother again and promised to come back for a visit after she was settled.

Archie still looked like he couldn't believe she was there, but just answered, "Alright."

When Rita walked by the room later that night, she could still hear Archie and the other boys chatting. It seemed like she might have added some excitement to their day and they were all having trouble settling down. She hoped he would get some sleep, and she was happy to be in the same place as him after so long apart.

The next morning, Rita showed up for her job promptly at six am. It wasn't easy work as the main kitchen prepped all the staff and patient meals, but Rita did not mind the hard work and was relieved to have a job.

She was the newest of all the workers so was given the basic drudgery work, peeling veggies and keeping dishes washed up. There were six other workers in the enormous kitchen, and they all had their own duties to fulfil. The main cooks and assistant cooks were all older; one even as old as her grandmother. There were a couple of girls not much older than her, but she was by far the youngest and they all regarded her suspiciously. They wondered what charity case the doctors were helping now. They were used to seeing all kinds of workers come through for short periods to work for the Mission, some from very far away. However, the ones from more affluent families usually had better jobs, such as helping in the main part of the hospital and were better dressed. Rita was easy to spot as a local.

Rita remained quiet and did her job. One thing Nurse Jupp had warned her about was getting involved in idle gossip. She explained to Rita the fusses that women could have when working together and that if she were to get into any quarrels she could be sent home. Rita vowed she would not get sent home to be a disappointment to her mom and little Archie. She would work hard and stay quiet if it killed her.

CHAPTER 35: ARCHIE
ST. ANTHONY HOSPITAL, OCTOBER 1947

Archie could hear the approach of Dr. Salter was doing rounds at eight. Archie was quickly learning how to distinguish the approaching footsteps sounds and couldn't wait to share his exciting news.

"Sister Rita is here and she is going to take me home." I was so excited I was nearly shouting.

"Your sister?" asked Dr. Salter.

I was nodding and grinning so wide my teeth were chattering.

"Where is she?"

"In the kitchen peeling potatoes until I am ready," I said. I could not get the smile off my face.

The other boys were all listening to this conversation. "She didn't say she was taking you home," Reggie interjected.

"Well, she didn't say she wasn't," I snapped back. Sometimes Reggie really made me mad.

Dr. Salter looked concerned. "I'll talk to you later, is that alright Archie?"

Aside: Dr. Salter

When Dr. Salter finished his rounds, he went in search of Dr. Thomas to find out what was going on. The Mission in St. Anthony was undergoing a transfer in authority as Dr. Curtis was leaving for the winter and putting Dr. Thomas in charge. As such, Dr. Salter was taking over the tuberculosis patients to lessen the load on Dr. Thomas. Archie was currently the patient of Dr. Salter's, and he knew nothing of Archie being released to go home.

He found Dr. Thomas in his office going through administration files and from there got the complete story.

"I guess she hasn't had the chance to tell him that she is also here to stay," replied Dr. Thomas.

"Well, now he will need to be told," Dr. Salter stated.

He usually didn't tell patients bad news until it was necessary, and he had wanted to wait a few more weeks to give Archie the news. Considering, he added, "I will fetch Rita and maybe we can tell him together. Poor little lad, all his talk is about going home to his momma and family."

Dr. Salter sent for Rita the next day who explained to him that she had been so busy with her new job that she hadn't had the time to explain the situation to Archie. They agreed to meet on Monday morning to do it together. They both believed that it would be less upsetting for him if they were both there. He told her he would arrange for her to take an hour off work that morning.

"By the way, how old are you?" he asked.

"I turned fourteen on October 2nd, sir."

The doctor looked stricken. He knew she looked young, but figured for sure she would be at least sixteen. "Can you read and write?" he asked.

"A little, sir. My aunt is a teacher and she has been teaching me."

"Alright, miss. I feel you should be in school, so I will talk to Dr. Thomas and arrange for you to go to school as well. I will send for you on Monday morning to visit your brother with me."

"Thank-you, sir."

Archie

On Monday morning, Rita was summoned to my ward. Dr. Salter was already here. As Rita approached my bed, and I got excited. She had visited me every day and every day I felt just as excited to see her as the day before. I looked at the two of them and grinned a big grin.

"Archie, we have something to tell you," the doctor began as he pulled the privacy curtain around my bed.

"I know," I said happily with another big grin.

"You do?" said Dr. Salter as he finished securing the screen.

I was nodding fast by this time and my grin was getting larger. "I'm eight today and you came to wish me happy birthday. The nurse has been helping me cross it off on the calendar for the past two weeks. She said I would probably get a special surprise."

Rita and Dr. Salter looked at each other but neither spoke.

Rita finally dropped herself on the bed beside me and gave me a huge hug. "Of course, I came to see you to wish you happy birthday and to tell you as soon as I get a break from work, I am going to go get you the biggest candy you have ever seen."

"I would like to wish you a happy birthday as well," replied the doctor, as he pulled the screen back around the bed. He shook my hand and turned to leave. "You should get back to work too Miss Rumbolt," he said to Rita. It was strange to hear her called Miss Rumbolt.

Rita gave me one last kiss and turned to follow Dr. Salter out of the room.

Back in the room we all looked at each other bewildered. "Why did he pull around the curtains for that?" one asked. We all shrugged.

That night, we screamed in delight as a rubber ball whizzed through the air and hit the wall by Arthur and proceeded to bounce off various beds before it finally hit the floor. Rita was visiting with me. She had brought me a huge lollipop and some smaller candy for the other boys to enjoy. She must have used whatever money she had to make my day special. I loved her so much and was so happy she was here.

She was perched on my bed and now ducked as the ball whizzed by her head. She gasped in surprise and turned around.

We all knew who was behind it even before he came through the door. Tonight, following him was his lovely wife holding something that was draped with a cloth. She was shaking her head but smiling at the theatrics that her always husband caused. He introduced his wife to my sister Rita, and Rita shyly said hi.

"We come with a surprise for a special boy having a birthday," the doctor announced.

Everyone beamed at me and I just grinned. Mrs. Salter lifted the cloth off the platter to reveal a beautiful cake with blue and cream coloured frosting. On it was written 'Happy Birthday Archie' in blue frosting and it had eight blue candles. The doctor struck a match and lit the candles before he asked me to blow them out quickly before the nurse came and got mad about the sulphur smell.

As I was blowing, one of the boys yelled for me to make a wish. As soon as I blew out all my candles, I looked up and told them that I wished I was going home real soon.

Everyone laughed and the doctor said, "Not before you eat your cake."

Mrs. Salter dished up cake for everyone on little napkins sand she even handed a piece to Rita. It was delicious. We didn't get cake often, so it was an extra special treat. Mostly it was Jello and custard for desserts. The visitors didn't stay long as it was almost time for lights out. I heard Dr. Salter tell Rita he would see her in the morning. I thought it was the best birthday ever and slept soundly that night.

The next morning, both Rita and Dr. Salter again showed up to give me the bad news. This time, when the doctor closed the curtain, I knew something was up. I felt a sickening lurch in the pit of my stomach. I had seen doctors do this to other children when the news was bad. I didn't like it and put my hands over my ears.

"Go away," I cried.

"Archie, it's going to be alright," Rita soothed as she snuggled me. The doctor looked sad.

"Go away," I repeated. "I don't want anyone saying that Ma died." I started to cry.

"No, don't be silly," said Rita. "Ma is fine."

"Then who? Cack? Little Dot? John? Roy? Dad? Mill? Who?" I demanded.

Dr. Salter moved closer. "No one died Archie, but we do have some unpleasant news."

I didn't respond. I just stared at the doctor.

"I'm afraid you will be staying with us over the winter here at the hospital."

"What?" I looked at Rita. "You are going home without me?"

"I'm staying here with you. Ma didn't want you to be here alone this winter without any family."

As she spoke about Ma, reality set in for me. I wasn't going to see my mother or any of my family until at least next June.

"No," I screamed. "That's not true. You're lying to me. The steamer is still making trips, we can go, I will be better soon."

I started to thrash around the bed in frustration, sending my breakfast tray flying off my bed and under Arthur's bed. I was sobbing and thrashing so uncontrollably that Dr. Salter beckoned the nurse to give me some sedation, but not before Rita, who was trying to hold me, got a whiff of something very stinky.

As the sedative started to work, Rita told the doctor about the smell, and he quietly started to investigate. As I drifted off, I heard him say they would keep me sedated and would do more tests in the morning.

October 22 - The cast on the left knee has been removed because of an extremely offensive odour. There were five draining sinuses from the knee joint and one abscess which opened itself the day after removal of the cast. The patient is receiving UVL and will have to be put in a cast again.

On the lateral aspect of the right thigh there is a small ulcer which had evidently been considered an area of necrosis following streptomycin. However, the probability of this being a tuberculous sinus from the right hip must be considered and x-rays will be taken. RBS

X-rays.
Hip Joints:
The left femur shows considerable rarefaction. The right femur shows no rarefaction, but there is a very suspicious area about the right medial side of the epiphysis, between the neck of the femur and the head of the femur. The joint service at the head of the femur is irregular and the epiphysis seems to be definitely abnormal.

Impression: early tuberculosis - right hip joint.
Left Knee Joint:
There is marked rarefaction of the bone. The lower end of the femur presents a roughened, moth-eaten picture with much destruction of the epiphysis. There appears to be an abscess cavity in the shaft of the femur, lower end. There is a large soft tissue swelling which represents capsular and pus.

The lateral x-ray shows very much the same picture with much destruction. The patella is very much rarefied and the knee joint in the position of semi-flexion. RBS

After all the investigation had been completed, Rita slowly came to visit me looking very serious. Her eyes were red like she had been crying. All of the boys were sullen, Dr. Salter had been in to visit and to tell me about the tests.

"Archie," she said, sitting on the edge of my bed. "I was talking to Dr. Salter, and he told me about all of your tests."

I turned my head away from her and didn't speak.

"Archie, why didn't you say that you were in pain? The doctor said your kneecap is resting on your femur. He explained that it's just bones rubbing together," she said, her voice cracking a little.

I glared at her. My worst fears had come true

"The doctor said I'm getting a full cast done. I don't want the cast. I want to go home."

My chart for later that day read:

October 29 - Bilateral hip spica has been applied, down to and including the left foot. RBS

I was now in a full body cast.

CHAPTER 36: FANNY WALLMANS, ST. LEWIS BAY, FALL 1947

Fanny sat in a rocking chair near the old wood stove sewing. She had managed to bring the chair from Matthew's cove that fall. They had been here at Wallmans for nearly five weeks. The men had signed on again with the Labrador Development Company when they had finished fishing. More workers were needed on the north side of the bay this year, so that's where the families had settled. This part of the bay was not as cozy and sheltered as Tooth Cove, but it offered more work opportunities and had more people around. Fanny was fine with that.

Today, Mildred had taken the boys next door to Edith's to learn some lessons. Edith, who was now almost seven months pregnant, didn't go very far but she really enjoyed having the local children come around so she could teach them some reading skills. The men were all gone to work, and the only sounds to be heard were the fire gently cracking and little Dorothy playing quietly with a doll that she had been given to her for her third birthday last summer. The doll had arrived from Battle Harbour and had been brought over to Matthew's Cove by one of the sharemen who had gone to fetch supplies. It was plainly wrapped and addressed to Dorothy Rumbolt. The sender was still unknown, but Fanny had her suspicions.

There are some things that only a woman can see in another woman's eyes, and Fanny had seen the kind gentle look in Dorothy Jupp's eyes after Archie was taken away in June. The family had tried to stop at the hospital to see Archie when the ice had finally cleared out of the day and they were on their way outside again. Archie had already been sent to St. Anthony and Fanny felt grief stricken. It was Nurse Jupp who had calmed her and told her of the wonderful treatment he would get in St. Anthony and that he would hopefully be home by fall. It was like looking into the eyes of a mother, like Nurse Jupp was the one who lost a son, not Fanny. Although Nurse Jupp didn't have the reputation of being kind and gentle in the surrounding communities, Fanny was not mistaken in what she saw. It wasn't the pitying, condescending look that the merchants' wives gave her either. It was a look held between two women who both loved the same child. That's why, when the doll arrived a month later, Fanny knew exactly who sent it.

Fanny had a particularly difficult day a month ago on Archie's eighth birthday. Getting out of bed seemed almost impossible. Mildred was a great help that day, getting meals for the children and keeping the house. When Ern had returned home, he found her down by the beach, sitting on a rock, and half frozen. She couldn't remember how long she had sat there, but she did know it was still daylight when she wandered down there with tears streaming down her face. She never let the children see her cry if she could help it.

"Fan," he said, trying to be gentle. "You need to come back to the house now."

"Don't tell me what I need," she snapped. "You walk around every day like nothing's missing, like nothing is different, how can you do that when he is all I can think about? And now with Rita gone too, it's just more than I can handle some days."

Ern sat down beside her and looked off into the distance. It was a while before he found his voice. "I miss them too. Some days, I think my head will explode with all the thoughts that are raging in there. But then I remember that I have to keep going for you and the other children."

Out of the corner of her eye, Fanny watched as a solitary tear ran down his cheek. He quickly brushed it away, hoping that she hadn't seen it. He had to stay strong for them all. That's what men do.

"Come on," he said. "Your mother has a huge pot of rabbit on and I'm starved." He had held out his hand and she had gratefully accepted it. As he pulled her into the warmth of his trembling arms, she knew that she wasn't carrying this burden alone.

Fanny sighed from the memory. She had been feeling much better since that night. The dull ache was still there, but the panicky desperation had subsided. As she rose from her rocking chair to put another junk of wood in the stove, she glanced out the weather-beaten window-pane. There was a group of men walking home from the mill. Some were walking slowly with heads hung low, and some were chattering animatedly with their hands. She finished putting the wood in the stove and grabbed Ern's old jacket and went outside.

Her father had just come out of his house too and was striding quickly towards the men. "What's going on?" he asked as he approached.

One of the men who was hanging his head and walking a little faster than the rest looked up and replied that the company had just shut the mill down and sent them all home. One of the men who was talking animatedly shouted that, "The bastards don't even know if we are going to get our pay this month."

Arch asked them if they had seen his boys. The man replied that they were still at the mill arguing with the boss. "Bill is pretty pissed off," one of the said, and Arch knew what kind of a temper Bill could have if he was wronged. Arch went back into the house to grab his coat before heading to the mill.

He didn't get far when he saw them all returning. Ern, Bill, and Bob were on the way back and didn't look pleased. It wasn't until later that night that someone from the camp came to let everyone know that there would be no more work. The Labrador Development Company had gone bankrupt. It was November 15, 1947.

Although the families prayed that there must be some huge mistake, two weeks had gone by and there was still no word to the contrary. The pit prop boat had left a week ago with all the remaining wood and the men who would be returning across the ocean. The Newfoundland families who had come to the bay, and the Port Hope Simpson men, had packed up and moved back to the island and Port Hope Simpson. No food supply boat had been there for more than two weeks, and the local families were getting low on supplies.

Ern, Bill, Bob, and another local man travelled to Fox Harbour in early December to get food supplies. They had scraped together all the money they had and had decided they would use it up in the hopes of the company coming through with their paychecks before the situation got desperate. It was a very mild year, and no ice was forming yet. In Fox Harbour, the local employee who supervised the Fishery Products store in the wintertime allowed them to have the few supplies they requested, although his own supplies were getting low to feed his own family.

They returned to Wallmans and told their families that they would have to spare the supplies until more supplies arrived. The quick retreat of the Labrador Development Company had left a very desperate situation.

Two nights later, Fanny went to the woodpile to get an armload of wood and found Ern sitting behind it smoking a cigarette. "What are you doing out here?" she asked. "I thought you had gone to your fathers for a game of cards?"

No response.

She walked around and looked at his face which was illuminated by the moonlight. He looked grief-stricken and she started to panic. "What is it? Is it Archie? Tell me."

"No," he replied.

"What then?" she demanded.

He still remained silent.

"If you don't answer, I swear I will smack you with this piece of wood. You are scaring me to death," she threatened, waggling a junk of wood at him.

He looked at her sadly, "I just had to kill the dogs." He hung his head.

"What?" she stammered, allowing the few junks of wood to drop as her whole body weakened. "The dogs are gone? Even Lady?"

Until now, she had not noticed how deathly quiet the shoreline was. The dogs were always barking at something, but usually the noise of the children drowned them out. The quiet right now was deafening.

"Oh my god Ern, is our situation really that bad?"

Even as she asked, she knew it was. It had been two days since she had been to visit the dogs. The usual scraps had to be recycled, what little there was. Since the Labrador Development Company shut down, there was barely enough food cooked to go around to the humans, let alone the dogs, and they haven't had a seal in weeks. The last time she saw the dogs, they did look very poor, she had just hoped that they would all make it through this bad spurt.

She would mourn Lady the most. The children had never been allowed around the dogs very much, but little Archie had always been very fond of Lady, and Lady of him. Once when he was five, she found him sleeping soundly snuggled with the dog and it had been Lady that took him to safety when he got sick.

"The dogs were starving, Fan," Ern replied. "I couldn't watch them suffer anymore. It was the only thing to do, the right thing."

As Fanny sank to a seated position beside him and pulled her knees to her chest, she knew he was right. But that didn't stop the hurt or keep the tears away.

"We will get more dogs when things improve," he promised.

"I know," she sobbed. "How will we tell the children."

"I'll tell them tomorrow."

"Ern, what will we do? Will we be alright?"

"We will. We just have to get through this. At daylight tomorrow, me, Bill, and Bob are leaving to go further up the river to hunt. We will take some canvas and make a lean too for a couple of nights. We will leave what food there is here for the rest of yas. Just keep an eye on Edith because Bill will be worried."

"What?" she practically screamed. "You had this all planned and is just telling me this now?" She gaped at him as the realization of the whole thing set in. "This is sickening and no, we can't let you leave here without food," she protested.

"We will be fine," he said. "And the food here will last longer with us gone. We will find squirrels and jays. We will be fine."

Even as he spoke the words, he doubted himself, but he needed to reassure her so she would stay strong while he was gone.

CHAPTER 37: NUSE JUPP
ST. MARY'S HOSPITAL, DECEMBER 1947

Dorothy Jupp was in the upstairs nursery tending to a child that had been born the night before, when Hughlette came to get her.

"There is a gentleman from Fox Harbour wanting to see you," he said.

"Is he ill?" she asked.

"I don't think so," Hughlette replied. "I asked him to wait in the waiting area for you."

"Tell him I will be right down to him as soon as I finish here."

As she walked down the stairs, she saw a man in his mid-thirties waiting patiently in the waiting area. She had met him before and recognized him immediately. He kept the records for Fishery Products in Fox Harbour and she had met him once when he had brought a child to the hospital to be seen.

"Well hello, Mr. Poole, it's nice to see you again," she greeted.

"And you also," he replied.

"What can I do for you today?" Nurse Jupp asked, skipping pleasantries and getting straight to the point. This habit had served her well as a nurse.

George explained the food situation in Fox Harbour and in the bay since the Labrador Development Company left. "It's getting really desperate. The Rumbolt men were down yesterday, and I barely had enough to give them. And what I could spare, left my family short as well."

At the mention of the Rumbolt Family, she knew it had to be Archie's family. She asked about him often whenever she talked to staff in St. Anthony. He was still in the hospital recovering and no doubt he was worrying about his family.

"Have you contacted the Ranger?" she asked.

"He knows the situation and is doing nothing," Mr. Poole replied sadly. "I think the stores in Battle Harbour are just as low on food and wouldn't spare us any even if they could."

"I see," said Dorothy. "Well, I can't promise anything, but I will make some enquiries."

He looked relieved. "Thank you so much, Nurse Jupp. All I ask is that you try."

"You have my word," she said.

As he walked out and replaced his hat on his head, he felt confident she would do more than try. He had heard the rumours about little Archie Rumbolt and how attached she had become and noticed a flash of emotion when he mentioned the Rumbolt men. He also knew how well-respected Grenfell nurses were among the government officials, and that this particular nurse would move mountains to get food sent in so the people in the area wouldn't starve. That Newfoundland Ranger in Battle Harbour would just have put up with what he had just done. Somebody had to care about the people.

On December 15th, 1947, the *MV Codroy*, a ship that normally transported rum and molasses from Barbados to St. John's, steamed into Fox Harbour with a whole load of food thanks to the efforts of Dorothy Jupp and Joey Smallwood. This would not be the only time that Nurse Jupp used her position to influence the Newfoundland officials to alleviate the starvation in Labrador.

CHAPTER 38: ARCHIE
ST. ANTHONY HOSPITAL, FALL 1947

The whole ward of boys were solemn in the days following me having a full body cast on. They had known from all the conversations with me over the past few months that the one thing that scared me the most was being in a full body cast like Garfield, Reggie, and Arthur. Not only did it mean less mobility, but it meant I wasn't getting home this winter. I was going to miss the last run of the boat this fall and not get to see my family until spring. That realisation caused me unbelievable sadness.

Thank God that Rita was here. She came to see me every day and made sure I ate something. Since the body cast, I had no interest in anything, least of all food. Rita insisted that I needed to keep up my strength and grow.

"Strength for what," I mumbled. "It's not like I can go outdoors and run around. And growing." I said with an eye roll. "How can you grow while you are stuck inside a cast."

Arthur had assured me that as I grew, the cast would be changed. Arthur was the positive one. Reggie had said that the cast would be changed often because it would get all stinky while my body rotted inside it. Reggie was the joker, but I didn't find it funny. Garfield had started to cry and I had gasped at the horror of it.

"That's not funny Reggie," one of the older boys chastised him and tossed a pillow in his face. Arthur told him to stop being mean.

Reggie immediately felt bad. "Sorry," he mumbled. "I was just trying to get the little kid from Tooth Cove to laugh." He covered his head with his blanket for the rest of the night.

Another reason that I didn't like to consume any food was the fact that whatever went in had to come out and making my water and pooping with this cast on, was the most degrading thing I ever experienced in my young life. It was bad enough when I had to get help before this, but now my functions had to be done through an opening in the cast. I had to wear diapers and was changed like a baby. I would try to hold it in as long as possible, and sometimes an Aide would come by and get me to do it on a bedpan. Lots of times I would have to do it in the diaper and lie in the mess until someone came to change me. It was horrible and I hoped the cast wouldn't have to stay on for long. I could still remember Ma's gentleness and her loving ways when she took care of me and I longed for her touch and compassion. Sometimes Rita did it for me, but it still wasn't the same as Ma.

A week after my cast had been applied, there was a rush of activity about the hospital. From the bits and pieces of conversation I overheard, it seemed that the patients in the building a bit down the road from the hospital, generally called the annex, were being sent back to Labrador and northern Newfoundland for the winter as the annex wasn't winterized. The annex patients were the ones who just needed rest, so it just meant they would be moved to winterized hospitals to finish their rest. I overheard that everyone for Labrador was going soon on the last run of the *Kyle*.

I wondered if Rita would be leaving too. She never did tell me how long she was staying. She did say a few weeks ago that she was going to stay. I hoped she didn't change her mind. I really didn't want her to leave me, but I didn't want her to feel guilty about not staying with me either. I wondered if she was the one too sick to go home, would I stay with her? I decided I wouldn't because she was older and maybe she wouldn't stay with me either. The more I thought about it the angrier I became. I would end up being here at the hospital all winter while she got to go home. It wasn't fair. By the time Rita came for her visit that night I wouldn't even look at her.

"Archie, what has gotten into you?" she asked.

"He thinks you are going home tomorrow," replied Arthur.

Both myself and Rita looked over at him puzzled. "I never said no such thing," I retorted, directing my anger towards Arthur. This wasn't the first time I had witnessed Arthur make such an observation. It seemed that Arthur's lack of vision gave him extra super hearing. Maybe he could even hear thoughts.

"I heard all the same commotion in the hallways today that you did," replied Arthur. "And I also heard all your grunts about it. Now I know why. You think your sister is going home and you have to stay."

"Is that true Archie?" asked Rita. I didn't respond. I just looked away and held back my tears.

"I'm not going home," she said softly.

"Don't go staying cuz of me," I said, but still wouldn't look at her.

"I'm not staying because of you."

"You're not?"

"No, of course not. I love my job here and I am making new friends. I may even go out to a dance on the weekend," she smiled.

I turned to face her and smiled back. The next best thing if I couldn't go home was Rita staying with me.

In the weeks that followed, I began feeling more and more pain in my hip area and it caused me excruciating pain to move my bowels. The nurses and Aides would keep turning me over to even out the pressure of lying on one side too much, but the pain was getting worse. I had stopped eating so I wouldn't have to have the pain of moving my bowels. Dr. Salter decided to send me for an X-ray and was very dismayed at the result. It seemed I was going to take longer to heal than expected.

November 19 - The patient has developed an ischio-rectal abscess left side which became quite tense. This was incised and drained and a considerable amount of greenish pus was obtained. The abscess was packed with gauze. RBS

November 26 - Patient draining from ischio-rectal abscess. General condition somewhat improved since incision and drainage. RBS

December 10 - Patient's general condition much improved. RBS

By the time Christmas rolled around, I was feeling better and even helped with some of the Christmas decorating crafts. I loved the activity which consisted of cutting strips of paper, colouring them, and then glueing them together to form a chain streamer. I proudly displayed it around my bed.

CHAPTER 39: ARCHIE
ST. ANTHONY HOSPITAL, DECEMBER 1947

The whole hospital seemed more upbeat and livelier during the week leading up to Christmas. Even though I couldn't understand what it was all about, it certainly put me and the other boys in better spirits. The boys discussed it in wonderment as some of them had been in the hospital over Christmas before.

"Well sir," exclaimed Reggie, "what a goings on. Back home we go to bed, and when we get up Christmas is here. But just look at all this, a tree up and still no Christmas."

An Aide who was adding another small, coloured picture to the tree that Garfield had coloured, laughed. "It's because the time is so long for people who have to be here all year. We try to make Christmas last as long as possible to keep everyone's spirits up and to help them not be sad about not being home."

Reggie pondered this. "Back on the Labrador, we have lots of extra food and everyone visits. Mom makes a special cake."

Upon hearing that said, I looked up from my colouring and felt tears sting my eyes. Reggie noticed this. "What's the matter Archie?"

"Nuttin. Colouring is stupid, is all," I said as I pushed my book and crayon off the bed and covered my head with my blanket.

"Are you having any pain?" asked the Aide I heard her retrieve the colouring book and crayon off the floor and them back on the bed table.

"No, just tired," I mumbled. I only answered her because I didn't want the contrary ole nurse to come poking at me again.

"Alright, well, have a nap then. Christmas is in two days and if you want a present you have to behave," she said as she exited the room.

When Rita visited that night, I still had my head covered and had left my supper untouched.

"Are you sick again Archie?" she asked, concerned. She hated seeing me sick plus she knew that the abscess really taken a toll on me.

"No," I said from under the blanket.

"Then what's wrong with ya?"

"Nuttin."

"We were talking about Christmas when he got like that," replied Reggie, trying to be helpful.

"Were you tormenting him again?" accused Rita, glaring at Reggie.

"No," exclaimed Reggie.

"It's true," piped in Arthur. "He was just talking about food at Christmas and his mom's cake."

"Oh, sorry Reggie", said Rita. After a pause, she exclaimed, "Oh my! Mom told me the story of the cake."

Rita gently pulled the blanket off her brother's face. "Are you craving Ma's cake?" she laughed, trying to lighten the mood.

"The only thing I remember of Christmas is the smell of Ma's cake. I don't remember how it tastes, but I know I would like to have some," I said sadly.

"I know what you mean. The smell of Ma's cake baking always reminded me that Christmas would soon be here. It will always be one of my favourite smells."

She propped Archie up as high as she could and hugged him tight. "Oh Archie, this winter will go real quick and we will both go home in the spring."

Out of nowhere came the ball and the boys screamed with joy. Dr. Salter didn't come to the ward every night, but when he did, the ball came in ahead of him.

"How are all you fellas doing tonight?" he asked as he came through the door.

Rita picked up the ball and handed it to me to toss. I picked up the ball and regarded it solemnly.

"Well, are you going to toss it back or not?" asked the doctor.

"Archie is a bit sad tonight," Reggie added.

"He is missing his family," stated Arthur.

"Am not." I retorted. I hated this type of attention. The last thing I needed was to be regarded as a cry-baby.

"I know exactly what is wrong with you," the doctor responded as he walked towards my bed.

"What?"

"Your hair is getting too long and it's making you feel icky."

I looked up at him. I didn't want to say anything, but the nurse had been in a few days ago and cut everyone's hair. When I saw how funny she was making them all look, I refused to have mine cut. Dad always cut my hair and there was no way that grumpy nurse was getting at it.

"I like it long."

The doctor laughed. "Well, everyone needs a haircut for Christmas. How about if I cut it for you?"

I studied the doctor's hair. It was nice. I remembered how nice I felt after a haircut and figured Dr. Salter would do a nice one for me.

"Alright," I agreed.

While the doctor left to get scissors, Rita propped me up in a semi sitting position, which was difficult considering the body cast. "Try to sit as straight as possible so the doctor is able to do a proper cut. This is so exciting."

The doctor returned and put a towel around my shoulders to catch the hair and started to work. The rest of the boys and Rita watched in fascination while I just grinned.

When the job was done and the hairy towel taken away, the doctor stood back and admired his work. The other boys clapped and remarked how nice it looked on me.

I just blushed. "I wish I could see it."

"Well, then see it you shall," replied the doctor. Before I had a chance to respond and while the boys watched in amazement, the doctor scooped me from the bed and carried me to the bathroom.

While I stared at my reflection in the mirror, the doctor beamed. "You definitely look like a movie star." I had no idea what a movie star was but assumed from the tone of the doctor's voice that a movie star was a very good thing. "You are my little movie star," the doctor continued as I beamed.

I slept well that night. The doctor showed me such a kindness that I knew I would remember for the rest of my life.

CHAPTER 40: ARCHIE
ST. ANTHONY HOSPITAL, CHRISTMAS DAY 1947

I was nudged awake while it was still dark. "Merry Christmas," Rita whispered so she wouldn't wake the other boys.

"Merry Christmas," I replied sleepily. I really wasn't ready to wake up.

"I am on my way to the kitchen, but I had to come in to see you. Are you excited?"

"Yeah."

"I even have a present for you, but I will bring it up when I get a break."

At this my eyes flew open. "For me? A present? What is it?"

"It's a surprise," she giggled. She gave me one last kiss and off she went.

I tried to doze until breakfast, but Rita's visit had left me far too excited. Breakfast was fresh bacon and eggs, and the eggs were served in fancy egg cups. Maybe Christmas would be nice, I thought.

Just as promised, Rita showed up mid-morning carrying a plate with a cloth draped over it. "Close your eyes Archie if ya wants yer present," she said.

I did as I was told, but opened my eyes when Rita placed the plate under my nose. My eyes nearly popped out on my cheeks as I stared at the little cake on the plate. I looked at Rita with teary eyes. "It smells just like Ma's cake."

"That's because it is, you silly goose." Rita was laughing as she told me how Ma had made it for her to take with her to keep for Christmas, and how she had stored it in the hospital cellar all fall. The cook had allowed her to heat it in the oven before she brought it up so it would smell its very best, even though it was in perfect condition and smelling delicious when she had peeled off the cheesecloth this morning. She was very pleased with herself to be able to do this for me, as Ma would be wanting every detail when she told her about it.

"I don't have much time, so I am just going to cut it into five pieces so we can all have a piece before I go back to work." The boys were pleased by this.

"Can we cut it in six?" I asked.

"Do you want two pieces, you greedy little imp?" Rita smiled.

"No, I want to keep a piece for Dr. Salter."

Rita smiled and did as I asked. We all munched happily on our cake and Rita placed the sixth piece in a wrapper for me. "Your thoughtfulness never ceases to amaze me," she commented.

The days of Christmas passed quickly. From the delicious turkey dinner to the joyful carolling, it always seemed there was an event to keep us occupied and to have something to look forward to.

Just as Christmas was winding down and the hospital was returning to the daily humdrum of activities, an event occurred that seemed like all hell had broken loose. I had heard Ma say that phrase on occasions when there was a great uproar of frightful occurrences. People were grabbing their jackets and running towards the hospital exit. In our ward we all looked at each other frightfully as we watched the commotion.

"I suppose the Hospital is not on fire," remarked Reggie. The words had no sooner exited his mouth when an Aide entered and told them everything was fine.

"Well, it certainly don't look like it, the way people are taking off. What's going on?" Reggie asked.

"It's nothing for you boys to worry about", she replied.

"Well, it's too late for that cuz we are worried," Reggie shot back.

"An airplane went through the harbour is all."

We all gasped. We had never even seen an airplane before and now one was sinking in the harbour not far from us.

"We want to go see," I piped up.

"You know you can't go see," said the Aide with an eyeroll.

"Why can't they?" asked Rita as she came through the door of the ward out of breath from rushing up the stairs.

The Aide shot Rita a dirty look as Rita explained that a plane had indeed gone through the harbour but was being held on the ice by its wingspan. Rita turned to the Aide and said, "Let's put them on the one bed and wheel them down quickly to the entrance so they can at least have a quick look while most people are gone out." Rita tore off her jacket to ready herself for the excursion. "After growing up with a bunch of younger brothers, I know you boys would never rest if you cannot go have a quick look."

The Aide started to protest but quickly backed down when she saw the determination in Rita's face. They managed to get four of us onto one bed. Arthur declined as he wouldn't have been able to see it anyway and remarked that he would let us describe it to him when we returned.

We suppressed the urge to squeal in delight as the girls pushed us out the door and towards the front entrance. They parked the bed by one of the big windows and watched our excited faces as we stared wordlessly at the sight on the harbour in St. Anthony that day.

Hordes of people were near the shoreline of the harbour. Some brave souls had ventured out closer to the airplane, but most looked very sceptical about what could happen. Planes were so new to those parts and maybe it was heavy enough to break up the whole harbour.

The girls let us watch just long enough to satisfy our curiosity and then rushed us back to the ward before they could be caught. The excitement was enough to occupy our conversations for weeks to come. Even Arthur felt like he had actually seen it himself. I was so proud of my sister. It was the most amazing day that I was sure I'd remember forever.

A little later, Dr. Salter told us that the pilot, Captain Joe MacGillivary of Newfoundland Airways, was alright. He had been delivering Christmas mail, and both he and the mail were fine, except for being a little soggy.

CHAPTER 41: FANNY WALLMANS, CHRISTMAS 1947

True to their word, Ern, Bob, and Bill had set out on a hunting expedition. While they were gone, Arch, Charl, and Tim kept fires going in all three houses and made sure there was water in the barrels. Roy, being twelve also felt like one of the men in charge but John found him to be a bit too bossy and too big in his boots, especially when he not only bossed Cack and Dot but tried to boss him as well. There were a few fights, but Mildred always managed to keep them under control. She knew her mother was sick with worry again. Food was very short, but they managed to eat sparingly until the men returned. Luckily, there was no hard work being done to work up hearty appetites.

They arrived back after ten days looking worn and tired, but did have a few partridges and rabbits, and two porcupines that would be saved for Christmas dinner. They knew it wasn't going to last very long and were overjoyed when they got word that a boat full of supplies arrived in Fox Harbour. After resting up from their expedition, they made the trip to Fox Harbour to get supplies.

It was another mild fall with no snow or ice, so they were grateful to make the trip in a boat. With what supplies they were able to get, they felt they were good until after Christmas. This time, they had no money, but Mr. Poole had been instructed to give them each five dollars' worth of food. It wasn't much, but it would their families going for a couple of weeks.

On reflection, they don't know what they were thinking that year by remaining in the bay. They supposed they were confident the company would recover from its troubles and return, providing them with at least some cash to get them through the winter. After all, they still owed the workers their wages and they didn't want to forfeit those wages by leaving and returning to Matthew's Cove for the winter. There was also the fact that they hadn't had the time to gather the fish and ducks that were required to spend a winter on the outside.

Ern hadn't had enough left of his food allowance to get Fan the dried fruit for her Christmas cake, but Mr. Poole's wife, when she learned this, gave him a small bag from her own supply. She had heard about Fanny's two children being gone for the winter and felt she didn't need anything else to upset her at this sad time.

Fanny had been happy about the dried fruit, but wondered how she would ever repay all the kindness that had been shown to her this past year. This Christmas, she decided she would try to stop wallowing in self-pity and try to feel grateful for the people around her. As much as she missed her two children, she knew they were being taken care of and at least all her family was still on this side of the sod, which was more than could be said of a lot of families that were dealing with hunger and sickness.

Christmas passed solemnly. Candles were lit for Archie and Rita. The porcupine was cooked and all hands from the Rumbolt family ate together. Fanny was unable to eat any Christmas cake, but she prayed that this year Archie was well enough to eat some. She felt she would never enjoy the cake again.

In early January, on a calm civil day, Bill left to take Ethel to the St. Mary's Hospital. Their baby was soon due to be born and they couldn't take a chance on it being born in the bay in case there were complications. It was still really mild. A bit of snow had fallen but no ice had yet been formed. Bill decided that he would take the boat to St. Mary's and leave it there until the spring. He would acquire some dogs to come back as they had no dogs left in the bay for the winter. Hopefully, by the time the baby was born, everything would be frozen and good for travel.

Fanny watched as Roy and John helped them load the boat and snuggle Ethel in blankets while Bill positioned himself on the tot to do the rowing. The boys couldn't believe how big her belly was and hoped she wouldn't burst before she got to the hospital. It would be a long row, but if the day stayed fine, they would make it in a day. If they couldn't make it, there were inhabitants along the shore where they could stay for a night.

CHAPTER 42: ERN WALLMANS TO FOX HARBOUR, JANUARY 1948

After Bill and Ethel had gone, the men discussed making another journey to Fox Harbour for food. Supplies were really low again. With flour that year being $11.75 for a one –hundred-pound sack, $5 per family didn't go very far, especially when there were five children to feed. Ern would never say this out loud to Fan, but on some level, he was glad that Rita and Archie were away. At least they were being fed and it meant not as many mouths for him to worry about. It made him sick to his stomach to even think such a thought but it was what it was. Ern possessed a very practical mind.

Mill mostly ate at her grandmother's so that evened it up to six people in each household trying to live on $10 worth of supplies. If Bill was home, he would share his as there were just two of them, but he was gone now. Ern also wondered if he could still get Bill's share. It was worth a try. He silently cursed the predicament that the Labrador Development Company had placed him and his family in.

Three of them prepared to travel to Fox Harbour the following day and hoped that the women and children left home would make the supplies they had left last until they got back. Arch noted that the weather glass was getting low again and hoped it wouldn't get too bad for them to make a quick turnaround.

They decided to walk as they didn't want to chance getting the only boat they had left in the bay stuck in Fox Harbour for the winter. They also took one sled so they could take turns towing it if they happened to get extra supplies this time. At the last minute, one of Erns' buddies from the mill decided to go with them. Eugene Grady, everyone called him Hugh, was wintering in the bay like the rest of them. He usually went home with his family from Carbonear each fall after the fishing season, but this year decided to try his luck with the Labrador Development Company. What a disaster that turned out to be. He was just a year older than Ern.

Today was crisp and cool, and by the time they got to Fox Harbour Pond they were getting tired because they hadn't taken any breaks. They decided to stop and have something to eat. They reasoned that if they ate now, they would have a quick turnaround in Fox Harbour and head back home. Usually they spent the night, but with the weather coming in they wanted to get back as soon as possible.

They built a small fire to have a boil up and during the process they discussed the predicament of all the families that were left stranded by the Labrador Development Company. They had no food, the majority of the people residing in the Alexis Bay area were suffering. The more they discussed it, the angrier they became, and by the time they finished their tea and toast they were quite worked up. They decided that if that guy in Fox Harbour wasn't going to give them much food, then they were just going to take it. They couldn't put up with this much longer.

Unbeknownst to them, Mr. Poole, who doled out the food in Fox Harbour, was in the woods nearby cutting firewood and had overheard their conversation. He hurried back to Fox Harbour to get there ahead of them and to make sure he was prepared for when they came. He had seen a lot of anger in the past two weeks and knew how to deal with it.

Ern and the other three men arrived at Mr. Poole's house just as it was getting dusk, but Mr. Poole refused to go to the store as it had no lighting. He told them he would fill their orders in the morning. There was nothing they could do but spent the night. Ern, like the other men, was distraught about having left the family in the bay with very few provisions.

The next morning, Mr. Poole delayed them again by explaining that a month had not yet passed since their last visit and the rules were for $5 per month. He said the Ranger in St. Mary's would have to sanction it. He offered them his boat for them to go to St. Mary's. It was still quite mild and the trip would be relatively quick, but the men refused and got angrier. Mr. Poole made the trip himself and brought the Ranger back. The Ranger sanctioned the extra food, but said he needed his own orders for St. Mary's filled first. This delay not only cost the men another night, but a sudden storm came up and cost them yet another night. In the matter of 20 minutes, the temperature dropped drastically and snow and wind came with it. Ern was inconsolable and exploded in anger. It took Bob and Hugh to hold him back from attacking the Ranger and Mr. Poole. Bob was shocked as Bill was usually the one with the temper, but Bill was not here to be enraged this trip. He had never seen Ern this angry and hoped he wouldn't have too again.

The next morning, Fox Harbour dawned clear and cold. Everything had frozen over. The men hoped that the return trip would be faster without detours around bogs. It was hard to believe that everything had frozen so quickly, but this time of the year, the weather was very unpredictable.

They had a quick breakfast and left at the first sign of light. It was cold, so they just walked faster to keep warm. They had made it to Brownies Path in record time when Ern, who was in the lead, heard Hugh give a yelp. Ern swung around thinking that the komatik Hugh was pulling had jabbed his ankle or something, but what he saw was Hugh kneeling beside the komatik desperately trying to fix a flour sack.

"It's a quarter gone," Hugh yelped. He was desperately scraping the snow behind the komatik trying to scrape up what had come out of the bag.

Tim and Bob knelt to try to help him as Ern walked a bit back through the path to see how far back the trail of flour went. It went as far back as he could see and knew there was probably a lot gone.

"It must have hooked and tore in a stump," Ern commented.

"We have to go back and scrape it up," reasoned Hugh who was still on his knees, now with a tea mug trying to scrape up flour and pour it back into the sack.

"What the hell flames is gonna be the good of dirty flour full of grass and bushes," bellowed Ern. He had to make Hugh see sense as the man was reacting desperately.

"It's all right for you," Hugh shouted back. "You got lots of family who wouldn't see you go hungry. I have no one." Hugh continued his scraping.

Bob and Tim stayed quiet. They knew that Ern was desperate to get home as quickly as he could, but they couldn't help but feel bad for

Hugh.

"Well, I am continuing on. Keep at that foolishness if you want to." Ern turned to keep walking. He did feel a slight twinge of sadness for Hugh, but refused to let it take any more of his time.

Bob and Tim gently prodded Hugh to leave the wasted flour and promised to share some of theirs with him. Hugh reluctantly secured the remainder of his flour and followed them along the shoreline.

CHAPTER 43: FANNY WALLMANS, JANUARY 1948

The harder the wind blew, the faster Fanny paced in the tiny cabin. The children were trying to keep busy and stay out of her way as they recognized that she was extremely agitated. No bread had been made which only added to her extra time to pace. A pot of seal meat simmered on the stove but, without salt meat and paste it wasn't going to be very tasty. Regardless, they were hungry and they would make do.

Fanny was worried about food but she was more worried about where the men might be. This would be the third night since they left and Ern knew darn well when he left that food was running out and that bad weather was coming. Had they left in the storm and gotten lost? She feared the worst. Her panic drove her from bouts of extreme worry where she felt she couldn't breathe, to bouts of anger that he wasn't back before the storm. He had lots of time to be there and back before the storm. If he had come through that door during one of her bouts of anger, she would surely strangle him.

"Big deep breaths," she told herself. She had to stay calm for the children.

She set the table for supper. There were five places to set as Mill was at her mother's house. They had shared up the food. Only four at her mother's now, but little Dot and Cack only ate about the amount for one. She shared the food in the bowls trying to make it even for Roy and John, and half bowls for herself, Cack, and Dorothy. She never gave herself a full portion as she would eat what the children would leave on their plates so that food wasn't wasted. She never cooked extra for leftovers because there was rarely enough for the meals.

Roy watched as she fetched a hidden bun of bread from the cupboard and carefully carved it evenly among the children. This was the last of their bread, and from the howling of the wind it was clear that the men wouldn't be back with supplies tonight.

It was getting dusk when Roy saw them round the point and stopped to light a smoke.

"They're coming, they're coming," he shouted excitedly, then grumbled, "They managed to get smokes though and we here starving."

Fanny jumped up quickly from the floor where she was mending an old rug to keep busy. The past few days had been hell, and relief washed over her. She gave Roy a clout in the head as she passed him so that he wouldn't continue with his negative behaviour. She grinned as she saw the men heading for the shacks and quickly stogged the stove with wood to get the kettle boiled. She also pulled the bean pot over a damper to boil rapidly. As soon as the men arrived with flour, she would make some doughboys to drop in the pot. Everyone would sleep well tonight with a full belly. She dreaded the thought of what the night would have been like if the men hadn't returned for another night.

It would be another two weeks before they would hear the howls of dog teams headed their way to take them back to Matthew's Cove. Nathaniel and Leander Rumbolt had gotten word about the starvation going on in the bay area and the mild winter had left them helpless to go get their brother Ern and his family until now.

Bill was also with them. He had rounded up a team of dogs in St. Mary's and when the other two men stopped by to get him, he was ready. He had already decided he wasn't taking Ethel and his newborn daughter, Ivy, back to Wallmans for the winter. Food was way too scarce. At least on the outside there were ducks and seals to be had, as well they would be closer to Battle Harbour for supplies. When Fanny saw them coming, she let tears of relief stream down her face. She was so happy to have her brother come to take their family home.

CHAPTER 44: ARCHIE
ST. ANTHONY HOSPITAL, SPRING 1948

February 21, 1948 - Patient is beginning to drain through the cast on his left knee. This will have to be changed. RBS

February 21st 1948 - X-ray, Hips - The left hip appears normal. The contour of the head of the right femur is slightly irregular although the joint space appears satisfactory.
Knee joint - There is some slight improvement in the appearance of the joint surface of the left knee joint and marked rarefaction of the bones. No evidence of fusion. RBS

February 29th,1948 - Patient has developed a swollen, tender fluctuant area over the rin anteriorly on the right side which would appear to be a tuberculous abscess. This has been aspirated. RBS

Winter was dark and dreary. I was tired of being poked and prodded by the nurses and doctors. I just wanted to go home. Rita visited almost every day on her way back to her room. She had made some new friends and although I was happy for her, I was also a bit jealous that she got to go out and have fun while I was stuck in the bed.

Dr. Salter visited a couple of times a week with his ball, and his wife sometimes brought baked goodies to cheer us up.

The Aides tried their best to keep us occupied with colouring and reading plus we had a little radio that we would sometimes turn on and listen to music. Rita was very impressed by my reading and told me she figured I could do better than her. She had been attending the school nearby when she wasn't working in the kitchen.

Arthur especially loved the radio as he couldn't see to colour and read. He loved to sing and when the radio was not available, he would help us pass the time by singing songs. He would memorize songs and sing them softly every night while we were falling asleep. I will never forget that one particular night when he felt extra lonely and Arthur began singing the following song:

A Mother's Loves A Blessing

An Irish boy was leaving,
Leaving his native home,
Crossing the broad Atlantic,
Once more he wished to roam,
And as he was leaving his mother,
Who was standing on the quay,
She threw her arms around his waist,
And this to him did say,

Chorus:
A mother's love's a blessing,
No matter where you roam,
Keep her while she's living,
You'll miss her when she's gone,
Love her as in childhood,
Though feeble, old and grey,
For you'll never miss a mother's love,
Till she's buried beneath the clay.

And as the years go onwards,
I'll settle down in life,
And choose a nice young colleen,
And take her for my wife,
And as the babes grow older,
And climb around my knee,
I'll teach them the very same lesson,
That my mother taught to me.
Chorus

I thought my heart would break that night. As much as I tried to muffle my sobs, I knew the other boys could hear me. If they did hear me, however, they never said a word. I was thankful for that. All the boys would have lonely episodes at times, so we understood the importance of not drawing attention to them.

On April first, Dr Salter and sister Rita came to my room and closed bed curtain. I grinned. They couldn't fool me.

"We are going to try a removing your body cast to see how you make out," stated the doctor with his hands folded in front of him.

Rita was smiling with twinkling eyes and nodding foolishly. I couldn't help it. I started laughing loudly. I threw back my head and close my eyes and really gave them a show. I expected them to start laughing too but they continued to stand there eyeing me strangely.

Finally, Rita said, "Archie, don't you want that bulky ole cast off?"

"Of course I do," I responded. "But yer not gonna fool me no better than Reggie fooled me with a glassful of piss, instead of apple juice." I let out another hoot of laughter.

They were still regarding me strangely when I heard Reggie say, "I don't think they know its April Fool's Day."

Thats when sister Rita doubled over in laughter and Dr. Salter laughed until tears ran down his cheeks.

The joke ended up being on me, but I was ecstatic with the cast removal.

April 10, 1948 - Comfortable in new cast. RBS
April 20, 1948 - Patient comfortable in cast. Sinuses would appear to be closing. RBS

It seemed like spring would never arrive. The slow approach of winter that year meant that it would be well into April before the warm days dawned. However, when it did arrive it was blissful and well worth the wait, as the air got warmer, and the sun got brighter and stayed around longer.

We were finally allowed to get some fresh air on the balconies for an hour a day. There is nothing quite as special as the fresh air of spring after a long winter cooped up inside.

The first day I got to go outside and breathe the fresh spring air was very disappointing for me. I had expected it to be that same as home when I would venture out on a hot spring day. How I would savour the smells. At home, the snow would be starting to melt off the tarpaper roofs. The melted snow would plop onto the wooden plank bridges or in the cast iron water barrel on the bridge. All those heated smells would mingle with the spring air blowing through the trees. Ma would leave the door to the house open, and the delicious wafts of her cooking would seep into it all, creating the most luxurious scent that could be imagined. That was home and I had taken it for granted and as hard as my nose tried to conjure up the smell I so painfully missed; it just didn't happen. My eight-year-old vocabulary wasn't able to express my feelings so I kept my sadness to myself. I only hoped it wouldn't be too long before the boats started running and I could get back home.

CHAPTER 45: ARCHIE
ST. ANTHONY HOSPITAL, JUNE 1948

Eventually the boats did start running but I remained in the body cast.

However, there was a little ray of sunshine that came into my life that spring. Little Bart Webber from Spotted Islands came into the ward. He was affectionately called little Bart because he was the youngest and smallest kid that had ever been seen on that particular boy's ward.

Like all the rest who had first come into the St. Anthony Hospital, Bart was awestruck, shy, and lonely. I felt bad for the little fellow, so it became my mission to help him adjust to this strange place he found himself in. We usually remained quiet when a new boy was admitted as the loneliness and confusion of their first few days brought back sad memories of our own first arrival. Something in me felt the need to reach out.

"Where's ya from?" I asked.

"Spotted, on the Labrador." Bart kept his eyes cast downward as he spoke.

"I'm from the Labrador too, Tooth Cove."

"Never heard of it."

Everyone laughed; the uncomfortable silence was broken, and the chatter began. By the time the nurse came to wheel him away for his surgery the next morning, little Bart was feeling a bit better.

Hours later, little Bart was wheeled back into the ward and we gasped in horror at the sight. Not only was he in a full body cast but his legs were cast in a frog-like position. None of us talked that night as Bart's sporadic whimpering created a heavy sadness on the ward.

The next morning Dr. Salter explained his idea of having cast Bart's legs in that fashion but no explanation could relieve the heavy cloud that hung over the ward for the next few weeks. My own condition stayed the same.

July 3, 1948 - Patient doing well in cast. GWT

July 10, 1948 -Condition unchanged. GWT

"Hey Archie," Rita bubbled as she practically danced into the room. All the boys looked up from their lunch in admiration. Rita was a lovely looking young lady, and since they had all gotten to know her, they realised what a caring, loving soul she was also. I was so proud she was my sister.

"I'm just getting a little break and came to see how you were doing." She mopped her forehead and neck with a napkin. "This heat is perfectly rendering."

I rolled my eyes. "Do you have to be talkin like the ones here?"

"Don't be silly Archie. If I ever want to be somebody, I have to improve the way I talk."

"You were talking just fine before you ever came here. And besides, I am making out really good. I just have a regular cast on now and as soon as I get two good months I can go home before the last boat."

"That's wonderful," exclaimed Rita as she clasped her hands together and arched up on her toes. "I hear you guys are going outside today to watch the ball game."

I was a bit shocked by what I just scantily witnessed. From the past nineteen months of lying in a hospital bed with nothing to do but to watch expressions, I had learned a lot from people watching. By now I could tell, even before a doctor reached the foot of a patient's bed, what news he was going to deliver. It had become sort of a game for me. So, what I had just witnessed on Rita's face certainly did not jive with her physical gesture of happiness. But I left it alone. For now, I was excited about the ball game too.

The ball game was amazing. The doctors were playing against the local men. The men were sprinting and jumping in the hot July sun, stopping occasionally to mop their foreheads and drink water. Everyone was laughing and the crowds surrounding the field were screaming and cheering. I cheered really hard for Dr. Salter. One day I hoped to play ball as well as him. I had grown to really care for the doctor and trusted him to make me well enough to go home soon.

It would be a month later when Rita walked into the ward early one morning with Dr. Thomas. I knew instantly that something was up. Rita just stared at the floor as Dr. Thomas explained that the body cast would have to be applied again. "We thought your bones would fuse better with exposure to air, but unfortunately, we were wrong. I'm terribly sorry Archie."

I remained sullen as Rita tried to hug me, but I brushed her off and remained silent. As I turned my back to her, I had a weird feeling that she was not as upset about me not going home this time as she had been in the past.

10th August 1948- Hip Spica applied. GCW

CHAPTER 46: FANNY
MATTHEW'S COVE, SUMMER 1948

Fanny slowly walked the foot path back to her home after visiting with Ethel and the new baby. She really admired the way Ethel interacted with her daughter. She wished she had had the opportunity to learn to read and write so that she could be smart too. She wondered if being smart could have somehow protected her children more.

The days have been long and busy since that cold February day when they were rescued out of the bay. From digging their old house out of a snowbank, to gathering wood and food to survive the winter, the days had been exhausting. Then came chores to prepare for the fishery. The merchants were at it again. Charging the highest kind of prices for food and twine while paying the men the lowest kind of prices for the catch. There was no way to get ahead, no matter how hard you worked. It seemed Ern was always sad or angry, so she did not dare share her own feelings of loss and sadness with him.

Instead, she turned to the only thing she had available. Food. The children never finished off their meals, so she did it for them. It wasn't a lot of food, but it was a mindless habit that seemed to relax her. Sometimes. She could feel extra pounds start to pad her hips and thighs. She wasn't obese by any means but even a few pounds on her small frame felt like a lot. Just something else to feel guilty about. It never ceases to amaze her how there could be overweight women when there was so little food around.

Sometimes the sadness of having two of her children so far away overwhelmed her. During those times, she would trek out to Capstan Cove and discuss her sadness with Bella, the sister she had lost so long ago. She prayed Bella was watching over her nephew and niece and would keep them safe until it was time for them to return. Her heart ached to see them again.

Fanny was stirring a simmering pot of soup for supper when John burst through the door with a letter for her. She grabbed it and smiled as she noticed the familiar scrawl of Nurse Jupp's handwriting. Without even removing her apron she headed out the door for Ethel's house dragging little Dorothy along and John on her heels.

She was ripping open the envelope as she burst through the door of Ethel's house. Everyone stopped dead in their tracks as a ten-dollar bill slid from the folded piece of paper. Fanny handed Ethel the letter as John stooped to scoop up the money. Money was only given at weddings and funerals. Ethel's mouth hung open with shock. She didn't know what to say.

"Just read the damn letter," Fanny insisted. She didn't know what to make of the money. Ethel obeyed.

Dear Mrs. Rumbolt;
I hope this letter finds you and the children doing well.
I had been so positive that Archie was on the mend in July when I got word from the hospital that he was doing better. However, I just recently got word that the body cast has had to be reapplied. As such, it's very likely that Archie will have to remain another winter in St. Anthony. I am very sorry to have to inform you of this.
I have included some money in the hope that maybe you will be able to find the time to travel to St. Anthony to visit him before the last trip of the Kyle*. I can't imagine how difficult it must be to raise a family and have some money for extras so I pray that I may be able to offer some assistance.*
I know both Archie and Rita would love to see you before winter arrives.
Sincerely
Nurse Jupp

While Ethel had been reading, Fanny had sunk into a chair and was now holding her head in her hands and silently sobbing.

John handed the money to Ethel who was folding up the letter and watched as she replaced the letter and money back into the envelope. "Are you really going to St. Anthony Ma?" he asked.

"I can't believe they will be gone another winter," Fanny sobbed, completely ignoring John's question. No one knew what to say.

Finally, Ethel broke the silence. "Just go home and talk to Ern."

"The trap got all ripped up again today. Da is in the stage trying to mend it." John knew his father was in a bad mood about that but didn't want to say that.

Fanny knew exactly the mood Ern would be in over that. "I don't want anyone saying anything. I will tell him when the time is right," she decided.

It would be a few days before Fanny found the opportunity to tell Ern about Archie having to stay another winter. He was so saddened to hear the news. That combined with the poor summer they were having in the fishery, he felt so defeated. Fanny had expected him to roar about it, but it was like he had given up on having anything good happen to him. Ern also knew how devastated Fanny must be over this and he didn't want to make her feel any worse.

Two weeks later John could no longer contain himself. "So, Ma, are you going to go to St. Anthony or not?"

Ern looked up from his plate of stewed fish and waited for Fanny to respond. She didn't.

"What's going on?" he asked.

"Nothing. John, eat your supper."

Ern laid down his fork. "You're not sick, is ya Fan?"

"No."

"What will you do with the money?" piped up Dorothy.

"What money?" asked Ern. When Fanny didn't answer he bellowed. "What in the hell flames is going on?"

Fanny glared at Dorothy while addressing Ern. "When Nurse Jupp sent me the letter about Archie, she sent ten dollars in case I wanted to go to St. Anthony. I didn't pay it no heed cuz I wasn't going anyway."

"What did you do with the money?" Ern asked.

"It's still in the envelope in the room. I meant to send it back. I just forgot," Fanny admitted.

"You're damn right you are sending it back. We don't need no handouts from that woman," he stated firmly.

The conversation ended and the whole family was sullen for the rest of the night. The next day, Fanny had Ethel write a letter of thanks to

Nurse Jupp and sealed it in an envelope with the money to send back. Fanny knew she would have to put the idea of going to St. Anthony out of her head, but it was so difficult. For a brief moment, she had let herself dream about seeing her son and daughter this fall. It was now 16 months since she had seen her son and almost a year since she had seen her daughter. It was almost unbearable to have to let that dream go.

She walked out to Capstan Cove that night to sit in the quiet little cemetery and be with her memories. She heard a rustle behind her and turned to see Ern sit down alongside her.

"Did you want to go to see them?" he asked.

"I have the money sent back now," she said.

"That's not what I asked you," he pressed.

"There is no way I can go. Don't be silly."

"Just answer the damn question woman," he insisted.

"Of course I want to go you damn fool. I'd be pretty stupid not to want to see my own children after all this time," she shot back.

"Then you will go."

She looked over at him like he had just sprouted ten heads. He just kept staring ahead. "How in hell flames am I gonna to be able to do that. On a crow's tail?" she asked.

"I will find a way. I need to know that they are fine too."

With that said he stood and left without another word. She sat there for another hour while it grew dark, trying to figure out what just happened.

CHAPTER 47: FANNY
SS KYLE, FALL 1948

Fanny didn't know where she would ever find the time to leave her family to travel to St. Anthony. She could hardly imagine leaving them for a day, let alone two whole weeks. Mildred was so excited for her mother and told her to stop being so foolish, that she had left them each time she had to go have her babies.

"That was different." retorted Fanny. "I was sick then."

"You listen here," Mildred blazed. She shook one finger in her mother's face and stretched out her other arm with a finger pointed toward the mouth of the cove. "You are getting on that boat, and you are going to see Archie and Rita, and I don't want to hear nuttin else about it."

Fanny smiled. Mildred always had a quick temper just like her father. Rita was like her, slow to the boiling point but once boiled, they could match anyone. Fanny knew she was going to go but just had to justify leaving her other children. She would take little Dorothy, of course, but would really worry about little Cack.

"Watch little Cack, don't let him down by the land wash," Fanny said with tears in her eyes.

"Ma and I will not let him out of our sight," Mildred replied.

Fanny cringed every time Mill called her grandmother 'Ma.' She always hated that Mill didn't move with them when they moved into their own house years ago. At the time, Fanny was so busy tending to her own home and her younger children that she didn't protest and insist that Mill move with them. Plus, her own mother was still mourning Bella, and she didn't have the heart to take Mildred from her too. She had mentioned it to Ern a few times, but he just told her to stop dwelling on it. He was right of course, it could not be changed now, and there was no point in dwelling. Sometimes she wished she could think like a

The SS Kyle. *PANL IGA 17-84.*

man and not agonise over the children so much.

She just wished she could stop being in this sorry state she was in. She felt like she could never be happy again. As precious as her children in her home were, she was always mourning the ones that were gone.

"And make sure Roy puts his trap mitts up to dry in the night. You know how sore his hands gets. And don't go lettin John be going over to Trap Cove by himself."

"Mom! Stop worrying. Now get ready. The *Kyle* will be here any minute."

Fanny felt a tear run down her cheek as she went to her room to finish zipping up the little suitcase that Ethel had insisted she borrow for her trip. Her heart just did a little dance because Mill had just called her 'Mom.'

Ern and the boys were patiently waiting in the motorboat as she walked down the wooden walkway to the wharf. She was holding her suitcase in one hand and little Dorothy's hand in the other. The boys had long since raced down from Tilsey, a point of land that jutted out into the sea allowing an unobscured view, and announced that the *Kyle* was coming out the bay. As Ern helped them both into the motorboat, they heard the first blast from the *Kyle* announcing the ship's arrival. It would be another twenty minutes at least until the ship came to a complete stop and lowered the gangway. When the ship travelled from north to south you had to be right there when she stopped if you wanted to board as she didn't stay as long in each port as she did when going from south to north. The reason being there was very little freight going this way.

Fanny pulled little Dorothy closer, feeling a blast of cold fall air chill her as the boat rounded the point towards Battle Harbour where the ship would anchor. By the time the motorboat puttered to its destination, the *Kyle* had just dropped anchor. A dozen other boats were lined up near the gangway to either send or retrieve packages or send or retrieve people.

When it was Fanny's turn to head up the gangway, she solemnly took the hand of the Mate helping people aboard. Ern passed Dorothy to her and Rita carried her up the steps. The Mate followed behind, her carrying her case. Once on deck, she waved to the boys as their boat puttered away from the ship. She proceeded to the purser's office to pay her passage plus a bunk for her and Dorothy for the night and thought about how much flour and butter she could have bought for the cost. Guilt kicked in again, but she quickly put it out of her mind like Ern instructed her to do. She was going to see her children and the excitement of that was overriding everything else right now.

It was getting dark, and she doubted she would keep Dorothy awake to see the next two ports, so she took her on a walk around the ship and marvelled at the cleanliness and stateliness. The dining room had white tablecloths with stewards buzzing around them in their white coats. Everything looked so proper. Someone had left the door to their stateroom open, and she could see teak and mahogany decor, and the windows to the smoke room were the same shape as church windows. Little Dorothy had declared she was hungry when they passed the dining room, but Fanny explained she had brought food for them to eat. She didn't want to spend any more of her precious money than she had to.

They slept in the third-class women's quarters. There were about twenty or so bunks with little privacy screens. Fanny got Dorothy all settled next to her and she was asleep in no time. Fanny dozed a few times, but mostly she stayed awake with the anticipation of finally seeing her son the next day.

Fanny stepped off the ship and looked around St. Anthony in amazement. Battle Harbour certainly paled in size to this place even though at peak season in Battle Harbour there were hundreds of people around. She held tight to Dorothy's little hand for fear of losing her in the crowds that were assembled on the wharf to meet the *Kyle*. Dorothy whimpered and clung to her mother's dress while Fanny navigated the crowd holding her little suitcase in front of her.

Once Fanny burst through the crowd, she saw her. Walking fast but in a prim and proper fashion. Rita had never been the type to barrel along like Mildred who did everything in an expeditious manner.

As Rita rushed into her mother's embrace. Fanny felt a huge sense of peace, as if the world was being made right again. Both women were crying when they finally pulled apart and Rita quickly scooped up little Dorothy and swung her around as the little girl squealed in delight.

"I can't believe how much you have grown," declared Rita as Dorothy beamed with pride. "You should see what I have for you."

"I want it now," said Dorothy impatiently as Rita laughed. Dorothy may have grown but she didn't change.

"A little later? I kept a tray of breakfast for you Ma."

Dorothy pouted and Fanny shook her head. Her stomach was growling but she needed to see Archie first.

Rita took the case from her mother and led the way to the hospital. "I didn't tell him you were coming. I can't wait to see his face," Rita declared excitedly.

CHAPTER 48: ARCHIE
ST. ANTHONY, FALL 1948

I could hear Rita's footsteps coming down the hallway. I had learned to pick her footsteps from anyone else long ago as it always gave me such comfort when she visited. As she rounded the doorway as walked into the ward, I couldn't help but notice the wide grin on her face and the excitement in her eyes.

My head did a little bolt off the mattress, and I dug my elbows into the mattress by my sides to lift off my shoulders. I couldn't do many major moves because of the body cast, but I could sense something very incredible was going to come out of her mouth and I couldn't contain himself.

"I have a surprise for you," Rita beamed.

"Are we going home?"

"No, but the surprise is almost as good as that," she teased.

With that I watched dumbfoundedly as Ma walked into the room. I was in shock. Ma looked a little rounder, and I don't think I ever saw her without an apron on. Was it really her? My thoughts and emotions that now all collided in my head weakened me.

It's amazing, I thought. But where is Dad? Did he die? No, he wouldn't have died cuz Rita looked happy. They wouldn't have made this trip if Rita and I were going home so that means we are here for another winter.

The thoughts raged loud in my head until they were so loud I thought my head would explode, so I did the only thing an eight-year-old boy with no mobility could do to stop the madness. I lay back on the bed and pulled the covers up tightly over my head.

Mom and Rita rushed to my side and Rita pulled the privacy screen.

"Oh Archie, I've waited so long to see you, please don't be scared," begged Ma.

I couldn't respond but I felt myself make a little whimper.

"Archie, Ma came all this way to see you, now take down that blanket," Rita ordered.

I made a tiny head shake no as a response.

"Archie, if you don't take down that silly cover, I am walking out that door and not coming back, you hear me?" I heard mom say which caused me to whimper louder.

"I brought you something," she coaxed.

This got me to bring the cover down and expose my red, wet face.

Ma quickly scooped what little of my tiny body that was not casted into her arms and held me tight while gentle sobs shook both our bodies. Rita wiped tears from her own face while she plumped up some pillows behind me so I could be raised up a bit.

I couldn't believe how nice this felt. I had dreamt about Ma's hugs for so long. I took a big, long whiff of her scent, a smell he always missed but could never conjure up. It was a warm soft smell mixed with sunlight soup and molasses buns, and it said simply home.

Ma finally found the strength to pull away and grasp my cheeks in both her hands.

"Look at your handsome little face," she exclaimed. "Your baby looks are all gone and my little boy is being replaced by a young man. Look at how much you have grown." Her voice was hoarse and her nose was almost touching mine.

"Ma," I croaked. "What did you bring for me?" Ma and Rita let out a little laugh as Ma straightened herself. It was then that I realised my little sister was there.

My eyes widened and I gasped. "Is that little Dorothy?"

Dorothy grinned and looked down shyly. She had been witnessing the whole scene quietly. Her mother reached down and grabbed her by the waist and lifted her onto the bed.

"You musta doubled in size," I exclaimed and everyone laughed. I gazed at her admiringly. Her pudgy baby fat was disappearing, and she wore a plain little jacket over a dress, and little black shoes. Her curly hair was getting a bit longer and Ma had a ribbon in it. I was so proud to see her.

Dorothy grinned and peeked sideways at him. "Ma brung ya cake," she blurted out.

"I did," replied Ma, tearing her eyes away from me to get it out of her bag.

Ma's hands shook as she retrieved the cake from her bag. The last time I saw Ma was in Tooth Cove, the spring before last. She had been so skinny she looked a lot older than her 34 years but now she had filled out again and looked well. I was happy about that.

Ma handed me the tiny package wrapped in brown paper, and I held it to my nose and took a big deep breath.

"Christmas cake," I exclaimed.

Mom just nodded and took a deep breath and exhaled slowly. I unwrapped the package and broke off a small piece and popped it in my mouth.

"Want some Rita?"

"One small bite and I will wrap it up and have to cook and put it in the cold storage till Christmas for you," she offered.

My euphoric look quickly changed to sadness as I remembered I would spend another Christmas away from home.

"Don't look sad," said Rita, immediately reading my thought. "At least you will have some of Ma's cake to share with your friends."

Ma looked pale. "Rita, I need to go to the toilet."

Rita showed her mother where to go. By the time she got back to the ward, Rita had pulled the screen open again.

"If you three only knew how good it makes my heart feel to see you laughing and joking like old times," Ma said.

The visit went well, and Ma told me she was happy to see I had made some good friends.

She stayed with relatives in St. Anthony until the *Kyle* made the return trip. She came every day to visit but was only allowed to stay for short visits each time.

"I'm so happy to see where you are living, and I can't wait to tell your dad all about this place."

"Are ye moving in the bay this year?" I asked.

"No, my son. My bay days are over," Ma explained. "Looks like it will be Gin Cove till we get some land from the Mission to move in the harbour. I want the boys to go to school this year."

I really missed her after she left, but the visit really did me good. After that I still missed her, but it wasn't the same desperate feeling as before. Maybe I was growing up.

CHAPTER 49: FANNY
GIN COVE, SPRING 1949

Another Christmas and winter passed with mother and son living worlds apart.

Fanny and Ern had moved into Gin Cove, just outside of St. Mary's, and the boys walked over the hill every day to attend Princeton School. It was a harsh winter food wise. Wild game had been scarce this year, and the merchants hadn't stocked up enough food to last everyone the whole winter.

Fanny's father had obtained a radio and most nights the families would sit and listen to broadcasts. It was an exciting time as Newfoundland geared up to join with Canada. Fanny didn't understand a lot about it but from all the hoopla, it seemed that it would be a good move for people. Mostly, she just sat knitting while listening intently to hear hospital updates from the Gerald S Doyle News Bulletin. If there were any news or updates on Archie it would be announced using his initials 'AR.' Sometimes there would be a message, "AR doing well," or "AR had a cast changed today," or "AR and RR says hello to their family in Gin Cove." Fanny lived for those tidbits.

It seemed every day was a rush from dawn to dusk: cooking, cleaning, mending old clothes, and making new clothes from old rags. The youngsters were growing like weeds. Then every night she would grab her knitting and go to her mother's to listen to the radio.

Everyone had been really impressed how the Smallwood government sent planes to drop necessary food to residents in the area. Then in May, something exciting happened that even overshadowed the dropping and distribution of food in April. Roy burst through the door, from running all the way from school, holding an envelope. He was holding it out to her and breathlessly saying "open it ma, open it."

Fanny shrunk back. The sight of an envelope unnerved her.

"Ma, open it," demanded Roy once more, thrusting the envelope at her.

She took it because Roy looked excited about it, and she was just opening it when the rest of the children came in. They had all heard the news at school about the Baby Bonus and couldn't wait to see what was in the envelope. The children gathered around as she opened the envelope and pulled out the yellow rectangular piece of paper with her name on it and gasped at the amount.

"How much did you get?"

"What will you buy?"

"Can we get some candy?"

"I need new boots."

The children went on and on.

Fanny was mesmerised and shoved the cheque and the envelope into her apron pocket. "Go on outside and play while I get supper ready," she ordered.

At the supper table the questions began anew. Roy was relentless. "From all the talk today Ma, I figures you got $26." When Fanny didn't answer he asked again. "Well?"

"Eat your supper Roy," said Ern. He could tell Fanny was upset about something again and he knew better than to make her talk about it before she was ready. He found it strange though because from what he had been hearing all the other women were ecstatically happy today.

Later, when the kids were settled down for the night, he asked her. "So did you get $26?"

"No," was her short reply.

"I knew it," Ern growled. "I knew they would screw up someone's money. I guess we will go see the Ranger about it tomorrow."

"I got $41," she said as she rocked and knit, showing no emotion.

Ern gaped at her. "Well, what's wrong with ya then?" he asked.

"The extra is for Rita and Archie and they won't get to enjoy it."

"Look Fan, Archie and Rita have all they need and they would want us to have the same. Wouldn't it be nice to have extras for a change?" he argued.

Silence.

"Well, it don't make any sense to send it to them and you can't give it back," he concluded.

"I want my own radio so I can listen to it in my own house," she stated.

"Fan, a new radio is going to cost about $35, that's almost the whole cheque."

"But I will get another cheque next month," Fanny argued.

"While the youngsters go hungry this month," he retorted.

Fanny fell silent again. She would argue with him about anything, but not about the youngsters being hungry. Maybe she was being selfish.

Then came Roy's voice from the bedroom. "I heard at school that Sam Acreman is getting a new radio and selling his old one for $10."

Fanny looked hopefully at Ern as he sighed and looked away, silently giving his consent.

They got the radio the next day. Listening to the radio felt like the closest thing to having Archie and Rita home with them, next to them actually being home. The children were excited and pleased to learn that there were shows dedicated just for children, plus having music in their house was wonderful. Fanny never let them forget that they had it because of Archie and Rita.

Ern's concession was to dictate when the radio could not be turned on and that was mealtimes. Even though he would never admit it, it was nice to sit in his own home at night and listen to the radio.

CHAPTER 50: ARCHIE
ST. ANTHONY HOSPITAL, SPRING 1949

Another Christmas and winter had passed and for some reason this year didn't seem as bad as last year. I hoped I wasn't going to totally forget about what it was like at home though. That warm cuddly feeling I got when I thought about home was still there, but it didn't have the excruciating yearning it once had. The yearning had been replaced by thoughts of wanting to be home, but this isn't so bad.

I really enjoyed the other boys, most times, except for when I was the brunt of a taunt or joke. However, we all had their turns at being the brunt, so it all evened out.

Most of the chatter was about farts and poops and the older boys talked about pimples and girls. I thought that was gross. There were times when we all shared the same joke, like the time we passed around a jug for everyone to take turns peeing in and the last boy accidentally dropped it on the floor. Our hoots of laughter could be heard right through to the nursing station. The nurse who came to investigate was not impressed and there was no dessert for anyone in the ward that night. It was so worth it though. The prank stimulated lots of conversations and laughs and seemed to bring us closer than ever.

Over the winter, some of the boys that lived close to St. Anthony went home for a while, some went home to stay, and new ones came to the ward. It was a constant transition. Garfield had gone home but came back. Daniel went home and didn't come back. Transitions were sad and it seemed I never could get used to saying goodbye to my friends.

Winter turned to spring and then came the preparations for the return of the coastal boat. All through the wards there was activity again. Women with babies were finally going back to Labrador and some of the adults who had recovered from TB were also leaving for home. I was still in a body cast, so I knew I wasn't going anywhere. I wasn't as sad about it this year though. I knew I still had until October before the boats stopped running for the winter again.

Then another sad day happened. Dr. Salter walked into the ward without his ball coming ahead of him. He looked sad and hopeful at the same time.

"I have good news and sad news," he stated. We all listened intently.

"How can news be both good and sad?" asked Reggie.

"Well, the good news is that I am returning to Montreal. My time here is up, and although I am happy to be returning home, I am saddened that I will miss you boys."

There was silence and Reggie finally spoke. "We will miss you too. Will you come back to visit?"

"Probably not as it is a long way to travel and I expect to be very busy with my work there. But I promise to write and tell you stories of the big city," he said.

I glanced at Garfield and watched a tear roll down his cheek. I couldn't stand all this sadness and needed to lighten the mood so I wouldn't cry myself.

"Do you think you could cut my hair one last time?" I asked.

Everyone laughed as Dr. Salter grabbed a pair of scissors and a towel to wrap around my shoulders and gave me a haircut. While he cut, we chatted about meaningless things: the weather, the new nurse, what we had for supper, things like that in an attempt to avoid the inevitable. We knew that as soon as the haircut was done, he would be gone from our lives forever. Patients and staff coming and going was something we should have become accustomed to in a long-term hospital setting, but this doctor had occupied a special place in our hearts.

When he was finished, he shook all our hands and left quickly. That was the last time any of us ever saw him, but his kindness remained forever in our hearts and minds.

August 9, 1949. X-ray.

Hip: No definite abnormality can be seen in the hip joint, although there is some suggestion of slight flattening of the inferior surfaces of the head of the left femur.

Knee: There has been little change in the X-ray appearance of the knee. Some distraction of the joint space, and the medial condyle of the femur has a moth-eaten appearance and also the upper end of the tibia on the medial side is very rough. No abscesses are seen in the epiphysis.

Impression: TB Knee. GWT

August 31, 1949. Condition Unchanged. GWT

September 25, 1949. Condition Unchanged. GWT

October 26, 1949. Condition Unchanged. Patient is up and around crutches. GWT

November 5, 1949.

The Patient has been up and around in crutches for some time in a cast. It was decided to discharge him to the Orphanage where he will be followed from time to time.

Diagnosis: TB knee, active.

CHAPTER 51: RITA
ST. ANTHONY HOSPITAL, FALL 1949

Rita burst through the door of Dr. Thomas's office without knocking and with such force that the door banged off the wall.

"Where is my brother?" she demanded.

Dr. Thomas looked up from his writing, quite bewildered by the scene unfolding before him. Rita had come to work in the hospital two years ago and he had never heard as much as an unkind word from her. He was momentarily taken aback.

Then he realised what he had forgotten to do. With all the flurry of activity of comings and goings due to the last coastal boat today, he had totally forgotten to inform Rita about Archie.

"Well?" she demanded, her eyes ablaze.

"I'm so sorry Rita, I should have sent for you but it's been such a busy day and things happened so fast, and I need to be in surgery in a few moments. Can we talk about this a bit later."

"But the boat is still in the harbour and I need to go home with him. I need to get my things. You have to tell them to wait for me" Rita was panicking.

"Rita, that boat is only coming from Labrador now. That's why I have a patient awaiting surgery," he explained.

"But the boys in his room said he had left the hospital." Now Rita was confused.

"Yes, that's true. He has been discharged to the orphanage," he said.

"The orphanage?" Her response was barely an incredulous whisper. She felt her legs go to jelly, but she refused to give in and sit down. "The orphanage," she repeated with disgust.

"He will be fine there and will get to go to school with the other boys and..."

She didn't hear his last words because she was running out of the hospital, down the steps and across the roads and fields towards the orphanage.

She bounded the steps of the orphanage two at a time and entered a tiny porch making a sharp right turn and flew up the other four steps that led into the main area. As she entered, she came face to face with Mrs. Hodge who worked there as a house mother.

"Where is Archie?" Rita asked, breathless.

"You mean Archibald Rumbolt who was sent to live here today?"

"Yes," replied Rita, still out of breath from the run.

"He is on the second floor in the boys room awaiting supper," the house mother replied.

Rita bolted to the right and made the 180 degree turn up the stairs before anyone could stop her. Mrs. Hodge was tight on her heels. "You can't go up there," she cried.

By the time Mrs. Hodge got to the room, Rita was already sitting beside Archie on his bed.

"Are you ok, Archie?" Rita asked softly.

Archie nodded but kept staring at the floor.

"Miss, visitors have to have permission from the headmistress, you shouldn't be here," Mrs. Hodge said while looking uncomfortable.

"May I have just a few minutes?" begged Rita

Mrs. Hodge nodded but went to the head of the stairs to keep an ear out.

"Archie I'm so sorry I wasn't there with you today when this happened. What can I do for you?" she asked.

Archie continued to look down at his cast. All the boys in the hospital ward had signed it. "I thought I was going home," he said sadly. "I had seen the *Kyle* through the window and was so excited." Then the tears came and the heaving sobs.

Rita gathered him into her arms and held his frail quivering little ten-year-old body while her own tears streamed silently down her cheeks. Even Mrs. Hodge, who was keeping watch on the stair head, was sniffing loudly.

Then we heard the headmistress bellow that supper was ready and heard the scurry of the other children returning from outside. Mrs.

Hodge hurried into the room to help Archie navigate down the stairs and told Rita how to slip out through the other side of the building. Rita promised Archie she would be back later that evening.

Rita walked sullenly back to the hospital and slowly up the stairs to her room on the third floor. She wondered what she was going to do. Surely, they wouldn't keep her on in the hospital kitchen after she left so suddenly today and didn't return. There were lots of women needing work and no nonsense was tolerated. And did she want to stay there anyway? With Archie gone, what was the point of her being here?

But more than that. How could she leave him in that godforsaken orphanage? One of her friends worked there and the stories she had heard weren't good. One story that stayed with her involved a child who didn't like a particular meal and had vomited it back up and was forced to re-eat it. The children were mostly orphans with no place to go so they didn't know any better. But Archie did. He came from a good loving home he would surely suffer from the restrictions and the harsh discipline. She curled up on her bed in the fetal position. All the other girls were working or at supper, so she was alone. She needed to think.

She must have fallen asleep because a rap on the door awakened her and she bolted upright. "Dr. Thomas would like to see you in his office," one of the girls said.

The clock said 7:15 pm. Surely Dr. Thomas wouldn't kick her out of the hospital at this hour with nowhere to go.

She entered his office a lot more slowly than she had earlier that day. He was at his desk writing and nodded for her to have a seat while he finished up. He laid his pen down and folded his hands and gazed at her. He could tell she had been crying.

"I need to explain about Archie," he began. "I'm so sorry I didn't involve you, but it was all so fast. We needed the beds in the wards at the same time a bed became available in the orphanage."

Rita darted a disgusted look his way and he looked down, suddenly ashamed. "I know there have been stories about the orphanage and I will get to that. About Archie. He had been improving greatly recently but there is still active TB in his knee joint. I don't want to send him home like that away from medical care, but he is a growing mature young man, and I didn't want to keep him in the hospital any longer either. He has been in the hospital now two and a half years and he needs to get out and be more active. Do more things, while still being near the hospital. Do you understand?"

"I don't want him to be in that orphanage. I will find a place to rent and take care of him myself," Rita stated, stubbornly folded her arms signifying that her mind was made up. Although, she didn't have a clue what she was going to do. She just knew she didn't want him in that place.

Dr. Thomas smiled. He was so proud of the young lady she had become and the love she had for her brother. He couldn't believe she was still just sixteen years old.

"Are you laughing at me?" Rita growled. At this point she didn't care if she had to sleep under the wharf tonight. She came from a family that prided themselves not to be mocked.

"Of course not. That's why I have come up with a solution that may help," he explained.

Rita's expression turned hopeful; she had great respect for the doctor.

"I have arranged for you to start work in the laundry room at the orphanage. You will reside on the third floor there and you will be close to your brother."

Rita's mouth hung open. "I don't know what to say."

"Just say thank-you," the doctor smiled.

CHAPTER 52: FANNY
ST. MARY'S HARBOUR, FALL 1949

It was dark outside already and it was barely 5pm. She was trying to get the boys fed. She couldn't believe how much they could eat as they got older. One of her brothers had gotten a seal today, so all households were having a scoff tonight. Their home was not quite finished, but she was glad they were building in the harbour this year and not living out in Gin Cove. It would be a lot closer for the boys to attend school. And now that Cack and Dorothy were going also, her mind was more at ease.

A knock came on the door and Roy opened it and stepped aside as Hughlette entered.

"I have some news from the hospital about Archie and Rita," he said.

Fanny scooped the paste off the seal and put it in the heater of the stove so she could give Hughlette her full attention. Ern also stood up. The first thought that crossed Fanny's mind this time was that it can't be bad news or the minister would have come. She was quite relaxed but noticed Ern's clenched hands by his side. He could never fool her with his cloaked fears.

"Are they alright?' asked Ern.

"Yes, they are fine. I guess you knew that Archie had been out of the body cast for a while now and was getting around on crutches?" Hughlette asked. Fanny nodded as she had had a message at least a month ago.

"Well, Dr. Thomas felt he would be better off in the orphanage."

"My boy in the orphanage when he has a home to come back to?" Ern was not impressed.

"It's not like that, Ern. Archie still had TB and he is better off near the hospital but not in the hospital. Dr. Thomas feels he needs to be somewhere where he can have a more normal life as a boy but still be near the hospital if he gets sick again," Hughlette explained.

Fanny could sense Ern's anguish and gently touched his arm to sooth him. Ern turned away and grabbed his tobacco to roll a cigarette. Anything to keep himself from punching something.

"What did Nurse Jupp say?" Fanny heard herself asking.

"She was saddened, of course, that he would not get home again this winter but if he still has active TB in his knee, this is not a good place for him to be. Also, he will have access to a great education. The best teachers in Newfoundland are in St. Anthony." With this statement Hughlette has raised his eyebrows and tilted his head forward to affirm the importance of what he had just said.

Fanny nodded and wished she had had the opportunity to learn to read and write. She wondered who wouldn't want their child to learn. "What about Rita," she asked.

"Dr. Thomas got her a job in the laundry at the orphanage so she will be there with him. Plus, she will also continue to go to school," Hughlette said.

This made Fanny smile just as Ern struck a match to light his cigarette. Fanny drew a deep breath of relief just as Ern took a deep drag of smoke. She thanked Hughlette for coming and offered him some seal, but he said his mother was also cooking seal tonight and he best be going.

It was the middle of November, and the boats were doing their last run, so they hadn't really expected Archie back this winter, even though they had stayed hopeful. This confirmed that he would not be home. The meal was eaten in silence.

That night, in the stillness of their unfinished little home, Ern turned his back to Fanny still trying to process the idea of his children being in an orphanage. Desperately trying to rationalise how he could have been a better father and protected his children from living so far away.

Fanny had her own thoughts. She desperately missed her children but dreamt of them having a great education and someday returning home to be better than the Acreman's. Not that she despised the Acreman's, but that she admired them and felt they had wonderful lives that she could never aspire to. Sam's son Gordon lived next door to her and was married to a nurse from Boston who worked for the Grenfell Mission. Many times, Fanny's heart would ache with the thought that had she been born with the opportunity to become a nurse, she may have been able to hold her children closer and protect them. She now prayed that maybe, through all this heartbreak, her children would achieve what she could only dream of. She had to find the silver lining in all this, or she would surely go mad.

CHAPTER 53: ARCHIE
ST. ANTHONY ORPHANAGE, FALL 1949

There were days I had to pinch myself to ensure I wasn't dreaming. Life here in the orphanage was of far better quality than the hospital. The Headmistress could be mean, and the meals were not as good, but the freedom to wander the halls and to go out to school as opposed to a teacher coming to the ward was so freeing. There were days I felt like I had been let out of prison. Maybe it was just the leg cast instead of the full body cast, but whatever it was, I liked it.

I also had the freedom to see Rita whenever I wanted. If there were times she couldn't visit, I was able to hobble to the basement and chat to her while she folded and ironed clothes. Once, when the Headmistress was out of the building, she even sneaked me up to the third floor to show me where she slept.

On the second floor, where I slept, there were two wards of boys with a nursery separating the boys' wards from the girls' wards. Boys and girls had separate stairwells to use to go down to the first floor for the dining rooms and activity rooms. We could also exit the building from the first floor.

I wasn't long adjusting to my new routine. I paid attention and obeyed all the rules. I even faithfully swallowed the cod liver oil from the bottle on my nightstand. Some of the other boys thought it was disgusting and would pour it down the sink when no one was watching but I figured, if it would make me all better, I would drink it.

The days started early and were filled with school and chores. It was so tiring that at first that I was glad there were early bedtimes. Most times I would be fast asleep when Rita sneaked in for her nightly hug and peck on the cheek on the way to her room on the third floor. She would usually tell me about it the next day.

St. Anthony Children's Home, or the Orphanage. PANL VA 15c-73.3.

There were at least ten staff coming and going. Some worked full-time and some were part-time Aides. Some lived in the orphanage, some did not. It was a bit overwhelming at first trying to keep all the names straight, and I could never remember all of the Aides.

Rita had started as an aide in the laundry room, but she was a diligent worker and often worked alone. Next to the laundry was the kitchen which I quickly learned to stay away from as the cook could be a bit mean. Rita explained it was because the Headmistress was always warning the cook about cooking too much and giving extra to the kids. Rita also had told me that kids would get hungry because they didn't like certain things that were cooked and food would get stolen from the kitchen. The cook, therefore, always had to be grumpy so the kids would stay away.

Across the hall from the kitchen, and accessed by going under the staircase, was the workshop. Here is where handyman Ben Acreman spent his day working on little motors and fixing broken stuff in the orphanage. I liked Ben because he reminded me of Sam from my time at St. Mary's. Sam and Ben were brothers who had come from away nearly fifty years prior to work with Dr Grenfell, Ben had also explained to me that we were sort of related because his son, John, was married to my cousin, Marjorie. I really enjoyed watching Ben fix motors and build things. Someday I hope to be able to build Ma a big cabinet and fill it with pretty dishes or get a new motor for Dad's boat to make it go really fast.

On the main floor were the dining rooms. Staff and children dining rooms were separate. The staff one had sinks and serving dishes to serve the food that came up from the kitchen on the dumb waiter. The dumb waiter was a small elevator like hole between the floors where the cook could place food in from the kitchen in the basement and it could be raised to the first floor by a pulley. Staff also had a sitting area and beyond that there was a large room for group activities and socials.

This main floor area is where I could always find Mrs. Hodge, the house mother or Mrs. Brown, who worked in textiles and was responsible for mending and sewing. I had met Mrs. Hodge my very first day and taken a liking to her after she had been so accommodating to Rita.

Elizabeth Hodge had moved to the orphanage in 1938 after the sudden death of her husband left her with five small children. Her children grew up in the orphanage and she was taken on as house mother. She remained nice to me after she had witnessed my pain that first day and I grew to admire her. But she could be strict when she needed to be. She was determined that her children would have a good life despite the cruel hand they had been dealt with the death of their father.

Mrs. Brown worked in textiles. She had a proper sewing room on the third floor where she would teach girls how to sew and mend clothing, but most times she worked from a small room off the main area. Here she would do some hand sewing or knitting during the day, so she was always available as an extra pair of hands if needed.

I didn't see the Headmistress much but when I did, she was usually barking orders at the staff while the children cowered and stood back. It seemed like Headmistresses came and left frequently so no real attachments were made with the children unlike with the local staff. The Headmistresses were always the same: stern, no nonsense women who came from away with something to prove. I just steered clear and only spoke if I was spoken to directly. I addressed them as Miss or Ma'am and never knew any of their names.

My favourite people were the boys I roomed with and the friends I made. Of course, I would never forget my friends from the hospital but the bonds created at the orphanage were a bit different. Although there was prevalent sadness, it wasn't the same type of sadness of being stuck in a bed twenty-four hours a day. If you were mad with a certain boy, you just hung out with a different boy for a while instead of hiding under the bed covers until you were no longer mad. The sadness at the orphanage was because most of the children had no homes to return to, unlike the children that were hospitalised.

I made friends quickly as I was really good at being a great friend; a quality that remained with me throughout my life. Unlike most of the other children who had either been yanked from unfit homes or whose parents had passed, I had had the opportunity to watch and observe people for the past three years and learn how to act appropriately to ensure I thrived in whatever environment that was thrown my way. It was weird, but most of the time I didn't even realise it was happening. It was like I could sense someone's needs and yearnings and be more attuned. It was like a survival instinct to me, and I soon became endeared by the staff and residents at the orphanage.

The days started early with a quick washing of face and hands, then teeth brushing, and swallowing our cod liver oil. The house mother tried to watch while we did all this even though sometimes, she would get distracted long enough for the older boys to toss the oil or do a quick pretend teeth brushing. Then it was down the steps for a breakfast consisting of porridge and tea. Most times there was a glass of milk, and on special occasions there was toast, eggs, and juice. I ate whatever was put in front of me. The children that didn't would have hunger pains. I had known about hunger pains when food was short at home and I didn't want to feel that again.

Then it was off to school. The walk was excruciating at first with my cast and I lagged behind. It was also colder by then and I had to be bundled up. The older boys would offer to help, but I was too proud to accept any assistance. As time went on, I got faster and kept up good with the other boys.

Dinner time we returned to the orphanage and usually had beans or soup with bread. Everyone ate the bread but the kids who refused to eat the soup or beans were punished. Usually, the punishment was no desert which was a really bad punishment when there were cookies. Then it was back to school until three and chores at the orphanage after that.

The Hodge boys were known as the barn boys because they took care of the animals at the barn. I was usually sent with them with a bucket to collect the eggs. Other boys carried in wood or shovelled snow. The girls peeled vegetables or mended clothes or cleaned. Everyone had chores to do.

Suppertime was always some type of meat served with vegetables. Homework was completed and bedtime was seven thirty. The older boys would talk and laugh for hours but I found the new routine very exhausting. It wasn't until spring when the days started getting longer, that I would stay up too.

CHAPTER 54: ARCHIE
ST. ANTHONY ORPHANAGE, SPRING 1950

Another Christmas and another cold winter had passed. The orphanage had some really nice Christmas socials and a couple of winter ones. The socials were fantastic. Local guitar and accordion players would come in play and sing, and the staff and older kids would dance jigs and reels. The younger kids would bop up and down and clap. There would be fabulous food. Everyone would be happy and having fun. Those were magical times for me, and I vowed to someday learn to play the guitar and the accordion and own one of each for myself.

I did not, however, like the trudge to and from school each day. On level ground I could keep up with anyone, but ploughing through the snow was different. I made it through the winter without incident and was happy to see the weather warm and the snow recede.

I was also getting to know the boys a lot better and finally remembering all their names. There were the Hodge boys, who had been there the longest and actually made life in the orphanage seem normal, so I really looked up to them. Their father had passed a few years prior, and their mother was given a job at the orphanage, allowing her to bring her children. There were three of them, Frederick, Clayden, and James. Fred was the oldest, Clayden in the middle, and Jim was the closest to my age but still three years older.

Gordon White was also three years older with an older sister in the orphanage named Marjorie who slept on the third floor. She was just two years younger than Rita and they soon became best friends. The youngest White sibling was Gayden, who was six.

The Pinksen boys had a bit of an age gap, so Rod hung out with the older boys and Eric, the younger boys. Wilfred and Neil Beck spent time with Eric and Gayden. As I fell right in the middle of the two age groups

I either hung out with the older boys or the younger boys depending on the activity. Even with living with all of these boys, I would also play with Dr. Thomas' sons, Len and Parm, who lived in the doctor's house next to the orphanage. I tried to just be myself and it seemed that everyone loved my genuine demeanour and the fact that I could keep a secret and always had their backs when they needed it.

By the time the boats started running in June, I had settled into a routine. My roommates were fast becoming my family, and I no longer felt the extreme emptiness of not being at home with my parents and siblings. I was on the beach one day throwing rocks at gulls when I saw Rita walking towards me.

"Hey Archie, are you able to hit one?" she asked.

"Nah, they are too fast for me," I laughed. I noticed she was serious and turned to face her. "What's wrong?" I asked.

"I'm going home for the summer," she said.

"Me too?"

"No, sorry Archie, but Dr. Thomas says you still need to stay close to the hospital. But you have made lots of friends and you can pretty much take care of yourself. You will be fine," she replied.

I hung my head. I didn't want to admit it, but I would miss her immensely. Just knowing she wouldn't be around made me feel very anxious.

"When will you go and when will you be back?" I asked, looking at her.

"I am going in a few days, and I will be back before school starts," she explained. "Dr. Thomas said it wouldn't be a problem as they won't be as busy this summer with no school and there are the older girls at the orphanage will be free to help out."

"Marjorie is going to really miss you."

"Yes, she will because she will have to do the laundry by herself," Rita laughed.

"Oh no," I laughed with her. "No clean clothes for us this summer."

As we walked back to the orphanage, Rita held one of my crutches so we could walk arm in arm, while she remarked, "You know, you are probably going to have more attention while I am gone. Dr. Thomas said you can go play with his boys, Ted Patey wants you to go hang out with his young boy, and Clarence Johnson says he will bring you over to his place for some home cooking."

"They all know you are going?" I asked.

"Yes, I had to know you would be taken care of before I made up my mind. I've been feeling homesick, and I know Mom could use my help this summer with the cooking and cleaning. So I feel I should go."

I just nodded and wondered why I wasn't more upset. Three days later, I stood on the wharf and waved her off as she stood on the deck of the *Kyle* waving back at me with tears streaming down her cheeks. I would really miss her but the only thing on my mind was the fresh pork we were having for supper.

CHAPTER 55: FANNY MATTHEW'S COVE, SUMMER 1950

They had been in Matthew's Cove nearly a month now and Fanny was breathing deep unrestricted breaths. It was like she spent the winter holding her breath and when her feet touched the soil in Matthew's Cove she could finally breathe again.

She often wondered about why being in the bay made her feel so restricted. She had the same people around and she was free to walk and roam. Maybe it was because the colder months were spent in the bays, so you had to dress warmer to go out, or that the houses were built further back on the land, so you had to go further to escape prying eyes. Out here, once you went to the hill that separated Matthew's Cove from Trap Cove, you were practically invisible as all the houses in both coves. Then there was Tilsy, where you could go and feel the warm winds from the unprotected knob that jutted out from the centre of both coves. The sea and vegetation smells were also amazing. Ambrosia for the soul.

Of course, the life here was much busier when the men were fishing as they had to be kept clean, well fed, and when there were lots of fish, they needed help at the stage. However, the few stolen moments she could wander the hills or just sit quietly on her flat rock near Capstan Cove among the blooming alexander were heavenly.

The past winter had been a different busy with the boys attending Princeton School. Roy and John didn't want to attend the school on nice days. Instead, they wanted to help their father get wood and hunt, but the Ranger was strict about the boys attending school. Apparently, you could lose the baby bonus if your school age children did not attend. Archie's and Rita's money had gotten assigned to the orphanage, so Fanny's check was now just $26. It was still a great help that she didn't want to risk losing.

She had been sitting at the table one night making sure the boys completed their homework when Roy started in again about her learning to read.

"For heaven's sake, Roy, stop tormenting," she cried. Fanny was disgusted as she figured Roy was just trying to wiggle out of doing his homework.

"I'm serious Ma, you could learn this yourself from our books and that way you wouldn't need Aunt Ethel to read everything for you," he explained.

Fanny looked away. She always hated that she had to run to Ethel with all her letters. It would be nice to be able to read her own and have some privacy. Plus, Ethel was busy with her own family since Ivy was born. She glanced over at Ern, napping on the daybed, and was glad he didn't hear the silly conservation.

"I'm getting too old for learnin," she stated.

"You're not old Ma," said little Dorothy, who was quietly colouring.

"It's just as well you try it so Roy will shut up about it," came a voice from the daybed. He wasn't asleep after all.

Fanny grudgingly gave Roy a nod of approval and he set to work writing down all the alphabet for her to study. Fanny was secretly happy about Ern's approval and Ern was secretly happy that maybe Fanny would shift her focus to something else besides Archie and Rita. Over the winter, Fanny made small advances in her reading and learned at almost the same pace as Cack, who had just started school that year.

Another positive thing that occurred was that Dorothy Jupp had given Mildred some part-time work in the hospital as aide's helper. Mildred was a very hard worker, and this was a great help to the family. Fanny was already grateful that the nurse kept her updated about Archie and it seemed as if Nurse Jupp always found a way to interact with the family.

Mildred loved the work, and the nurse treated her well. Almost too well. Sometimes it was a bit embarrassing when Nurse Jupp would choose her to do some personal work for her, instead of choosing the girls that had been there longer. The girls would shoot her dirty looks, and Mildred would shoot a look back that told them they could get a fat lip if they messed with her. She had grown up among all boys and had learned quickly how to settle arguments, and it was never ladylike.

Mildred would be nineteen that summer and being the tomboy that she was, Fanny had given up wondering if she would ever get married and settle down with her own family. That's why it seemed strange to her when she saw Mill run up the path towards her house that sunny June morning.

"Hi Ma, just ran in to see ya before I head over to Mom's," Mill said.

Fanny cringed. She would never get used to Mill calling her mother 'Mom.'

Fanny quickly collected herself and gave her daughter a big hug. "Just out for a visit?" she asked.

"Nah, too many flies in there for me. Nurse Jupp said I could take the summer off and go back in the fall," she answered.

Fanny knitted her brow in suspicion but didn't say anything. It wasn't until later that day as she was headed to the stage to get a fish for supper that her suspicions were confirmed. There was Mildred, bold as brass, headed to her grandmother Abigail's house with a brand-new dress on.

Ern found Fanny seated on her rock with her arms wrapped around her knees, quietly staring out to sea.

"Alright woman, what is it now?" He knew something was up if she was sitting out here at night. The days were still getting longer so it wasn't yet dark, but darkness was approaching. When she didn't respond he tried a softer approach. "Fan, I'm really tired maid. Let's just go home and go to bed."

"That's all you minds is the damn bed," she snarled. "That's all every man minds."

Ern's jaw dropped. "Woman, what's you gettin on with now?"

"Where do you think Mill is at tonight?"

Ern shook his head trying to make sense of this. He had just assumed she was sad about Archie again. "Wha?" he asked, dumbfounded.

"She is off beating around with that Ken, that's wha" Fanny snapped.

"For god's sake Fan, Mill is a grown woman, and Ken is a good man," he said.

"Good men don't go chasin after their nieces," she argued.

"Fan, my sister Maime has been gone for nearly 9 years. There is nothing wrong with this," he explained, patiently.

"He is old enough to be her father," Fan retorted stubbornly.

"That's not true Fan. Maime was fifteen years younger than me and Ken wasn't that much older than her. And I don't think he is doing all the chasing either."

Fan laid her head on her knees. She knew he was right.

"This is none of our business, Fan." He jumped the little gorge and sat beside her. He knew she was crying.

Finally, she spoke through her sobs. "This was the summer I thought we would finally be all together again. I know it would only be a matter of time before Mill would hitch that vagabond and move away. He can never stay in one place for very long. I figured Rita and Archie would get home this summer, and we would be a family for the summer."

Ern put his arm around her and pulled her head to his shoulder. "Rita will be home soon for the summer and maybe even before summer is over Archie will be home too. And I wouldn't bet on Mill moving anywhere, you know how stubborn she can be."

Fanny smiled at this. She did know how stubborn Mill could be, but she also knew that when Mill gave her heart to this man, she would follow him to the ends of the earth. As for Archie, she knew he was doing well but she also knew it was very doubtful that he would get home before the end of the summer, but she loved that Ern always tried to give her hope. Her heart ached for him every day. Maybe she just had a fit about Mill because this was something she felt she could control. However, she didn't even have control of the fate of her ten-year-old, let alone the fate of her nineteen-year-old.

CHAPTER 56: RITA
MATTHEW'S COVE, SUMMER 1950

It was a joyous day when Rita arrived home on the *Kyle*. Fanny had made Rita's favourite soup. Plain salt beef soup because Rita was always picky about wild meat.

The supper table was alive with chatter about St. Anthony, the hospital, the orphanage, and, of course, Archie. Rita tried her best to tell them as much as possible while eating with Dorothy snuggling as close as she could get.

Mildred arrived a bit late but ladled up a bowl of soup for herself and sat down. "The Queen made it home, did she?" she said.

"Mildred!" Fan snapped.

"I'm only joking Ma," Mildred replied, but everyone knew she wasn't.

Rita gazed at her sister while inhaling deeply. "You are looking well Mildred," she said.

Mildred rolled her eyes and stuffed a crust of bread in her mouth.

Rita knew the family was eagerly awaiting more stories, so she ignored her sister and kept talking.

Later, Rita had lovely visits with her s of grandparents that night. By the time she set off for home it was getting dark. Mildred met her in the path.

"So, do you have a boyfriend over there?" Mildred asked, a sharpness in her tone.

"No, I work a lot and there are strict curfews," Rita responded.

"I guess you heard about me and Ken," she preened.

Rita stopped and faced her sister. "Yes, do you think that is wise, Mildred?"

"Just listen to you and your fancy words," Mildred snarled.

"Well, I've been over there for three years. I can't help it if I talk differently now." Rita started walking again.

"It should have been me that went with Archie," Mildred said.

Rita stopped again. "What?"

"You heard me," Mildred said, eyes blazing.

"You were needed here. Ma knew you would be way more of a help to her than I would have been," Rita explained, voice raised.

"Well, there wasn't any big ole party for me when I came out from St. Mary's last week," Mill countered.

"There wasn't any big ole party for me either. It was salt beef soup and you can probably make it just as good as Ma anyway. You know you are a way better cook than I am," Rita shot back.

Fanny was just putting her dish towels on the line so they wouldn't go fousty overnight when she overheard the shouting. She was about to bawl at them to stop when she saw Mildred sink down to sit on a rock and put her face in her hands.

"I just wanted to be the one to go with him. I miss him so much," she said sadly.

"It wasn't all good times over there you know," Rita said softly. "I worked hard, and we both missed home a lot. Sometimes I was so jealous that you were home with the family, and I was the one over there."

There was a silence as Mill considered what Rita had just said. She had missed Rita and now that she was moving on with her life with Ken, she felt that they had missed out on a lot of sisterly bonding. She hated what this TB had done to her family and now she would probably be gone before they could all be finally united. It was probably easier to just be mad.

"Oh, I certainly wasn't jealous of the likes of you then," Mildred snapped as she stood and strutted back towards her grandparents' house.

Fanny sighed. She had so hoped those two would have finally gotten along. It was hard enough on them not growing up in the same household without them having to go through all this with their brother. She was so mad sometimes at the damn TB and what it had done to her family.

CHAPTER 57: FANNY
MATTHEW'S COVE, SUMMER 1950

The summer slid by fast after that. The girls hardly spoke two words to each other. They both picked up some odd jobs at Gradys, across the cove, but made sure they were on opposite shifts.

By the time it came for Rita to return to St. Anthony, Mildred had announced she was moving to Goose Bay with Ken. Fanny was heartbroken. Another child would be gone.

"Mom, I'm not a child anymore," Mildred protested.

Upon hearing Mildred call her mom, Fanny sniffled even more. "It's like I never owned ya. You slept at Mom's all the time, and now you're moving away."

"For god sakes Fan," interjected Ern. "You seen her every day. What difference did it make where she slept?"

"I'll be back to visit, Mom," said Mildred, glaring at Rita. "And I won't wait three years either."

"What's that supposed to mean?" Rita said, taken aback.

"You could have come home for visits if you had really wanted too," Mildred stated.

"That's not true," Rita protested. "Archie would have been devastated if I left, even for a few days. I was only able to come now because he is older and getting more independent."

At that, Fanny started to sob. Her boy was growing up and getting more independent without her being able to watch any of it. It was beyond cruel.

"See what you are doing? You are making Mom cry," Mildred shot at Rita.

"Ma, I'm so sorry. I didn't mean..." Rita never got to finish because Ern had had enough.

"Girls!!" he bellowed. "Enough! What in the hell flames has gotten into ye two this summer?"

The girls both hung their heads, and the rest of the children were quiet. Even Fanny's sobs dried up at this outburst.

"This is going to end here tonight, or no one goes anywhere," Ern ordered.

"Well, none of this would be happening if you had let me go with Archie instead of Miss Fancy Pants there," Mildred argued.

"What is your problem with me, Mildred? I haven't done a thing to you. I can't help the way I talk or dress."

"I bet Archie hasn't changed," Mildred challenged.

"Yes, he has. We both had to," Rita said and then more softly, "to survive."

Not even Ern responded. He just turned his back on them and stared out the window. It seemed like so long ago since he had had any control over what was happening to his family.

Fanny broke down again. Her son would be a stranger to her by the time he came home. She saw the change in Rita in just three years. Archie had been gone for almost four and had left home when he was much younger.

For a few moments, the only movement in the room was the gentle heaving of Fanny's shoulders as she tried to hold back sobs from the younger children. Little Dorothy sidled up next to her to leaned against her.

Finally, Roy broke the silence. "Look, Mildred, I know you think you suffered by not being the one to go with Archie, and Rita, I know you felt you suffered because you were away from home but you guys need to stop thinking of yourselves for a while and look at the real sufferers. Ma and Archie. Ma has lost a child, and Archie will eventually come back here a stranger because he left so young. And if you think the rest of us don't miss him every day you are sadly mistaken. Now, let's stop all this foolishness and make sure that whenever Archie does come home, he has a united family to come home to."

Still gazing out the window, Ern took a deep breath as his heart swelled with pride for the man his son had become.

No one knew what to say to that and were a bit ashamed when they realised he was right. Mildred was the first to kneel beside her mother and wrap her arms around her, Rita followed suit and soon they were all in one big ball around their mom and stayed that way until the sobs stopped.

CHAPTER 58: ARCHIE
ST. ANTHONY ORPHANAGE, SUMMER 1950

I had a few miserable nights after Rita left. It was so hard to sleep knowing she was not in the building. After a few nights of restlessness, I figured one of the boys must have told someone I was having a difficult time because the next day, after dinner, I got called to Mrs. Brown's room.

Mrs. Brown was responsible for clothes mending and knitting. The door to her small room on the main floor was always open so when I popped my head in, she told me to come right in. She motioned to a chair, and I sat down.

She was organising her different skeins of wool on the shelves. She wore a dark, ankle length dress with a lighter bibbed apron over it. It was the same outfit she had worn every day for the past nine months since I had been here. I wondered if she had only one outfit or just a bunch of the same ones.

"Choose a colour wool," she said.

"What?" I asked confused.

"Choose a colour wool you want to work with. The headmistress has instructed me to teach you how to knit."

"Why?"

"Well, it's a more relaxed time of year with school out for the summer and not as many winter clothes needing mending so I have the time to teach you," she explained.

"I meant, why me?"

"It seems you are at that in between age where you are too young to go off with the older boys and too old to play with the younger boys. Plus, it seems you have been a bit sad since your sister left," she continued.

"But why knitting? Why not woodworking with Mr. Acreman?" I asked.

"Well, it seems that the new headmistress has this newfangled idea of knitting helping with math skills." Mrs. Brown rolled her eyes.

"But I'm good at math."

"Look, I don't question what they tell me to do. I just do it, and if you know what's good for ya, you will do the same. Now pick a colour" she ordered.

I picked blue and before long I was knitting a scarf. I was to spend thirty minutes an afternoon with her and had to have ten rows completed each day. I soon found that I would much rather be outside with the younger boys so I would rush to complete my rows before bedtime. In less than two weeks, I was sleeping well again. Mrs. Brown then told me to leave my knitting in her room and work on it at my leisure because she knew the older boys had been tormenting me about it when I had it in my room.

The only one in my room who had said anything about the knitting was Rod, but that wasn't even much. I didn't mind. I looked up to Rod as he had always stood up for me and helped me whenever I needed help ploughing through the snow. Rod could be a real hard ticket when he wanted to be, but he was always good to me. Sometimes it was really funny the stuff he would do.

I will never forget the hot July day that Rod started flicking peas at the other boys in the dining room. Mrs. Hodge had caught him doing it and told him she was taking him to see the Headmistress. He replied that she would have to catch him first. He started to run but she caught him by the shirt collar. He didn't miss a beat. Quick as a flash he knelt on the floor and reached up and pulled her bloomers to her ankles and was up and running up the stairs before she even realised what just happened. As she tried to run after him, she tripped and fell as her bloomers were holding her ankles together. We all hooted with laughter that quickly went quiet when the Headmistress showed up.

Rod was punished but maintained it was totally worth the punishment and the boys had laughed about it for months afterward.

CHAPTER 59: ARCHIE
ST. ANTHONY ORPHANAGE, FALL 1950

Rita returned before the end of August, and I was ecstatic to see her. After mid-August I made the trek to the wharf every time the coastal boat arrived and searched the crowd for her. Then at last, there she was. She squealed in delight when she saw me, and I beamed my biggest ever smile.

As we walked back to the orphanage together, I wanted to know all about my family and all about the fishing and berry picking. We berry picked on the hills in St. Anthony, but it just wasn't the same as back home. I remembered all the sea smells and the taste of the berries, and it was very different over here. As she rambled on about Roy, John, Cack, and Dorothy, I listened intently to all the funny stories but found I couldn't conjure up their faces. This made me sad. Then she told me the news about Mildred moving to Goose Bay and I thought my heart would break. I was happy that Mildred had found someone to love, but the thought of everyone not being there when I was finally able to go home deeply saddened me.

As I laid in bed that night with all my knitted goods from Mom and Grandmother tucked next to me, I allowed my tears to stream into my pillow. I was jealous that Rita had been able to go home to see them all, but I still hadn't given up hope about getting home before the last boat. Lots could happen in the next three months. Just before I drifted off to sleep, a vision of Rita that had been nagging me came into focus. It was a sad, wistful look that I prayed wasn't because she felt she had been obligated to come back here with me. Now, on top of my other sadnesses, I felt guilty of causing Rita to suffer also.

I didn't see Rita much for the next few days as she was catching up with her work and with Marjorie and her other friends she had made over the past few years. She waved to me whenever she saw me, and I was glad she looked so happy. Maybe the fleeting sadness I saw in her wasn't because she had to come back here at all. I made a mental note to ask her when the time was right.

Right after school started in September, there was talk about another boy coming from Labrador. That made me perk up. I wondered if it could be Bart or Arthur from the hospital. I hadn't seen either of them in a long time and I missed them.

It was becoming a rare occurrence in the past year to have new people come to the orphanage to live because of homelessness or neglect due to being part of very large families. The Hodge boys said it was because of the baby bonus and that relatives were taking children in to live with them for the money. The only new children that showed up there now were mostly older kids who could get a better education in St. Anthony than in their tiny communities.

Then came the day that the new boy was brought to their room. He was given the bed next to me. His coat and skin colour were like the boys from Northern Labrador, but his round eyes and wavy hair suggested otherwise. However, those things were not discussed among my age group. The boys' name was Winston, but everyone called him Wince. He was quiet and he shyly kept his head down, only looking up to acknowledge being introduced to the other boys. He didn't talk much for the first few days, but quickly became loved due to his friendly demeanour. He never uttered harsh or mean words, laughed at all the jokes, and stayed out of quarrels. He was a lot like me but different in that he didn't feel the urge to fit in like I did. He did tell me that he didn't grow up with a lot of people around, just his mom and dad, and that he enjoyed being alone when it was quiet. I didn't feel so bad leaving him after that and tagged along whenever I could with the older boys, while Wince only went occasionally.

Whenever the older boys went on long treks I was left to associate with the younger crowd. I enjoyed them because they were not as serious, and they looked up to me the way I looked up to the other boys. Wince also declined spending days with the younger boys, preferring to do things alone. Lots of times, he and I would just chat and once Wince got to know me better, he asked a lot of questions.

"What happened to your leg? Where are you from? When did you get here? Who is Rita to ya?"

I thought all the questions were funny and it was nice to hear Wince chatting. I had heard him cry for many nights when he first arrived, so it was nice that he was getting along. I noticed though that no why or how questions were asked. I figured that Wince had gotten the same talk as I did on arrival. No talking about your past families was a general rule at the orphanage. It seemed that talking about this really upset a lot of the children and everyone was instructed that if we wanted to talk about it, we should talk to an adult or the minister. For now, this was our home and there was lots to do and talk about while we were here besides the things we couldn't control.

It was a very different adjustment for me as the boys talked about this stuff all the time in the hospital. Rita quickly explained to me that children in the hospital were there because they were sick and they had families to go home to, but here at the orphanage, most didn't have any families to return to. For some children, like me with my TB leg, the reason was obvious but if anyone was there because they had been orphaned or neglected, it was not known. This was terribly sad, so I didn't speak of it again.

CHAPTER 60: ARCHIE
ST. ANTHONY ORPHANAGE, FALL 1950

School continued without incident that fall while I awaited news on my leg. It was still in a cast, but I was getting around on it really well. I knew the doctor had to pronounce me well and give permission for me to return home. My constant requests to the Headmistress asking when I would get to see the doctor were starting to make her angry, so I stopped asking so much. The last boat would be leaving in November, and I wanted to be on it. The last time I had asked a question I had gotten this response.

"Young man, I have no control over when the doctor determines he will see patients," the Headmistress scolded. "If you were sick, I would take you to the hospital, but I can only assume that the doctor wants you to heal more inside that cast until he is ready to do further investigation. This is the fourth time this month you have asked me and if you ask again, you will be punished. Do you understand?"

I had nodded my head sadly and retreated to my room. I didn't eat supper that night and when Rita dropped by to visit, I refused to talk to her or even look at her.

"Everything will work out," she had said in a soothing voice. I had told her earlier that I was going to ask the Headmistress again. She had warned me against it but we both knew I had some of our mothers' stubborn streak in me.

"Don't you even care if we get to go home or not?" I flipped to face her.

"Of course I care, but it does no good to worry about it," she soothed.

"Isn't that what you were worried about when you came back here a few weeks ago?" I demanded.

"I don't understand what you mean."

"You looked like you were sad to be back here and it's all my fault." I flipped back towards the wall again. I was glad my bed was in the corner so I wouldn't have to face anyone.

Rita was quiet for a few minutes. Then she sat the other way on the bed with her back against the headboard like she couldn't keep herself upright with her own strength.

"I can't believe you picked up on that. Maybe Mildred should have been the one to come with you. She is older and maybe more motherlike than me." I heard Rita start to cry so I flipped around again.

"I don't want you to be sad because of me. You should go on back home. I'm fine. I may even get home on the last boat," I said.

"No, you silly imp. I love it here." We were both speaking in hushed voices even though I knew the other boys could hear it all.

"You don't miss home?" I asked.

"Of course I miss home, but I like it here too. Plus, I am making some money and getting good schooling. I may even be a nurse someday," her happiness was clear in her voice.

I beamed at that. Rita would make a wonderful nurse. "Then why were you sad?" I asked.

Rita drew in a deep breath and let out a long exhale before she spoke. "Mildred is mad at me because she should have been the one to come with you three years ago," she started.

"But someone had to stay and help Mom," I interrupted.

"Mildred thinks that someone, should have been me."

"But Mildred was better at that. I love you Rita, but you can't cook for beans," I laughed.

"You brat," she retorted while smiling. Then in a serious tone, she said "She is ready mad at me, Archie."

"But she never would have found the love of her life."

Rita smiled. "Hey, I'm the one supposed to be cheering you up."

"Actually, I do feel a bit better that you are not sad because of me."

"Now go to sleep. I have to get up to my room before the headmistress catches me." She gave me a quick peck on the cheek and then she was gone.

As Rita's footsteps retreated, a muffled whisper came from the next bed. "You are so lucky to have so many people that love you."

"Thank you Wince. Sorry to have kept you awake."

I could only think happy thoughts that night as I imagined the family back home that I loved so much. I could still hear Wince's muffled sniffles as I drifted off to sleep.

CHAPTER 61: ARCHIE
ST. ANTHONY ORPHANAGE, FALL 1950

I turned eleven on October 20, 1950. As was customary in the orphanage on your birthday, I had a cake with candles and the cake was shared for dessert. No one had to ask what I wished for as everyone knew how badly I wanted to go home.

Clarence Johnson had brought me over a pair of knitted socks and Rita had given me two dollars as she knew I liked to have a bit of money to buy candy sometimes at the Grenfell Store. However, I had been saving my money for a while now and had saved five dollars that I was keeping to buy something for Mom before I left for home. I had his eye on a brooch at the store and I was hoping it would still be there when I got the news. It had a big purple gem surrounded by sapphires. I knew mom would love it as she never had many nice things. Rita said times were getting a bit better at home now, but Mom still did not own anything very fancy.

Ria told me later that week that Mildred and Ken had gotten married, and they were expecting a baby. She also added that they were moving back to St. Mary's for the winter. This was the best news I had heard in a long time as it meant that all my family would be home when I was able to go.

Finally, the day came when the Headmistress told me I would not be going to school that morning as the doctor had sent for me.

I was taken to the X-ray room in the hospital and then to the doctor's office to await results. Dr. Thomas smiled at me and asked how I was feeling and how I was enjoying the orphanage. I replied that I was feeling fine and that I had made a lot of friends at the orphanage so I was enjoying that as well. However, I admitted that I was looking forward to getting my cast off and heading home for the winter. That's when a serious look came on the doctor's face.

"Archie, I'm afraid your knee is still not healed," he said softly.

"I'm sure it will heal over the winter. I can even rest on it if I need to because my family lives close to the school at St. Mary's now, and I have two older brothers that can pull me on a sleigh if they need to." I stopped for a breath and noticed the doctor's expression had not changed. I started to feel sick.

"I'm not getting home again this winter, am I?"

"I'm so sorry Archie," he consoled. "I wish I had better news, but we can't chance you going back to Labrador with active TB in your knee. Without being near a surgical hospital, you could lose your leg, maybe even your life if the TB were to spread."

I couldn't speak. I was trying desperately to hold back the tears. There was so much going on in my head right now that I thought it would burst.

The doctor noticed my dilemma and offered to send for my sister.

X-ray 30th October 1950. TB process is present in the left knee joint. There is no fusion of the knee at present. Destruction appears to involve the femoral condyle on the medial side particularly. There has not been much change during the past few months. This boy should be kept in a cast and watched carefully. GWT

Rita and I walked back to the orphanage in silence.

She walked me to my room and told me to rest for a while before dinner. She was going to send Mom a letter telling her the news. I imagined Mom reading the letter and I started to cry. She would be so upset.

"I'm so sorry Archie. I know how badly you wanted to go home."

"I feel like I may never see home again," I sobbed.

"Of course you will. You have made a lot of progress since you came here. Remember the dreadful body cast?" she reminded.

"Mom is going to be so sad."

"Yes, she will. But how sad would she be to have you home and you got sick again?" she asked.

I considered this and decided Rita was right.

That night after lights out, I heard Wince whisper my name.

"Archie, you still awake?"

"Yes," I replied.

"I know you are sad, but I am happy you are staying. You are like a brother to me now and I would miss my Labrador brother."

"I was really looking forward to hunting some rabbits and partridges this year," I said.

"I used to enjoy that too. I'll tell you some stories tomorrow, if that is alright?" he asked.

"And I will tell you some too."

I couldn't help but smile in the darkness.

CHAPTER 62: FANNY
ST. MARY'S RIVER, FALL 1950

Mildred, Ken, and the letter from Rita arrived all in the same week. Fanny was really worn out from all the emotions she was feeling. So happy one moment, sad the next, then excited to be a grandma, then furious with the TB. It was exhausting.

When the time came to plan a little celebration for Mildred for the next week, Fanny was distraught. Ern was so busy helping Ken make a house livable for him and Mildred that he didn't notice the state of his wife. Aunt Liz noticed and even though she wasn't the type to interfere, she decided to have her say.

"Do you realise you just put onions in all the mustard salad? You know Roy don't like that," Liz pointed out.

They were making salads for the celebration supper. It was a Friday afternoon, so the children were all in school except for Dorothy. Mildred had taken her for a walk.

"Well, I guess he is just going to have to learn to like them," Fanny retorted.

"Fan, this isn't like you. You always cater to the food the boys like. What's wrong?" Liz asked.

"Nothing."

"It's about Archie and Rita not coming home again this winter. Isn't it?"

"Yes, but I don't want to talk about it. This is supposed to be a happy occasion for Mill. I don't want to be making a fuss and spoiling it for her," Fanny said, avoiding the question.

"Well, you shouldn't be spoiling it for yourself either. It could be a lot worse, you know."

Fanny thought about little Bella and immediately felt guilty, but even that guilt didn't ease her pain. "I can't help it. I just feel sick every time I think about it," she cried.

"The doctors know what is best. You don't want him coming home and getting sick again, do you?"

"No," Fanny sulked.

"Then, just start concentrating on the children you have here and let the doctors take care of Archie. The damn TB can't stay in his knee forever. I want to see him coming back with both legs intact, kicking a ball and going to his rabbit snares by himself."

Fanny slumped into a chair. There were no more tears left in her; she had expelled them all last week. The manner in which she dropped into the chair made did her more cognizant of the fat that was beginning to cushion her butt and hips. Stress had previously ruined her appetite, but recently the stress had been increasing it. Her mother noticed it too.

"You're not in the family way again, are you Fan?" Liz asked, suspicious.

"No," Fan glared at her, flabbergasted at this thought. "There will be no more babies for anyone to snatch from me."

Aunt Liz nodded at this statement. "It's for the best anyway. You have enough to look after now, and you will soon be a grandma." She grinned a grin so big that Fanny thought she would crack her face.

"And you will be a great-grandmother," Fan reminded her. They both giggled at this and got back to work preparing the meal. The first thing Fanny did was boil some extra potatoes to make another mustard salad without onions.

CHAPTER 63: ARCHIE
ST. ANTHONY ORPHANAGE, WINTER 1951

X-ray OPD - 3rd February 1951
There has been definite improvement in the X-ray appearance in the left knee, and healing is taking place in the epiphysis of the femur. There is no bony evidence of fusion though the joint space is destroyed and the cartilage has completely disappeared. GWT.

Rita had accompanied me to this appointment, and we practically bounced back to the orphanage after hearing the good news. The fact that the TB was retreating was great news. The doctor had also discussed the implications of what was going on in the joint space, but all we had heard was the regression of the TB. We were solely interested in leaping one hurdle at a time, and we considered the retreat of the TB to be the major hurdle blocking me right now.

Even though there was an excruciating cold wind, we were still grinning like fools when we entered the orphanage. All the other children were still at school, but Mrs. Hodge and Mrs. Brown met us in the entrance and were just as excited as Rita and I to hear the news.

"Go sit at one of the dining tables and I will get you both a hot cup of cocoa," Mrs. Hodge offered. She was always so kind to us and today she kissed the top of my head.

Mrs. Hodge was just pouring the steaming cocoa into two mugs for us when the Headmistress appeared.

"What have we here?" she demanded to know.

"Archie and Rita just returned from the hospital and it's really cold out, so I was getting them a cup of cocoa" Mrs. Hodge said.

"What do you think this is, a hotel?" the Headmistress snarled.

"I just thought…" She started but she didn't get to finish.

"You are not paid to think. Now get back to work. And Rita I suggest that you head back to work also. Archie can go to his room to await dinner and make sure you go back to school after dinner."

Rita and I could hear Mrs. Hodge apologising as they hurried up the stairs to their rooms, their cocoa untouched.

"Why does she have to be so mean?" declared Rita.

"Maybe she misses her mom," I guessed.

"I bet her mom doesn't miss her then. What kind of a mom raised such a mean person anyway?"

This new Headmistress had shown up on the last coastal boat. It seemed she was from a long way away and very young with something to prove. She was strict, stern, and I couldn't think of a single person who liked her. It was also obvious she hadn't spent much time around children. Most of the Headmistresses who came and went were spinsters and most of them were a bit mean, but this one certainly was extra mean.

It seemed that this winter, the older boys were always in trouble, but then again, they were always up to no good. It all made for some good ole laughs though. I craved to do some of the things the older boys would do. They didn't do really terrible stuff, just what Mom would call devilish stuff, and I could definitely see my brothers doing similar things. Like switching out salt and sugar, hiding people's boots, and the occasional theft of food from the kitchen. I spent a lot of time with Wince that winter as Wince had no interest in mischief, and I couldn't run very fast with my cast on.

Then in late March, on a warm sunny day, I was called downstairs. There in the entrance with a big round belly, looking like it was about to burst, stood Mildred, grinning from ear to ear. She looked older than I remembered, but it had been four years since I had seen her. She was a small woman, like Mom, but with Dad's firm features. I wanted to run and jump into her arms, but I wondered if I would hurt her belly.

"Archie," she exclaimed hoarsely, her voice filled with emotion. "I need a big hug." She rushed towards me and crushed me into her arms and against that big belly.

She was crying openly now but I was still in shock and having a bit of fear about hurting the belly.

As I pulled away the questions poured out. "Where did you come from? How did you get here? How long are you staying? Did I hurt your belly?"

Everyone laughed and for the first time I noticed the man next to her. I had seen him before. He was Alfreda's father and he was smiling broadly at me. Alfreda was two years younger than me and was my first cousin.

"Didn't Rita tell you I was married and having a baby?" Mildred asked. "The baby is due soon so I had to come over here to be near the hospital to wait, and no you can't hurt my belly, the baby is well padded in there." Mildred gave her belly a few pats to show me. This time I had to laugh.

"But why here and not St. Mary's?" I asked.

Mildred waived a hand and said, "They just wanted to take extra care of me. Really make sure nothing goes wrong."

I had heard that sometimes women came down to St. Anthony if they were afraid there could be problems. Nurse Jupp was good, but the doctors were in St. Anthony.

"Come on, get your boots on and walk to the Grenfell store with us. I need to get some wool before we head out to Uncle Eric's," Mildred invited.

Ken gave me ten cents to choose my own candy to buy and Mildred let me choose one of the wool colours for her. I chose blue wool, my favourite colour. It was nice to be with them. It felt different when you were around family and shared a common bond. It's like certain ties can never be forgotten by the heart.

When it was time for her to leave to go to Uncle Eric's in Great Brehat, I started to feel sad and wished she could stay.

"I will be back soon for a checkup, my little sweetheart. So don't you worry, I won't be gone long. I can't believe how much you have grown. Mom would love to see you. You know she still cries every day." Mildred wiped away a stray tear while Ken put his arm around her shoulder and kissed the top of her head. "I guess I cried my own share of tears too," she smiled as she wiped her face.

"I'm sure I will be home by the first boat," I declared.

I got to see Mildred a couple of more times before she left for home with her newborn son. Mildred had knit me a cap and mitts out of the blue wool, and I really loved them. Rita took me to the hospital to see the baby before Mildred left. I will never forget peering into the tiny bundle of blankets and seeing the little pink face.

"Archie, I have something to tell you," Mildred started.

I looked at her with wide eyes not knowing what to expect.

"We all love and miss you so much at home that I decided to name my son after you. This is little Archie Stead."

CHAPTER 64: ARCHIE
ST, ANTHONY ORPHANAGE, SPRING 1951

The weather was warming every day, and the days were getting longer. I was happy to finally get to spend more time outdoors again but there seemed to be a deeper sadness since Mildred had been here. I had noticed how lovingly she looked at her son and it reminded me so much of how Mom had looked at me before I left home. There had been long periods that I couldn't even conjure up Mom's face, but now that I had a mental image again, it seemed impossible for it to fade away.

Life at the orphanage had suddenly become mundane and I felt like I was missing out on exciting things that may be happening back home. I imagined my family getting ready for fishing season and moving out to Matthew's Cove. I could envision Mildred bundling little Archie up tight in lots of blankets and sitting in the bottom of the boat with him, so wind wouldn't take his breath away or make him cold. Like I had seen Mom do with little Dorothy so many years ago. Little Dorothy would soon be seven and I hadn't seen her in three years. Little Eric Pinksen had just turned seven and every time I looked at him, I couldn't believe that little Dorothy was probably that big already. Sometimes, when I was feeling extra lonely, I would compare my siblings to the ages of the boys I lived with. Tonight, I pretended Wilfred Beck was Cack, that Jim Hodge was John, and that Rod Pinksen was Roy. I slept pretending I was back home.

Then came the talk of the coastal boats starting again, and I wondered if my next doctor's visit would determine the TB had gone and I would go home. I asked the Headmistress about when I would get to see the doctor and she was so angry that I would dare to waste her time with such nonsense, that I was sent to my room without supper that night.

Archie Rumbolt, Wilf Beck, and Gaden White in St. Anthony. From the Wilfred Beck Collection.

As I lay in bed with my head turned to the wall and my stomach growling, I heard Rod and some of the other boys discussing sneaking to the carrot cupboard. I knew that they weren't really hungry. It was just some devilment they did to pass the time and make dares with one another.

However, I not only felt hungry but felt mad about having been sent to my room without supper for just asking a question. I flipped over and sat up to face the other boys.

"I'm going too," I stated.

Wince glanced a warning at me to not do this. "Archie, stay here with me and they will bring back a carrot for you. You know you can't run on the stairs as fast as them."

"I'm going," I replied forcefully and firmly.

Wince turned away, he didn't want to argue with me.

Rod and the other boys grinned. I didn't get to have much fun, and it would be nice to see the cupboard. Besides, if we got caught, no one would punish me on my crutches. Other times, when the older boys tried to get me to join them, they argued how they had seen the older ladies take a pitying interest in me because of how long the TB was lingering.

The boys jumped off their beds and headed towards the stairs before I had a chance to change my mind. Rod and one of the older boys were ahead, I was in the middle, and two more boys were coming behind. They didn't want me to be at the back of the line.

Everything was quiet as we navigated down one flight of stairs to the main level and rounded a corner to descend the second flight of stairs to the basement. The carrot cupboard was directly under the basement stairs.

While Rod worked the latch, one of the boys thought he heard a sound and as soon as Rod had the door opened the last boy pushed us all inside. We stifled our giggles as best as we could and then went silent to listen. We didn't hear anything so Rod went to work untying one of the brin bags that held the carrots. As he passed each of us a carrot, we heard the noise again, but not before I had sat down on a sack and hungrily bit into the carrot. One of the boys went up to check the door, but it wouldn't open. Someone had jammed the door from the outside and we were trapped inside.

I later learned that it was Ben Acreman. He had been working in his workshop when he heard us on the stairs. How many times had he warned Rod that they would be caught, and they needed to stop that foolishness? He intended this time to teach us a lesson and had jammed a broom under the latch and went to get the Headmistress. He figured we needed a good tongue banging to smarten us up.

He had found the headmistress in the sitting room. She stomped past him to descend to the basement while he followed. He didn't want to miss this.

We all cringed as we heard her approach. She was already yelling as she removed the broom, and we heard it clatter as she flung it across the floor. Rod was the first to brush past her and head for the stairs followed by the other boys. Me, I was still fumbling with my crutches, and I was the last one to start moving.

Infuriated even more that the boys did not heed her command to stop, she started to chase us. She grabbed the first thing that came to her hands, a barrel stave from a broken barrel lying at the foot of the stairs.

"This can't be happening," was my first thought. "You all know I can't run."

But I had to. I had to run or at least I had to try. By the time I raised myself from the huge sack of flour I was using as a seat, the bigger boys had fled. Eric was younger than I and hadn't gotten far but was still ahead of me as I hobbled round a corner to head up the first batch of stairs.

Blood pounded in my ears, and everything seemed to go in slow motion. I had gotten to the third step when I saw Eric round the corner to head up the second batch of steps. "No!" I screamed to him. "Please don't leave me."

I watched him pause briefly before he turned to slowly make his way back down to me while leaning down to extend me his tiny hand. I knew it. I knew he wouldn't leave me.

There were other noises too, but I couldn't understand them. They were muffled and unrecognisable due to the loud pounding in my ears and the slow motion of the scene.

That's the moment when all went still. I saw Eric's eyes widen in horror at something behind me and I saw a silent scream form on his mouth. I tried to process what this meant. As I tried to turn to view what Eric was seeing I felt a massive slap at the back of my leg forcing my whole body to slam hard against the steps.

I don't know how long I have passed out. A minute, an hour, a day? No, maybe just a second because I could hear Eric whimper as he scurried up the next batch of stairs. My head pounded with the impact and I could taste blood. I could hear movement behind me. Curiosity and fear took over. With every ounce of strength I could muster in my arms I grabbed the edge of a step and pushed my body into an upright position.

The second chop of the barrel stave came harder this time causing me to spin uncontrollably and face my attacker. I almost couldn't believe my senses. I heard the sickening crack as my cast burst open exposing my battered leg and saw the pure evil of the Headmistress I now faced.

In that moment, remember the minister preaching in church about the evil that existed in the world and how he hoped we would all be good little boys and not have to witness it. I wasn't a good boy though, was I? I let hunger get the best of me and now I was being punished.

As the concrete basement floor loomed up at me to welcome me into the cold hard realm of death, I could see my Ma's tear-streaked face and smell her fresh raisin buns.

The last sensation I had was of falling... falling... falling.

I could hear yelling. Ben yelling for Rita. Rita and Marjorie yelling for me. She came to me, to the bottom of the stairs and tried to help me up. I heard the Headmistress, still in a rage, ordering Rita to go to her room. Rita ignored her and continued to help me. The Headmistress still had the barrel stave in her hand, holing it like a weapon.

"You did this?" Rita hissed at her.

"He was stealing carrots," she said smugly.

Rita pulled me into a sitting position and Marjorie bent beside me as Rita pulled herself up to face the Headmistress.

"You woolly headed son of a bitch," Rita spat. Rita didn't anger very often but when she did, nothing scared her.

"How dare you speak to me like that. I told you to go to your room," the Headmistress ordered.

"It's not me that's going anywhere," Rita fired back. "You won't be here after tomorrow. I can guarantee you that."

Rita and Marjorie carried me up the stairs while the Headmistress stormed off wordlessly. The other boys were silent as Rita settled me into bed and laid beside me as I whimpered. It was getting late, so she decided to wait until morning to get Dr. Thomas. As I drifted off to sleep, I moaned, just loud enough that Rita could hear, "I just want to go home."

I was still lying helplessly in bed the next morning when Dr. Thomas showed up. The other boys had gone off to school. They had told me how sorry they were, but I had assured them that I had gone with them willingly and what happened was not their fault. Wince had not said anything, but I noticed he had been crying.

Dr. Thomas examined me and told me I would be admitted into the hospital right away for x-rays and another cast application. He then sent for the Headmistress.

Dr. Thomas noticed that I cowered as she entered the room and stood at the foot of my bed. She stood straight and composed and looked the doctor straight in the eye. As Dr. Thomas addressed her by name, he informed her that she had not been hired to abuse children. He told her to go pack her bags and to be out of the orphanage by noon.

That was the last time Rita or I saw the woman. I was sent to the hospital that day and ended up spending the next two weeks there on bed rest.

June 8, 1951
Patient admitted for cast removal and X-ray.

P.H. This patient has been in Hospital; on several previous occasions (see case history #22299) for tuberculosis of the knee. Knee has been in cast for two years and child is living at the Orphanage, and is brought into hospital from time to time for X-ray examination and re-application of cast.

Interval History: Patient has felt well since last admission and gets around well with his leg in a cast.

P.E. Well developed and well-nourished boy who is gaining weight and looks healthy.

E.N.T.: Negative
R.S.: Negative
Heart: Negative

Local condition: Cast removed and knee examined. There is some dryness of the skin due to the cast. Knee is not fused.; has about 10 to 15 degrees motion. There are several healed sinuses and one small granulating area in front of the patella, which may be a pressure sore due to the cast or a new sinus.

Impression; Tuberculosis, knee. GWT

Rita visited me every day while I was in the hospital. The boys had even made a card to send over to me. Rita told me once how she had seen the Headmistress chop at me with the barrel stave, but after that it was never spoken of again. Dr. Thomas had done what was in his power to do and hopefully it served as a warning to other Headmistresses who showed up here.

X-ray 22nd June 1951

There has been very little change in the X-ray appearance of the left knee since January. The joint space is destroyed. Tuberculous process also involves the spiphysis of the femur particularly, and of the tibia on the medial side. Surgical interference may be necessary in this case. GWT.

"How is Mr. Archie Rumbolt doing today?" asked Dr. Thomas as he entered the ward. Rita was already there as the hospital had sent for her to hear the report.

"I'm good," I smiled. The doctor seemed in good spirits so I could only assume the news was good.

The doctor sat on the edge of the bed and explained that the tuberculosis was still present and that it was still a waiting game. They would apply a new cast, and I would be free to go back to the orphanage. It would be checked again in a few months.

I looked at Rita with terror in my eyes, willing her to say something.

"I'm afraid Archie doesn't want to go back there," she told the doctor.

"Is this true Archie?" Dr. Thomas asked.

I nodded yes but kept my head lowered while I fought back the tears.

"But the Headmistress is gone, and Mrs. Hodge is in charge until we get a replacement. You like her, don't you?" he reassured.

Again, I nodded.

"So, you still don't want to go back?"

This time the head shook no.

Dr. Thomas glanced at Rita for an explanation.

"Archie has been having nightmares. I think he needs to go home," she said.

This time Rita cast her eyes down. She didn't like to talk out of place to a doctor. Especially a doctor who had done so much to help them. I looked at her gratefully.

Dr. Thomas considered this. "I don't like the fact that I would be sending him back to Labrador with active TB. However, it is contained, and travel is much easier in the summer."

While he pondered aloud, Rita and I held our breaths and didn't interrupt.

"Alright," he said as he looked directly at Rita. "If we do this, I will have to make you aware of proper sanitation at home and what to look for if Archie were to start getting sick."

My eyes grew big, and Rita nodded. We both couldn't believe what we were hearing.

"I'm not making a decision right now. I need to consult with another doctor, and will make a decision by Monday. In the meantime, you will remain in the hospital," he said.

25th June 1951
Patient discharged home for two months to return in the fall for further check ups. New cast applied to leg. Condition unchanged.

CHAPTER 65: FANNY
MATTHEW'S COVE, JUNE 1951

When the *Kyle* sounded its horn announcing its arrival at Battle Harbour, Fanny thought she would jump clean out of her skin. She had been beside herself with excitement ever since she got the news on Monday that her children were coming home, even if it was for just two months.

She hadn't stopped cleaning and baking and pacing. It's been almost three years since she had seen Archie and almost a year since she had seen Rita. How much bigger were they? Would they be so accustomed to better living conditions that they would think poorly of the family now? Would they think of her as stupid after being around all them smart doctors and nurses for four years? What if she couldn't cook as well as the orphanage people? What if Archie got sick again? Her mind raged on and on until she was nothing but a pile of nerves.

Last night the tensions had erupted.

"No Fan, I am not going to Battle Harbour to get more apricots," Ern was adamant.

It had been more than four years since he had seen his son, but he knew apricots would not be the main thing on his son's mind when he got home. He needed Fan to relax and enjoy the time, not to be rushing about the house baking like a mad woman.

Fanny folded her arms across her chest. She didn't trust herself to speak.

"You got enough pies and buns and cakes made to feed an army. Slow down maid. He is going to be happy just to be home. He won't be caring about food," Ern said.

"Archie loves apricots, and I have them all used up," she cried. She couldn't even look at Ern at this point. It was like he wasn't at all excited, or happy or anything. Damn men don't care about anything.

"Alright," Ern finally conceded after a few moments of awkward silence. "I'll get another pound when I go to Battle Harbour tomorrow."

"You're acting like it don't matter that your son is coming home tomorrow after being gone for over four years," she scolded.

"You knows it matters, woman. But he will want to come home to the normal place he left, not a home to be fussed over. He will want to go play with the other boys and sneak cigarettes and all the other stuff the boys do. Fan," he paused, only realising himself what he was about to say, "he will soon be twelve years old. He is not a little boy anymore." The last of his words came out just barely a whisper and hit him like a ton of bricks. While he had been busy struggling to keep his family alive his son had left as a boy and was soon returning as a man.

He looked over at Fan, who was still gazing through the window with her arms folded.

He left and went to the stage.

The next morning Ern and the boys had checked the nets and made a quick stop to Battle Harbour for supplies. Fan drew in her breath as she opened the bag. Ern had purchased five pounds of apricots.

It wasn't long before she heard the putter of the motorboat coming back into the harbour with Ern and the children. She splashed her face with cold water and ran down the bank to the stage, followed closely behind by Mildred and her mother. Bob and Charl were already there.

Dorothy was snuggled next to Rita on one of the tots while Archie sat in the cuddy with Cack and John. Roy stood next to his father at the engine, looking very mature. Ern beamed her a smile and she smiled back.

She gave Archie and Rita big hugs and hurried everyone up to the house for dinner. The chatter was incessant. "Will you have to stay in the house? What is St. Anthony like? Does your leg hurt? Do you have a girlfriend?"

"Children!" yelled Fan. "Let him eat and rest. You got lots of time to ask him stuff."

Fanny and Rita dished up the beans while the children and Ern gathered around the table. "I think we will be eating beans for a month," laughed Roy.

Archie looked over at the two pots on the stove. "Is that two pots of beans?" he asked.

"Yes," Fanny nodded nervously. "I remembered you like beans and couldn't decide whether you would prefer baked or boiled so I made both."

Archie's eyes grew big and he looked at Rita who stifled a giggle.

"What?" demanded Fanny as she looked quizzically at Rita.

"That's about the same amount of beans that are made for sixty people at the orphanage. Not many kids there like beans."

"Not many kids anywhere like them," said John.

Fan looked disappointed and placed a bowl of baked beans topped with crispy salt pork in front of Archie. As Archie spooned the beans and pork into his mouth, he closed his eyes and let out a moan.

"Are you alright?" his mother asked.

"I am now. This is definitely a taste of home. Mmmmmmm. The cook at the orphanage can't make beans like you ma," Archie smiled, and shovelled in another mouthful.

Fanny shot a quick told ya so look at John before she beamed at Archie and went back to slicing bread.

CHAPTER 66: ARCHIE
MATTHEW'S COVE, SUMMER 1951

It was so exhilarating to be home. I couldn't run fast over the hills like my brothers, but I could go at a nice steady pace when I wanted to. A lot of times at night, when Roy and John would be done with fishing, they would take me in the wheelbarrow and go over the hills for hours to Trap Cove or up on Tilsey.

When the pussy willows bloomed, me, Cack, and Dorothy would go pick bunches for Mom, and both grandmothers. They loved that, and arrange them in old baby bottles to use them as centrepieces for the table. They would always have some goodies baked and a sweet cup of tea for us.

I also loved visiting little Archie. He was still so tiny, but Mill would let me hold him, and if he didn't wiggle too much, I would sit with him awhile. Sometimes I would go with Rita to Banningtons across the cove. Bannington had a small business and Rita worked there for the summer cleaning and baking. The owner would occasionally have me fetch some water or wood and pay me some small coins. The summer seemed to be rushing by so fast.

One night while Roy was giving me a ride to the lookout on Tilsey in the wheelbarrow, we stopped for a break.

"How do you like being home, Archie?" he asked.

"It's a wonderful vacation. I feel so special," I said honestly.

"A vacation?"

"Yeah, because I know I have to go back," I explained.

"Are you sad about that?" Roy always asked the difficult questions.

"I don't know," I admitted.

"Do you like it better back there?"

"I don't know." This was making me very uncomfortable.

"You don't know if you would rather be in an orphanage or here with your family?" Roy was shocked and I felt immediately guilty.

"I don't know," I repeated.

"I hope Ma never hears you say that. It will break her heart," he said.

"You won't tell her. Will you?" I asked, worried.

"As long as you don't tell her I smokes," Roy smiled as he lit up a cigarette. "Want a draw?"

"Sure." I took a deep drag and coughed and urged while Roy laughed.

"It's been a hard time for everyone, Archie, but Ma especially." Roy gazed off in the distance while he took long drags on the cigarette.

"I missed her too and I thought coming home would be the same as it was before I left," I paused. "Everyone is so much older. It's like time passed without me."

"You grew up too though." Roy smoked and we both pondered silently.

"I think it's time to ditch 'Archie,'" Roy laughed.

"What?"

"You are almost grown up and still using that baby name," he explained.

I considered this and agreed he was right. The more I considered it, the more I liked the idea. There couldn't be two Archies anymore. Better to let the baby be the only Archie now.

"I can't wait to tell everyone," I grinned.

"Archie," came the booming voice of my uncle Norm as walked up the hill.

Roy quickly stamped out his cigarette as Norm gave a chuckle. "I'm not stupid ya know."

Roy looked Norm in the eye. "I never said ya was. I bet you were smoking at my age."

"I certainly was," laughed Norm, as he ruffled Archie's hair. "How's my favorite nephew?"

"I'm good," I grinned, silently hoping Uncle Norm hadn't seen the drag I took on the cigarette.

"I don't want you tellin Ma about me smoking either," Roy said to Norm through clenched teeth.

"Look boy, I don't want no sauce from you. I never tattled in my life."

Roy did not respond.

"Whatcha doing Archie?" Norm asked.

"You will be the first to know," I grinned.

"Know what?"

"I'm changing my name to Arch, seeing there is another little Archie." I puffed out my chest to look as proud as a peacock until Norm cast his eyes down and slowly took a seat on a rock.

"Dad would be proud," he said sadly.

"Uncle Norm," I started, but my breath caught in my throat. "When Rita told me that Grandfather died, I was in a full body cast and I was already so sad I wasn't able to be more sad. I feel so bad about that now." I blinked quickly and looked away.

"That's understandable, little one."

"Grandmother still looks sad though," I said.

"She is fine enough, and I think she will be so happy about you being Arch," Norm smiled.

"Do ya really think so?" I grinned from ear to ear. "Let's go tell her next."

"Alright," laughed Norm as he scooped Arch up and deposited him back in the wheelbarrow.

"Uncle Norm," I smiled. "You are my favourite uncle."

Norm puffed out his chest proudly. "Maybe you won't say that after this fast ride."

Norm ran with the wheelbarrow and Arch screamed while Roy ran along beside them begging Norm to slow down.

At home, that night, I decided it was time to announce my news. Everyone was silent.

"Fine by me," said Cack and they all laughed.

Except Mom. "I'm going for a walk," she said.

Ern looked at the door after she left but did nothing.

"I'm going to go for a walk with her," said Rita and she left.

CHAPTER 67: RITA
MATTHEW'S COVE, SUMMER 1951

Rita caught up with her mother and they walked silently to Capstan Cove. Fanny hopped out on her rock and Rita sat on a smaller rock with the crevice between them.

Finally, Fanny broke the silence. "I missed the four of the best years of a little boy's life. The years where they grow into a man. The years that they learn to do things for themselves. I wasn't with him to make sure he did his schoolwork, or to protect him when the big boys were tormenting him." She started to sob.

"Stop that, Mom. You are being foolish now. You had a whole family to care for and Archie was fine. He had me."

"He should have had me," she whispered.

"And what about the other children, who would they have had?" Rita asked.

"I should have kept him home."

"Kept him home to die? A lot of kids have died from this, Mom. You did the right thing. It was the only option," Rita reassured.

Fanny just sobbed.

"Mom? Would you prefer he died?" Rita asked her.

Fanny stopped and turned to face her like she had lost her mind. "Are you cracked?"

"Well, it seems to me that you had two choices and if you feel you made the wrong choice then obviously you wish him dead."

"If you dare say that to me again, I will slap you silly," Fanny blazed.

"Well, you stop talking crazy talk Ma," Rita was mad too by this time.

After another silence Fanny spoke. "Tell me about what happened before you came home."

"How did you know about that?" Rita asked quietly.

"He told Roy and Roy told your father. I don't know if I want him to go back there," Fanny admitted.

"That woman is gone now."

"What if there is another one?" Fanny asked.

"Then I will take care of that woolly-haired bitch too," Rita grinned.

Fanny smiled. "I could hear Mill say that but not you."

"I was so mad Ma," Rita gazed out over the ocean, remembering that night and almost couldn't believe herself how quickly her anger had flared.

"Actually, Mill would have punched her. She would have laid her out like cold junk."

"Yup," Rita laughed. "She sure would have. Come on Ma, let's go home and see Arch."

She reached for her mother's hand, and they walked back arm in arm.

CHAPTER 68: ARCHIE
MATTHEW'S COVE & ST. ANTHONY, FALL 1951

I couldn't believe how fast the summer had gone. I had thoroughly enjoyed being home. My brothers were considerate young men and Cack and Dorothy were adorable. My mom's cooking was amazing, and her warm soft bosom was just as I had remembered. She could still make everything better. I was so sad to be leaving but everyone kept saying that maybe I would go back and get checked and my knee would be all better and I would be back again before the last trip of the boat.

However, as much as I loved my family, there was some feeling that kept me yearning to be back in St. Anthony. I hated it when I felt that, but I couldn't help it. I missed Wilfred and Neil and Rod and Jim and especially Wince. Everything was orderly back there. I enjoyed school and even enjoyed my chores. I loved my family, but sometimes I felt I didn't belong anymore. Even after the bad that had happened, I still yearned to go back. It was daunting to think about and I couldn't imagine voicing it out loud to anyone.

The day Dad's motorboat puttered out through Matthew's Cove to the awaiting *Kyle* anchored by Battle Harbour, my feelings were so scattered. I felt like I had smoked a whole cigarette belonging to Roy. Mom sat beside me holding me tightly. I could literally feel her grief and sadness.

"Ma, I could be back again before the last run of the *Kyle*. Don't be sad," I said.

Mom wiped away a stray tear and nodded. "I know," she said.

When the *Kyle* docked at the wharf in St. Anthony, Marjorie and Wince were waiting for us on the dock.

"I'm so happy you are back Archie," said Wince. He grinned widely at me while Marjorie and Rita embraced in a hug of giggly joy.

"Actually, I am Arch now." I said as Marjorie arched her brows and Rita shot her a wink.

"My little brother is all grown up now, apparently," Rita smiled.

"I don't care what you are called, you are still my Labrador brother," beamed Wince.

I felt a bit weird as we entered the orphanage for the first time since June, but my fears quickly vanished when I met the new Headmistress. She met us at the door and brought us to the sitting area for tea and buns before sending us to our rooms to rest until supper. She apologised for the actions of the last Headmistress and assured me and Rita that it would not happen again. I felt certain that Dr. Thomas had instructed her to welcome us and say that, but nonetheless, it was comforting to hear.

I had the same bed next to Wince. Wince assured me that he had made sure no one else had been put in it. Two of the older boys had moved out over the summer and one more had moved in, but mostly everything was the same.

As I sat on my bed and chatted with Wince, Wilf, Eric, and the other boys, I felt a strange sense of homecoming. It was like I had just got back from a vacation to a strange land. I felt very disturbed by it, so I didn't say anything, however, it felt really good to be back.

I saw Dr. Thomas and had an X-ray just after school started, but there was no change, and the doctor said it was unlikely that I would get home this winter. I felt strangely indifferent about this and by the time my twelfth birthday rolled around, Rita felt compelled to question me about it.

Because I didn't dine in the same room as my sister, I was allowed to take my cake on a napkin and go eat it on the steps of the orphanage with her. It was a beautiful evening and through mouthfuls of cake Rita said "Arch, I haven't heard you mention going home before the last boat this fall. I figure the last boat will be in a couple of weeks."

I silently kept savouring my cake and looking straight ahead.

"What's wrong? Did something happen while you were there?" she asked.

"No," I said.

"Did anyone torment or hurt you?"

"No." I tried to busy myself by brushing crumbs off my pants.

"Then what in the hell flames is going on?" Rita asked in an irritated tone.

I glanced sideways at her and knew I had better answer, but I felt so ashamed of my feelings. "It's like I feel more at home here." I hung my head.

We sat in silence for a while until finally Rita spoke. "I felt the same way when I went home last summer but just assumed it was because I was older. I have so much love for my family, but we have been gone for so long."

I couldn't believe we were both feeling the same emotions of guilt and shame were. She took a deep breath and continued. "At first, I thought they had all changed but then I realised that it was me who had changed. I felt so bad about it that I didn't tell a soul. Then this past summer when we went home together, I knew you were feeling the same."

I glanced sideways again and saw her place her face into her hands. All I could muster was to nod my head.

"This has changed us both, Arch. I have just turned eighteen, so I know I won't go back there to live. But you have so much time left back there. The hunting and the fishing and you will get your feelings back for your family."

"I love my family to pieces," I replied hoarsely.

"Of course you do, my love. This is a very confusing time for you. Your body is changing into a man, and you are questioning where you belong. When you finally get home for a while and know you don't have to come back here, you will feel different. I promise."

She put her arm around my shoulders and gently helped me to my feet. "Come on, let's go back in. It's my turn to help with the dishes."

CHAPTER 69: ARCH
ST. ANTHONY ORPHANAGE, WINTER 1952

Construction started on an American Military Air Base during the spring of 1951. This base was part of the early warning radar system, DEW, in response to the post-war cold relationship between the Soviet Union and the United States. As a result, Christmas saw the most musical and high-strung party in generations. Military men brought not only their musical instruments and trays of delicious food, but also wrapped gifts for all the children at the orphanage. As everyone ate and danced, I sat close to the musicians and watched them in awe as they entertained the crowd. I especially enjoyed the guitarist and fell in love with the music that was being created. I vowed someday I would have my own guitar.

What I hadn't noticed that night was the dark-haired handsome man that took a liking to Rita and danced almost every dance with her. Rita later told me she was enamoured and giddy by the time the night was over. I was glad that she was happy. She said she liked to get her feelings all sorted in her head before she could share them with others.

Just before spring that year, Rod was being his rambunctious old self and tormenting the boys when he blurted out "So your sister got a boyfriend, huh Arch?"

"Stop talking shit Rod," I retorted.

"It's true," Rod laughed.

"It's not true and quit saying stuff about my sister." It seemed I was growing the Rumbolt temper as I got older, and the anger blazing in my eyes told Rod to back off.

Later that night Wince whispered to me, "Don't be mad but I think Rod was right."

I was silent as I knew that Wince would never lie or torment.

The next day after school I went looking for Rita. She confirmed the rumours were right, but the relationship wasn't serious. "We go for walks sometimes and we went to a movie one night. He said he would like to meet you, and he is coming to the Easter social. I would really like you to meet him, Arch. He has become very special to me."

"What's his name?" I asked.

"Wayne, Wayne Chiodo," she smiled.

I laughed. "That's a funny name," I giggled.

"Wayne says our name is funnier, Rum-bolt." As she laughed at the memory of Wayne saying this to her, I saw a twinkle in her eyes that I hadn't seen there before.

"Seems like you like him very much," I said.

"I do Arch. I adore him."

"Then I can't wait to meet him." I smiled.

When Easter Monday arrived, the hospital and the orphanage were in high gear preparing for the Easter Time. There were raffles, a soup supper, and a dance to raise money, but the highlight was the easter baskets that were auctioned off to the highest bidder. They had a variety of candy and toys from the Grenfell store and some even had a bottle of rum. The main feature in each basket was the homemade cookies or buns from the single ladies that worked for the Mission. Whoever was the lucky highest bidder got the first dance with the lady whose cookies were in the basket.

Rita hated baking, but said it was for a good cause. It seemed everyone was making tea buns or raisin cookies, so she opted to make something different. She decided to make Mom's molasses pork buns. When she saw the finished product, she wished Mill had been around to make them for her. They were really hard and dense, but she didn't have time to make another batch.

Later, after all the soup bowls had been washed and stacked away from the supper, we gathered in the main hall to begin the dance. I hadn't let Rita forget that she had promised to introduce me to Wayne if he showed up. Rita hadn't seen Wayne in a few days and didn't know what his work schedule was for today. That's why she gave a horrified gasp when she saw him approaching carrying the basket that she remembered placing her buns in earlier that day.

"Wa-y-ne," she stammered, her face turning a bright pink.

I looked at her in shock. "That's why he paid so much for that basket," I thought, having watched the auction.

As Rita looked at the plate of buns sitting in the basket with only half of one eaten, Wayne chuckled, "Rita, when we eventually get married, it won't be because of your baking, O.K?"

As I doubled over in laughter at this while Rita turned crimson and hid her face in her hands. "Rita, you didn't try to make Mom's lassy buns, did ya? Can I try one?" I asked Wayne.

Wayne held out the buns and I took one and bit into it. My face grimaced as I chewed. "This is not Mom's lassy buns. You made them wrong."

At that, Rita grabbed the half-eaten bun from me and the remaining plate of buns and tossed them in the nearest garbage.

"I'm sorry Rita," Wayne apologised with a smile. "I was just joking, please forgive me." He turned to me. "So, you are the handsome little brother I have heard so much about. I'm Wayne, your future brother-in-law." He held out his hand for me to shake.

"You are awful sure of yourself for someone who just criticized my baking," Rita said with a serious face, but I knew that she was the one teasing this time.

Wayne gave a nervous chuckle till Rita finally laughed to show him she was joking. "What else was in the basket?" she asked.

"Just some candy and toys. Would you like something Arch?"

I grinned and searched through the basket selecting a tiny toy guitar. "Can I have this?"

"You sure can," Wayne smiled.

The next day all the children from the orphanage went sliding. We had the whole week off for Easter. Rita went along to help out.

"Do you think you will marry him?" I asked her.

"He is a very nice man Arch, but I won't be marrying anyone till you are home and settled away," she explained.

"That might give you time to learn to bake," I laughed.

Rita laughed too. "Arch, that was so embarrassing. I wonder what I did wrong. I made the buns and cut up the pork and added it, just like

I saw Mom do."

"Did you fry the pork and add some of the grease?" I asked.

"I was supposed to fry it?" Rita looked shocked as I laughed. I had watched Mom do it a few times last summer while Rita had been busy working across the cove.

"Oh Lord," she exclaimed as I laughed louder.

CHAPTER 70: ARCHIE
ST. ANTHONY ORPHANAGE, SUMMER 1952

The rest of the spring passed without incident and before I knew it another school year was done and I was off to the hospital for a checkup and X-ray.

"Well, you still have the presence of active TB in your knee, Archie. I'm thinking maybe you should stay here at the orphanage this summer and rest. I know you have a large family at home that will inhibit you from obtaining proper rest." Dr. Thomas replaced his medical instruments back on a tray while he awaited a response from me.

When no response came, he said, "I wouldn't be so concerned if Rita was accompanying you, but unfortunately she has decided to stay on here for the summer."

I looked up, wide eyed. "Rita's staying?"

"I'm sorry, she probably hasn't had the chance to tell you yet."

"I'll stay too," I said.

"You are sure about that?" he asked.

"Yes, I am sure." I looked the doctor in the eye to confirm.

Later, I found Rita in the laundry room. "How come you didn't tell me you were staying?"

"I'm sorry Arch. I was going to tell you tonight. It came up suddenly and I had to make a quick decision."

"Is it because of Wayne?" I asked.

"Mostly yes. I don't really want to leave here for two months. I really like him, Arch," she smiled softly. "What did the doctor say?"

"That I still have TB, and he would like me to rest here this summer."

"I'm so sorry Arch. I would have travelled home with you and came back if you wanted to go home. Maybe it's all for the best huh?"

I turned my back and bounded up the stairs without responding or looking back.

That night, Rita suggested we go outside for a little visit in the fresh night air. We sat in silence for a few minutes on the steps of the orphanage.

"Dr. Thomas said that if you were going home, he would consider letting me go," I finally said.

Rita sighed. "Arch, if you really want to go home and that's the only way, I will go with you. I already told you that you are my priority."

"But I don't want you to go just because you think you have to," I said miserably.

"I don't think I have to. I want to do whatever makes you happy. You have been sad for way too long, Arch. I don't want you to be sad anymore. Wayne will understand. He loves me," she smiled.

I was silent again.

"Just tell me what to do and I will do it. If you want to go home, then home it is," smiled Rita.

"That's just it. I don't know if I want to go home or not." I slouched almost to my knees.

"Arch, look at me," she said firmly as she turned my shoulders towards her. "You have been gone from home now for five years. Of course you feel close to this place and the friends you have made. You were only seven years old when you came here. Almost half your life has been in this place. Don't you dare feel guilty about wanting to stay here."

"It will break Mom's heart if I stay here," I said.

"Arch, you are not better! If you chose to stay here after you were better, of course it would break her heart. But truthfully Arch, until you get better, I think Mom is fine with you being here."

I nodded but was too upset to speak.

"So, tell me truthfully. Do you want to go home or stay here this summer?"

"Stay here," I mumbled hoarsely.

The summer whizzed by. I rested as per the doctor's orders but also had some fun times outside with the orphanage boys and some of the local boys. I especially enjoyed playing with Ted Patey's son and Dr. Thomas's sons. I also had visits from Clarence Johnson and went to his house for an occasional meal. And of course, I spent time on occasion with Rita and Wayne.

Then towards the end of the summer, the Headmistress left and a new one came to take her place. This made everyone nervous as the new one reminded us a lot of the nasty Headmistress we had only a year ago. However, because of this, Dr. Thomas kept close observation, and she seemed to be fine.

By the time school started, I was ready for the routine again. I had another appointment with Dr. Thomas in October and Dr. Thomas seemed confident that the TB was slowly shrinking and hopefully by spring it would be gone. I again had mixed feelings but also felt that by the time spring came I would be itching to get back home, however terribly I would be missing my newly made family here.

CHAPTER 71: ARCHIE
ST. ANTHONY ORPHANAGE, FALL 1952

Then in November something sinister started happening. It seemed to start so slowly that no one really noticed until it became so intrinsically unbearable that everyone in the orphanage was being affected by it. It concerned the nursery.

The nursery was right next to the boys' ward and held the babies and toddlers under five. There weren't many children there but there were enough to be aggravating at times when they would constantly cry, and the criers would usually keep the others awake. So, some nights it could get really noisy.

It had gotten less aggravating to me after the birth of little Archie more than a year ago. I could still remember little Archie's tiny face and had spent some time with him the summer I had been home in Matthew's Cove. The past year was pretty good. The kind young headmistress would sit in there for hours sometimes, and sing to them and rock them when the house mother wasn't available. However, since she left, the new Headmistress didn't have the same patience. She would yell and scream at the babies, causing them to cry terrified cries. This was way more unbearable to the other children than the regular cries.

Yelling didn't reap a favourable response which only served to further infuriate the Headmistress. She began by placing them on a cold stool at the end of the hallway, past the boys' ward, where the staircase landing was located. They would cry themselves to sleep there and not disturb the other babies. When this ceased to work, she would strip them naked and put them there. Sometimes the horrifying screams would be unbearable, but we would not interfere for fear of repercussions.

Many nights the Headmistress would just walk away for hours while the little baby would finally drift off into a fitful sleep and tumble off the little stool. I craved to go take that baby into my bed and snuggle it, but having been institutionalised for so long, I knew this would have dire consequences. Sometimes Rita would use the boy's staircase come down from her room on the third floor and put the baby back into its cot.

It was a rough few months that left a lifetime of scars on us boys. I never did know if the punishment had worked and made the babies more obedient or if one of the staff had reported the Headmistress and she changed her ways. Whatever it was, I was happy when it ended.

CHAPTER 72: ARCHIE
ST. ANTHONY ORPHANAGE, SPRING 1953

The sweet fresh smell of spring was in the air when I was brought to the hospital to see Dr. Thomas for the last time.

March 28th 1953
Seen in OPD. Cast removed and x-rays taken which appear to show fusion taking place spontaneously. Cast is being left off for one month. The knee seems clinically solid.

"You are doing so well Archie that I could probably put you on the next plane going to St. Mary's," the doctor said.

My eyes widened. These were the words I had waited for for nearly six and a half years. It was like some lifelong fantastic dream had finally one true. So why was I hesitant to be excited? Had so many disappointments over the past six years made me doubtful or did I not want to go back at all? I was so confused.

Dr. Thomas continued. "I am thinking that maybe you should finish out your school year and return when the boats start running. How do you feel about that?"

I nodded, still in shock.

Dr. Thomas, realising what was happening, immediately lowered himself into the chair next to me and softened his voice. "I'm so sorry, Archie. I know this is a sudden a shock to you. For the second time in your short lifespan, your world is being turned upside down. I have seen dilemmas like yours many times even involving much older people and involving people who have been here for much shorter periods of time than you have been."

I nodded sadly but was encouraged that the doctor understood.

"Everyone calls me Arch now," I said.

Dr. Thomas gave a small chuckle. "Then Arch you will be to me also. I am so proud of the young man you are becoming, and all the staff here will be sad to see you leave. But we are so happy that you have healed and are finally going back home where you belong. That's another reason why I feel you should wait till June. You will have adjusted to the idea and have prepared yourself. Do you understand what I mean?"

I nodded while my eyes brimmed with tears. "Thank you very much for healing me."

"You are kindly welcome. It makes me very happy to have success stories like yours. Not everyone has fared so well with the disease, but everyone on staff here has contributed to our war against the disease."

I nodded and smiled.

"From having known both you and Rita for the past few years, I feel very confident that you have a wonderful family to return to. Now then young man," the doctor changed his tone again to signify that their conversation was coming to an end. "What is the first thing you plan to do when you get back to the orphanage without a cast on?"

I grinned. "The very first thing I am going to do is find some pants that actually fit me instead of the two sizes too big ones that I have needed to fit over the cast."

We both had a great laugh at this.

I was halfway back to the orphanage before I fully realised the freedom I felt without the cast. Then I realised the fact that I was truly and surely going back home for good. Not just a summer and then leaving. I was going home to stay. I suddenly felt so light and free that I broke into a run and ran the rest of the distance to the orphanage.

As I shot into the orphanage and hurled myself down the basement stairs, I could hear the house mother shouting at me to slow down.

Majorie and Rita were folding sheets when I burst through the laundry room doorway. "I need pants," was all I could manage through deep gasping breaths.

They both looked at me like I had ten heads. "Pants," I repeated.

Rita shook her head in disbelief. "Arch, your cast is gone."

I grinned, bobbing my head up and down affirmatively. "And the TB is gone too."

Rita made a huge gasp and put both hands over her face. "Is that true?"

"Yes," as I grinned a huge toothy grin. Rita grabbed me and gave me a huge bear hug while Marjorie danced with delight.

As Rita pulled away with her eyes full of tears she said, "I thought this day would never come. And now that it has, it don't even seem real."

"I know," I said. "It does feel strange. Can I have some smaller pants now?"

Marjorie went to the clothing shelf and selected a pair of pants she thought would fit as Rita helped me remove the large pants.

"I still have a small dressing, and I have to use salve and a leg sock till the skin gets tougher. It's still kind of niche from being under the cast for so long. And the doctor says my leg will always be straight, but I don't mind that." I rambled away while they helped me into a better fitting pair of pants. I couldn't believe how much better it felt and I couldn't wait to see the other boys.

The girls and I giggled and talked about all the years we had dreamed of this moment. Marjorie commented on how strange it was that we lived in an orphanage for so long while we had family at home awaiting their return. There were others, of course, over the years who had stayed to recover from TB, but none that had stayed there as long.

When I entered the boys' ward, I walked as straight as I could. No crutches and wearing fitted pants. All the boys could do was stare with their mouths hung open.

"Well, say something," I demanded.

"Did they forget to put your cast back on?" asked Wilf.

Everyone laughed even though young Wilf was quite serious. We all knew the Mission rarely forgot anything.

"Are you all better Arch?" asked Wince, nervous but hopeful.

"Yes" I screamed. "Thanks be to Jesus." I had whispered Jesus as I didn't want any grownups outside the dorm room to hear. I had heard Dad and my uncles say it many times and I had always wanted to say it myself. Now I finally had an occasion to truly celebrate so I had let it rip.

Everyone laughed and cheered, bringing the Mrs. Hodge up the stairs to investigate. She was as happy and excited as the boys. Pretty soon word had spread throughout the orphanage and I became a bit of a celebrity for a few days. I thought back to when Dr. Salter had told me that I was a movie star and wished I was able to tell him about my recovery.

Later that night I laid awake, too excited to sleep. I could hear the gentle snores of the other boys and sometimes tiny whimpers from the babies in the room next room. I thought about how I would miss all those sounds that I had come to associate with comfort. I wondered if I would still be sharing a room with all my brothers when I returned home or if I would be just sharing with Cack? I wondered if I would have to go to bed as early as I did here?

As my thoughts continued to spin, a small whisper pierced the darkness. "Arch, are you still awake?"

"Wince, you are still awake too?" I asked.

"I will really miss you Arch," he said.

"I will really miss you too Wince."

The next few months passed without incident. The last of my lesions had healed and the skin that had been so niche beneath the cast had toughened up so I no longer needed the leg sock. Best of all, I was astonished about how quickly I could manoeuvre with the straight leg. Anyone seeing me navigate the area would not have guessed I had spent the last six and a half years in a cast.

By the time June rolled around, I was getting quite used to the idea that I was truly going home. When the older boys talked about how jealous they were I would beam with pride that I had a family to go to. That said, seeing Wince and Will looking sad would tear at my heartstrings.

On my last visit to the doctor in early June, I was told frankly about how lucky I was to have survived. A lot of folks weren't so lucky as many had not won the battle with tuberculosis. Plus, I had lived in a place where the majority of the children had no family to return to, so I was doubly blessed. The doctor told me that I probably wouldn't realise how blessed until I was back home with my family. All I could think about that day was that somehow I felt I had two families.

As I walked aboard the *Kyle* in late June amid the flurry of migratory fishers and families making their spring trip to Labrador, I was happy I had had the past three months to get used to this idea. Rita toggled behind me with my suitcase. Her and Marjorie had stuffed it full of clothes for me. Rita even sneaked in a cute little dress for Dorthy.

Rita had been very sad since she had finally admitted to me that she wouldn't be going home. We had both cried a lot that night. I got mad and said I wasn't going home either. Rita had gotten mad and said she would go home and be an old maid. Finally, through the sobs, and seeing how much she truly loved Wayne, I decided that maybe I was being selfish. If I had learned anything the past six years it was that I had no control of most events in my life and that I should be grateful for all the people who had contributed to making it easier for me. Rita had also sacrificed nearly six years of her life for me and it was time for her to find happiness in her own life.

Rita found the area with bunks and put my suitcase on it. Some folks had gotten off in St. Anthony to fish from there so there were empty bunks. Two nurses going to the coast for work in Indian Harbour would accompany me and several other patients to their destinations.

When the first blast sounded signalling the first warning that the ship would soon be leaving, Rita and I made our way back on deck.

"I guess I better get off so they don't leave with me," she laughed.

"Alright," I replied. "Come home to visit soon, O.K?"

"I will be home for a visit as soon as I can," she said as she gave me a big bear hug. "You are almost as big as me now, Mom won't know you." She turned quickly and left but I could hear her sniffling.

I was on the way home now and the excitement was setting in. I watched as Rita ran down the gangway and onto the wharf and then made her way back to the orphanage. She stopped on the grassy bank and turned and gave a big wave. Then she was gone.

The second blast sounded after the gangway had been secured to the side of the boat. I heard my name called from the wharf and looked down to see the boys from the orphanage waving wildly to me. I jumped up and down and waved both arms and kept my eyes on them until the *Kyle* had pulled away and they were no longer in sight. For many years to come I would not forget little Wince who had remained still with his arms wrapped around his body while the other boys had waved.

During the crossing, three other Labrador boys were also travelling home. Guy Penney, Hughlett Clark, and Aaron Clark. We had fun exploring the ship and having some laughs but as much as I enjoyed their company I just couldn't wait to step ashore in Matthew's Cove.

CHAPTER 73: FANNY
MATTHEW'S COVE, JUNE 1953

Fanny paced the floor. This was the day she had prayed for and now that it was finally here, she felt like every nerve in her body was pulsing wildly. Cack and Dorothy had gone out to Tilsey earlier and watched until they could see the smoke from the *Kyle* rising in the distance. Ern and the children were puttering out through the cove in the motorboat when the first blast sounded. She stayed home to get a meal ready, or at least that's what she told the family. She really needed to get her nerves under control.

They were still in St. Mary's when they got word from the hospital that Arch had a good report. The cast was off and there was no TB left. She was dizzy with happiness that night. Mill was still home and the whole family would be together again soon. She couldn't wipe the smile off her face. When her and Ern went to bed that night, she felt like all the stars in the universe had aligned to finally bring her good fortune. Her heart was full.

Now, as she placed her hand on her growing belly, she wished they had been more careful that night. Little Dorothy would be nine years old in a few weeks and now here she was in the family way again. If Arch hadn't been so cruelly snatched away from her for so long, maybe she would feel differently. She just couldn't stand the thought of bringing another child into such an unpredictable world. Added to this, there was a young man coming on the *Kyle* who hadn't lived with them for six and a half years and she hadn't seen in two years. It was her son, her flesh and blood, that she had agonised over for years. Now that her deepest prayers were coming true, she felt like that precious bond she had with her son all those years ago had vanished. There was no way she could handle starting a whole new batch of agony with another child.

By the time that the second blast sounded signalling that the ship was preparing to leave, the motorboat was puttering in through the cove. Fanny moved the pot of soup off on the hot end of the stove and forced her wobbly legs to carry her down the hill to the wharf. Roy and John were just helping Arch out of the boat by the time she got there. She first noticed the fitted pants but, when he raised his head to look her in the eye, she couldn't hold back the emotions for another second.

His face was angling into a man's face, but his eyes told her that he was the same little boy she nursed and snuggled for the first seven years of his life. He ran to her, and she gave him a big hug, maybe holding on too long because he wiggled out.

"I smells partridge soup," he said. She felt ashamed for a moment that her clothes always smelled like whatever she was cooking but dismissed the shame for happiness.

Everyone laughed and Fanny quickly dried her eyes and followed them up the hill.

"No more reason to cry now Fan," said Ern as he fell into step with her.

Her hand went instinctively to her stomach but she remained quiet.

With Arch home, the summer went by quickly. Fanny watched him as he had some trips to the fishing grounds. He seemed to love everything about home and even exclaimed about the smell of the codfish. He was helping this year with the washing and salting while Roy and John did the heading and splitting. Fanny heard Ern tell him that it was good to have him home and her heart swelled with pride. At the end of a long day, Arch would tell Fanny how her cooking the best thing ever.

CHAPTER 74: RITA
MATTHEW'S COVE, SUMMER & FALL 1953

Rita came home for a short visit at the end of August. Marjorie had come with her, and everyone was so happy to see them. They all sat around the oil lamp that night and listened to Rita's stories of the orphanage while they nibbled the delicious shortbread cookies she brought home. She told them that the secret ingredient was the real cow's butter.

Rita told everyone how both herself and Marjorie had fallen in love with airmen from the base and planned to move to the States with them that fall. The whole family was sad but she promised she would visit as often as she could. She said if she didn't like it, she would be back to stay. Wayne was a good man and would never force her to live there against her will.

The next morning after the boys had left, Rita helped her mother with the chores. "Momma, you are awfully quiet. Is everything alright?" The words had no sooner left her mouth when she realised the problem and gasped. "You're having a baby."

Fanny looked away so Rita wouldn't see the tears that were springing to her eyes.

"Mom?"

"Yes," Fanny croaked in barely a whisper.

"Aren't you happy about it?"

This time Fanny faced her, eyes all ablaze. "What in the hell flames is there to be happy about."

Rita was shocked into silence.

"I just turned forty-one-years-old. I'm getting too old to keep having babies. This child is going to be younger than three of my grandchildren." Mildred had given birth to her third child in May. She sighed deeply and continued. "Archie came back this summer to live and I barely know him anymore. Every day I live in fear of something happening to another one of my children and now I was stupid enough to get myself in this state again."

"Mom, you are far from old and the mission almost got all the TB cleaned up now and there are good medicines to help people. What happened to Arch will never happen again."

"I'm sure there will be something else, some other new sickness." Fanny slumped into a chair. She didn't cry. She was all cried out from the past few months. She just felt tired.

Rita sat beside her and rested her head on her mother's shoulder. "Everything will be fine Mom. I wish I could be here to see my little brother or sister though."

"I wish you didn't have to go away. Are you sure he is worthy of you Rita?"

"He is a good man, and I will soon be twenty so it's time I settled down," Rita laughed.

Fanny sighed. She had no more words for her grief.

"Oh," declared Rita. "I have something for you." She disappeared into the room she was currently sharing with Dorothy and returned with a little box. "This is for you."

"For me?" Fanny asked.

"Yes. It's from Wayne and I, but I have to give some credit to Arch as he had his eye on it in the Grenfell Store for a while. After he left, I realised that he had never been able to save enough money for it, so Wayne and I bought it together. We wanted you to have something petty in your life. You deserve some beautiful things Mom."

Fanny slowly opened the little box and gasped as she peered down at the beautiful brooch inlaid with precious stones. "I love it," she said as tears sprang to her eyes. "Where would I ever go to wear this?"

"You could wear it every day to remind you of the beauty in this world."

"My children remind me of the beauty in this world everyday," Fanny said absently and then realised what she had just said.

"And now you have another beautiful baby on the way," smiled Rita.

Fanny kept staring at the brooch. "I saw one of the ladies in Battle Harbour wear a purple one, almost like this but not as pretty."

Rita laughed, "It's actually violet, Mom. I loved it because the colour represents the happy things you dream about for the future. It's also the colour of royalty and means faithfulness and spirituality." Rita paused to take a breath, "We are all going to be fine, Mom."

Fanny could only stare at the beautiful brooch. "Violet," she whispered. "What a beautiful name."

CHAPTER 75: FANNY
MATTHEW'S COVE, SUMMER 1954

Fanny was enjoying a quiet moment with her knitting while Violet slept in the next room. The men and boys were fishing, and Dorothy was off playing with friends.

Her mind flashed back to a year ago when her whole world seemed to teeter on the verge of collapse. Her distraught thoughts of impending doom continued throughout the fall. Even after they had moved into St. Mary's for the winter, it seemed to her that her whole family had been disjointed. Rita and Mill had moved away, Roy was practically an adult at 17, Dorothy was gone with Olive every chance she could get, and Arch, John, and Cack were always off doing their own thing. It was like they were all living separate lives under one roof.

She had become more and more distant. Everything grated on her nerves, and she was snappy. She caught Arch looking at her sadly one day and she was so ashamed she asked him if he was alright. It was just before he turned fourteen and it was taking every bit of strength she had to make his birthday cake. It was the first cake she had made for his birthday since he was seven.

"You seem sad all the time Ma," he said.

"I'm just tired," she responded.

"I can finish making the cake for you if you want," Arch offered.

Fanny smiled at that. "Wouldn't be very nice for you to make your own birthday cake."

Arch grinned too. "Nice to see you smile Ma."

"I've missed making you a lot of cakes," she said.

"Well, nothing stopping you from making six more cakes then," laughed Arch as Fanny swapped at him with a spoon.

On his birthday, he had one big cake surrounded by six small cupcakes. Everyone laughed and celebrated. It was just a tiny window of happiness for her that fall before she slipped into her depression again. Ern was worried but couldn't understand how she could feel sad now that Arch was home and healthy. She felt like no one understood her, so she just kept her feelings to herself.

When Violet was born on December 4th, 1953, Fanny peered down into the beautiful little angelic face and wished she would soon feel better but it just wasn't happening.

Also, the thought of going home with all the work of a little baby and still needing to tend to a family that were only home long enough to eat and mess up the house, was more than she could bear. Then, when she would become cognizant of her thoughts, the guilt and shame of having those thoughts only added to her misery. Until Arch had been whisked away, she had probably been the happiest mom alive when it came to caring and tending to her children. She hated how she felt.

When the day came for her to go home from the hospital, strange things began to happen. Little Violet was practically whisked out of her arms the moment she entered the door. For the next few months, she would barely get Violet long enough to feed her and she was soon put on carnation milk which meant Fanny rarely held her at all. The boys and Dorothy cooked, washed dishes, swept, mopped, and doted on the baby. The only thing they refused to do was laundry, especially pinning it on the line.

"God forbid any girls see them pinning clothes on the line", Fanny would chuckle to herself. She actually loved pinning clothes on the line and the fresh clean air was a bonus. She always prided herself on how well she could maintain her white clothes. Most women struggled with this, but not her.

It was heartwarming to see the love the children had for their new sibling and slowly Fanny felt like her family was intact again and her mind began to heal. When Clarence celebrated his twelfth birthday in March, some family dropped by and asked how she was coping through this long old winter with a small baby.

"I don't think I had a baby," she replied. "I think my boys had a baby and I just became chief cook and bottle washer," she grinned.

Everyone laughed and had a great visit that night. Later, as Ern snuggled into her back and nuzzled his nose in her neck he whispered, "It's so good to have you back."

"Lord dying b'y, I've been back for three months."

"No maid, your body may have been back but it's good to have the old Fan back," he said.

"Who ya callin old?" she shot back as she smiled in the darkness.

That was five months ago, and Fanny still smiled at the memory. There was no doubt that God had sent Violet to her to be the glue that mended her broken family.

Violet started to awaken, and Fanny rushed to grab her so she could have the child's last few sleepy moments with her in the rocker before she fully awoke. Violet was still beautiful and petite at nine months old and as Fanny gently rocked her, Violet reached out to grab the brooch Rita had given her a year ago.

"Purdy Ma," Violet said.

"Not as pretty as you, little one," Fanny replied and Violet snuggled in again. Fanny smiled at yet another memory, the memory of Arch's face when he saw the brooch that Rita had brought a year ago.

For the remainder of her life, as her family expanded with grandchildren and great-grandchildren, she would never forget the healing power of children in families. She cherished every child she was blessed with, and every child that came into her world felt blessed and special.

EPILOGUE

The Grenfell Mission continued its assault on tuberculosis until well into the 1970s when widespread access to the disease fighting drugs became available. Tuberculous, or TB, is a bacterial infection that has affected humans for thousands of years. In the early 1900s, an understanding of the disease led to the development of new drugs to combat it. Although mainly affecting the lungs, it can also affect the bones, joints, lymph nodes, brain, and nervous system. Left untreated, TB is fatal in fifty percent of cases.

Newfoundland and Labrador saw an unusually high number of cases in the early to mid- 20th century. It was never discovered whether this was due to lack of nutritious foods or long winter months with cramped living spaces, but the fight was real, and the battle kept the Grenfell Mission very busy.

The doctors that cared for Archie have been prominently portrayed in Grenfell accounts and their own writings; however, Dorothy Jupp has never been popularised. As described by Iona Loreen Bulgin in her 2001 thesis, *Mapping the Self in the "Utmost Purple Rim": Published Labrador Memoirs of Four Grenfell Nurses*, Ms. Jupp, in her time, was seen as too independent and headstrong in the male-dominated world of the Grenfell Mission. Her direct contact with Joey Smallwood regarding the food shortages, for example, did not win her any accolades among the hierarchy of the Mission. She eventually retreated to the North Coast of Labrador where she finished her nursing career in Nain. She retired in 1974 and moved back to England where she died on July 7, 1986.

After visiting the Rumbolt family, it would take Dr. Anthony Paddon another five days to reach Cartwright, and by September of 1947 he was working out of North West River and another doctor was tending the Cartwright area. It would be 40 years before Dr. Paddon and Archie would cross paths again. This was at a combined council meeting in Happy Valley-Goose Bay where Dr. Paddon humorously asked "Are you the Archie that I travelled by foot, by boat, and by dog team to save his life?"

Dr. Robert Bruce Salter would return to Toronto in 1949 after two years with the Grenfell Mission. Eventually, he would become famous for a procedure called the Slater/Harris fracture which specialised in congenital hip fractures. Although he had left Newfoundland, he continued to consult with Dr. Thomas regarding Archie's progress.

As the executive director of the Grenfell Mission in St. Anthony, Dr. Gordon W. Thomas was a gifted, caring doctor who did a full range of surgery as well as balanced a heavy administrative load. Dr. Thomas retired in 1979, but, as he retired, oversaw the transition of the International Grenfell Association properties to the government. This transition finished in 1981. Dr. Thomas was also awarded the Order of Canada for service to the people of Newfoundland and Labrador on June 26, 1970.

St. Mary's River would become Mary's Harbour in 1955 with the coming of the Post Office. In 1968, the year-round settlers in the Battle Harbour area moved into Mary's Harbour under the Resettlement Program. With the collapse of the Fishery in 1992, most homes were left and not returned to abandoned. The Battle Harbour Historic Trust was able to revive the outlook for Battle Harbour and some locals were able to maintain their homes in the Matthew's Cove. Arch never did return.

Arch's family was very fortunate that it they did not lose anyone to death with this terrible disease, tuberculosis, and the six and a half years they spent dealing with a disjointed family eventually made them closer. Ern succumbed to heart trouble in 1974, and Fanny lived another fifteen years and passed peacefully in her easychair in 1989. Five of the brothers and sisters are still living and talk to each other often. John passed away in 2016 at seventy- seven years, Rita passed in 2018 at eighty- five, and Roy passed in November 2021 at eighty- five. Mildred celebrated her ninety third birthday this past summer and has the sharpest mind of them all. Sadly, the son Mildred named after Arch died suddenly at age forty- eight.

Fanny and her daughters at a family reunion in the early 1980s. Left to right: Dorothy, Mildred, Fanny, Rita, and Violet. From the Rumbolt Family Album.

Fanny and her sons at a family reunion in the early 1980s. Left to right: Clarence, Roy, Fanny, John, and Arch. From the Rumbolt Family Album.

Arch did have opportunities to see his old friends a few times years after his experiences in the International Grenfell Association hospitals and orphanage. He and Bart Webber stayed friends for the next 74 years. Bart did eventually heal and was sent home, but the two stayed in touch. I finally met him at the Residential School Apology in November 2017, and the joyful interactions between Bart and Arch told me everything I needed to know about the bond they had forged 70 years prior. Bart passed on February 7, 2023.

Arch and Bart together in Goose Bay in 2017. From the Rumbolt Family Album.

In July 2019, Arch visited Cook's Harbour on the tip of the Great Northern Peninsula, about an hour's drive from St. Anthony, to visit Garfield Warren. The two had a wonderful visit, and went to the old orphanage in St. Anthony. The building is now privately owned and turned into rooms for rent. The main layout hasn't changed much, Arch said, and he had his picture taken ascending the stairs where the Headmistress had broken his cast many years ago. Sadly, Garfield passed away from a sudden illness in May 2020.

In November 2017, Arch went to the Residential School apology at Goose Bay. The apology, made by Prime Minister Justin Trudeau, recognized the fact that the schools associated with the International Grenfell Association and the Moravian Mission had issues of abuse, neglect, and language and culture loss that was particularly impactful to

Arch and Garfield in July 2019. From the Rumbolt Family Album.

Arch at the base of the stairs where he was attacked. The carrot cupboard was under the stairs. From the Rumbolt Family Album.

Arch meeting with Prime Minister Justin Trudeau in 2017. Left to right: Labrador MP Yvonne Jones, Prime Minster Justin Trudeau, Arch, Marie Rumbolt, Arch's wife. From the Rumbolt Family Album.

the Indigenous peoples of Labrador. The St. Anthony Orphanage and Boarding School was recognized as one of those residential schools. The Grenfell Mission operated with the support of the Government of Newfoundland prior to 1949, and after 1949, operated with funding provided by the Government of Canada to the province to meet the educational needs of Indigenous students in Labrador.

Arch with Tony Obed, the face and heart of the Residential School court case. From the Rumbolt Family Album.

This book is the Archibold Rumbolt story. Over the years, he told me about his experiences, and I have done by best to share his story. I was pleased to hand him a printed draft of this book in 2025 so that he could see his story in print. Arch, my father, was shaped by his years with the Grenfell Mission. Years later, he would get his guitar and would play at his hometown gatherings. He and his uncle Tim, who played the accordion, would have a little land called "Uncle Tim and I," a play on the Newfoundland band of *The Mummers Song* fame, Simani.

Arch was always a softie when it came to discipline and his children could usually get anything they wanted with a few tears. It was the same for his grandchildren. His grandson was so attuned to his pop's intolerance for crying that he would hold his breath in screams to get what he wanted around Arch. I knew the worst that would happen is that the child could pass out and then automatically breathe again, so I refused to be manipulated. I remember scooping up my son one day while he was in the midst of one of his tantrums and going to the bathroom, away from my father, and locking the door. Arch banged and cried at the door. I never knew the full extent of why my father couldn't handle hearing children cry until I learned his story and learned about the crying babies at the orphanage.

Arch in his element in the late 1970s, playing his guitar to entertain partygoers at a dart league banquet. From the Rumbolt Family Album.

THE RUMBOLT FAMILY TREE

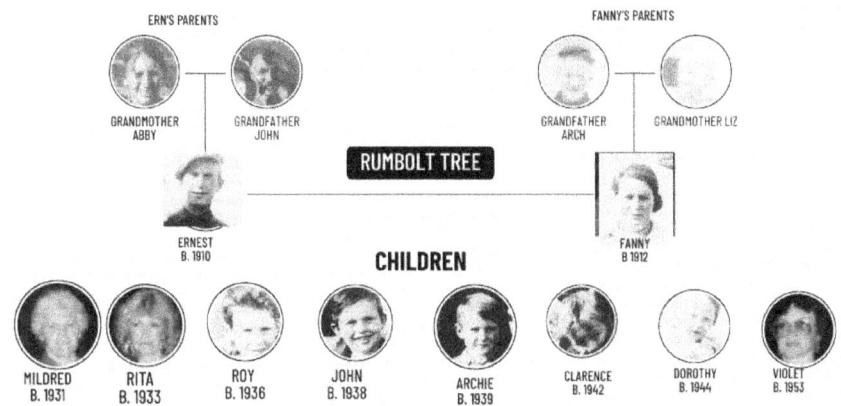

MAP OF THE AREA

Those photos show the area of where Tooth Cove actually is. No one has lived there for more than seventy years and it has grown over to the point that you would never tell that it did hold several families during the time of the Labrador Development Company.

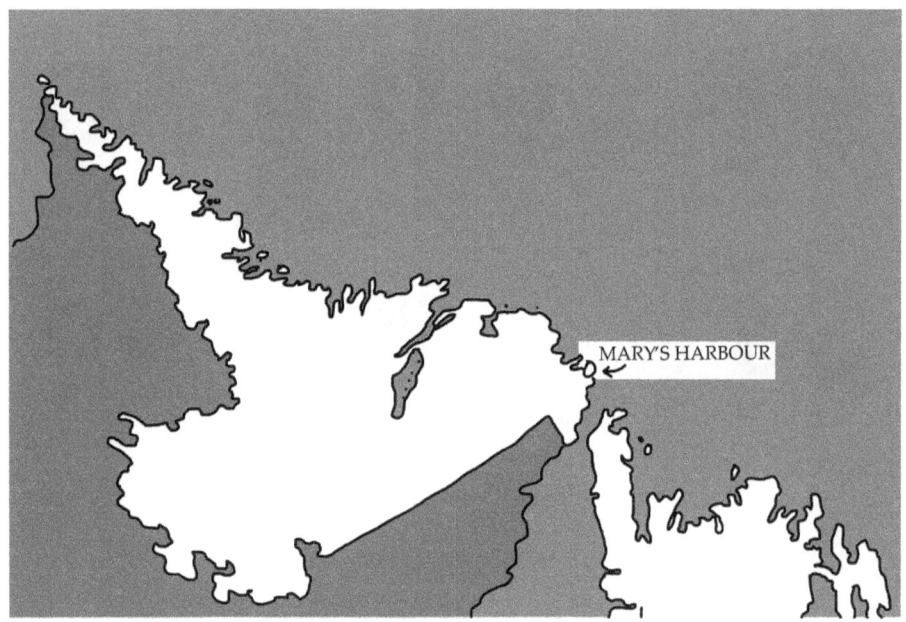

Expanded map of Labrador and part of the island of Newfoundland, illustrating the location of Mary's Harbour.

Zoomed in view of the complex Labrador geography (above).

Illustrating the distance between Matthew's Cove and Mary's Harbour (below).

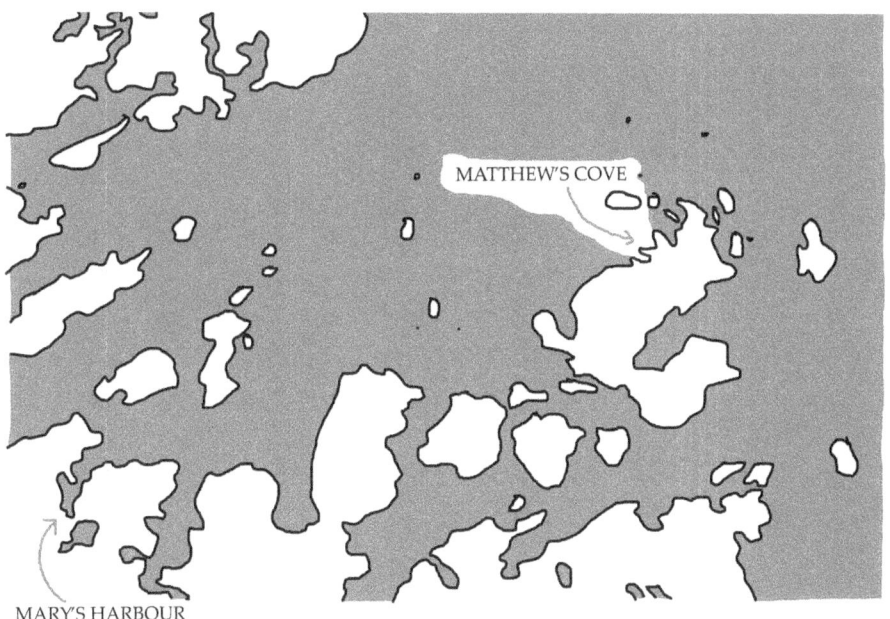

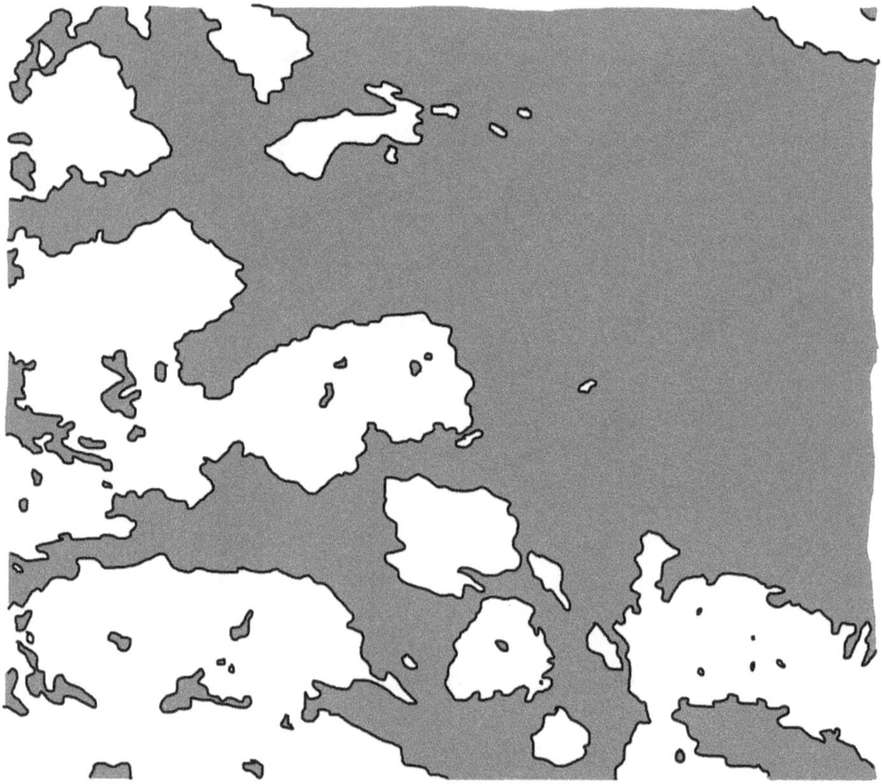

Illustrating the distance between Tooth Cove and Mary's Harbour (below).

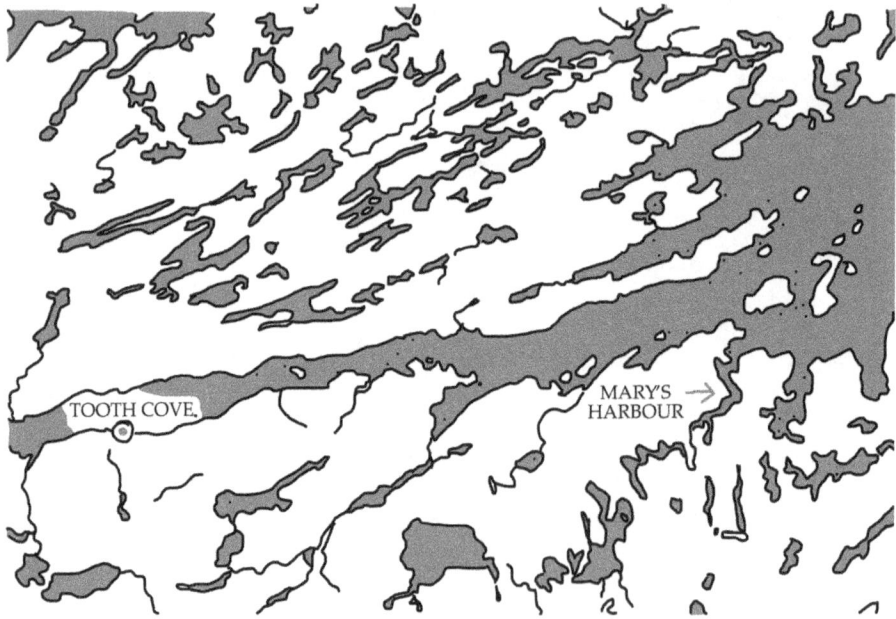

NINA RUMBOLT-PYE

Nina has resided in Mary's Harbour, Labrador her entire life with the exception of time in St John's completing a Political Science/English Degree with Memorial University.

Nina has been an active Nunatukavut (NCC) member for nearly 30 years spending half that time on the Governing Council. She currently serves as an Employment, Skills and Development (ESD) Policy Committee member for student funding as well as recently appointed one of the three Board members of the newly formed Nunatukavut Citizenship Committee.

Since retiring from Canada Post, she has been working as a Licensed Substitute Teacher at Bayside Academy, St Lewis Academy and St Mary's All Grade.

Among her notable volunteer work is Town Mayor, Harbourview Manor Co-Chair, Labrador Regional Appeals Board Member (For Municipal Disputes), and Youth Justice Forum. She is also a trained peer facilitator with Empowering Indigenous Women (EIW) and a PHASE instructor with the Canadian Junior Rangers. Her current passion is in helping Indigenous people make connections to communities through genealogy.

Nina has also been recently appointed Chair of the Board of Empowering Indigenous Women (EIW), representing all indigenous women across the Province of NL. She also currently sits as a Board Member of Writers NL and Them Days Magazine.

This is the first of three of creative non-fiction novels documenting her family historical legacies within the Residential School System.

Nina currently lives in Mary's Harbour, on the coast of Labrador with her husband of 40 years, her chihuahua, Mishka, and two cats Uapusk and Autumn.

www.ingramcontent.com/pod-product-compliance
Lightning Source LLC
Chambersburg PA
CBHW021144160426
43194CB00007B/685